CHANGING BRITAIN
1850 - 1979

Donald Morrison
(Principal Teacher of History, Kemnay Academy)

Elliot Morrison
(Assistant Head Teacher, Oban High School)

David Cooney
General Editor
(Principal Teacher of History, Hunter High School)

Pulse Publications

Acknowledgements

The authors and publishers would like to thank the following for permission to reproduce copyright material. [Publishers are followed by their authors in parenthesis].

Adam & Charles Black *(Sir David Lindsay Keir)*; Alfred A Knopf *(RR Palmer & Joel Colton)*; Allan Sutton *(Keith Laybourne)*; Allison & Busby *(John McLean & Nan Milton)*; Barrie & Rockliff *(P Rowland)*; Batsford Books*(Sarah Harris, Jennifer Harris, Alistair Wisker, Peter Lane, DH Aldcroft, M Bruce, R Eatwell)*; BBC Books/Publications *(Angela Holdsworth, the Listener)*; Bodley Head *(C Chaplin)*; Calder Books *(JP MacKintosh)*; Cambridge Educational *(Diane Atkinson, Caroline Lang)*; Cambridge University Press *(JH Clapham, James Kellas, HV Emy)*; Collins *(TG Smout, Sir R Coupland*; Croom Helm *(WJ Mommsen)*; Dryad Press *(Sue Mayfield)*; Edinburgh University Press *(JM Wolfe)*; Edward Arnold *(JR Hay, E Royce)*; Fontana Books *(R Black)*; Greenwood Press *(Sir David Milne)*; Hamish Hamilton *(GM Guddeford)*; Harrap *(Pauline Gregg)*; Heinemann Books *(John Ray)*; Hutchinson Radius *(James Hinton)*; Hulton Picture Company (pages 17, 28, 34, 51, & 77); John Calder Publishing *(John Mercer)*; John Donald Publishers *(Ian MacDougall (ed)*; Jonathan Cape *(T Dalyell, P Addison)*; Livingstone Publishers *(T Ferguson)*; Longman Group *(DG Wright, Hyman Shapiro, H Drucker, G Brown, V Cromwell, E Midwinter, RC Birch, Paul Adelman, A Wood, RJ Cootes, P Thane, CJ Bartlett, C Cook, J Stevenson)*; Macmillan *(AJ Taylor, D Fraser, N Lowe, Henry Pelling, R Skidelsky, Arthur Marwick, D Butler, J Freeman, JR Hay)*; Mainstream Publishing *(Angela Tuckett)*; Manchester University Press *(Richard Taylor, Nigel Young)*; Martin Robertson Oxford *(Philip Norton)*; Methuen *(LCB Seaman)*; Molendinar Press *(K Webb)*; New Left Books *(Tom Nairn)*; Open University *(H Cowper et al*; Penguin Books *(David Thomson, AJP Taylor, Alan Sked, Chris Cook, Arthur Marwick, Margaret Forster, Winston Churchill, J Stevenson, Walter Greenwood, George Orwell)*; Pluto Press *(Harry McShane, Joan Smith)*; Professional Books *(H Calvert)*; Punch Cartoon Library (pages 59, 101 & 103); Reprographia *(B Wolfe)*; Routledge *(John Roebuck, Lindsay Mackie, Polly Pattullo, Elizabeth Wilson)*; Scottish Council of the Labour Party (page 11); The Scottish Office (page 122); University Paperbacks *(GDH Cole, Raymond Postgate)*; University of Wales Press *(Keith Robbins)*; Unwin Hyman *(WL Burn, RM Titmuss, E Royston Pyke, Christopher Harvie, James Kellas, K Morgan, David Vital)*; Wayland Press *(Patricia Owen)*; The Welfare History Picture Library (pages 10, 65, 75 and 87); Gordon Wright (pages 108 and 113); Wheatsheaf Books *(James Hinton)*; WII Allen *(P King)*; Wiedenfield & Nicholson *(M Bruce, M Richter)*.

Contents

1	Britain in 1850	3
2	The Labour Movement	6
3	Women	25
4	Peace Movements	43
5	The Growth of Democracy	53
6	Laissez Faire & its Critics in Late Victorian Britain	62
7	The Liberal Welfare Reforms 1906 - 1914	73
8	The National Governments of the 1930s	84
9	The Arrival of the Welfare State 1945 - 51	96
10	Scottish Nationalism 1850 - 1979	105
11	Scottish Devolution 1850 - 1979	118
	Bibliography	127
	Index	128

Published and Typeset by **Pulse Publications,** 26 Burnside Gardens, Glasgow G76 7QS

Printed by **Holmes McDougall,** Edinburgh

British Library Cataloguing-in-Publication Data
A Catalogue record for this book is available from the British Library

ISBN 0 948766 11 5

© D & E Morrison 1991

1 Britain in 1850

Britain in 1850 was going through a period of rapid social and economic change. Both in the countryside and in the towns, new ideas and new technologies were being put into practice. In the countryside for the previous hundred years, the agricultural revolution had been working to improve the quantity and quality of food grown. Farm labourers were no longer needed in such vast numbers due to the introduction of new and more efficient machinery. As a result of these forces, there had been a massive movement of people from the small rural communities and villages into the growing towns and cities. By 1850, agriculture and industry seemed to be in perfect balance with half the population of Britain living in the country and the other half living in the cities.

The displaced farm workers were attracted into the towns, hoping to find employment in the new textile factories. However, finding work did not always lead to a better quality of life. The growing industrial towns simply could not cope with this rapid influx of people. In 1850, most towns lacked adequate sanitation. A typical factory worker would have no piped-in water or toilet in the house. He or she would have to share the outside privy with several other families. Drinking water was likely to be polluted by sewage or industrial effluent. Inside the 'back-to-back' or tenement, furniture would be sparse and the rooms dimly lit, damp and ill-ventilated. Overcrowding was also a great problem. Many families had to share the same house.

"The conditions of most industrial towns were so appalling that they seemed to many people to be hell on earth. The smoke-belching factories crouched beside the foul canals and rivers which supplied the water for both factories and people, and also acted as the main sewer which was expected to carry off all kinds of refuse including industrial and human excrement, dead dogs and cats, and the blood and bones of slaughterhouses. Around the factories clustered the small, mean terraces of workers' houses which curved across hills and through valleys, the jutting ribs on the diseased bodies of these towns."
(John Roebuck *The Making of Modern English Society from 1850* p3)

Not surprisingly, disease spread rapidly in such conditions. Epidemics of cholera spread throughout the country in 1831-2, 1848-9, 1853-4 and finally in 1866-7. Ten thousand people died of cholera in Scotland in 1848-9. In addition to this, Scotland suffered an epidemic of typhus in 1846 and 1849. Generally, the industrial workers were worst hit by such visitations. Children of all classes were also very vulnerable. In the 1850s, infant mortality stood at 160 per 1,000 ie. one in every six infants died in childhood.

Expectation of life at selected ages 1850 and 1979						
Period	At birth		At Age 15		At age 65	
	M	F	M	F	M	F
1850	39.9	41.8	43.2	43.9	10.8	11.5
1979	69.6	75.8	56.2	62.1	12.4	16.4

Table 1.1

Note that, between 1850 and 1979, the most dramatic improvement in life expectation was for children up to the age of 15 years.

UK Population 1851			
England and Wales	Scotland	N. Ireland	Total
17,928,000	2,889,000	1,443,000	22,260,000

Table 1.2

The 1851 Census provides a detailed insight into the main occupational groups in Britain.

Principal Occupational Groups in Britain in 1851 in order of size		
	Male	**Female**
Total population	10,224,000	10,736,000
Agriculture: farmer, grazier, labourer, servant	1,563,000	227,000
Domestic service (excluding farm service)	134,000	905,000
Cotton worker, every kind, with printer, dyer	255,000	272,000
Building craftsman: carpenter, bricklayer, mason, plasterer, plumber etc	442,000	1,000
Labourer (unspecified)	367,000	9,000
Milliner, dress-maker, seamstress (seamster)	494	340,000
Wool worker, every kind, with carpet-weaver	171,000	113,000
Shoemaker	243,000	31,000
Coalminer	216,000	3,000
Tailor	135,000	18,000
Washerwoman		145,000
Seaman (merchant), pilot	144,000	
Silk worker	53,000	80,000
Blacksmith	112,000	592
Linen, flax worker	47,000	56,000
Carter, carman, coachman, postboy, cabman, busman etc	83,000	1,000
Iron worker, founder, moulder (excluding iron-mining, nailshardware, cutlery, files, tools, machines)	79,000	590
Railway driver etc., porter etc., labourer, plate-layer	65,000	54
Hosiery worker	35,000	30,000
Lace worker	10,000	54,000
Others	553,000	200,793

Table 1.3 (Source: J H Clapham *An Economic History of Modern Britain* p24)

Table 1.3 shows quite clearly that most occupations were by tradition male or female dominated - men were builders, tailors, railway workers and shoemakers; women were domestic servants, dressmakers and washerwomen. The exception to the rule was the textile industries. They had been given a new lease of life by the technological revolution in the processes of spinning and weaving. Power driven machinery could quite easily be supervised by low-paid women and children.

Textiles, coalmining and iron were the new, rising industries. By 1851, cotton workers were the third largest occupational group in the country and textile work in general

3

Working population of Scotland by broad industrial group, 1851-1901 (000s employed)							
Year	Metals	Textiles & Clothing	Other Manufacturing	Agriculture & Fishing	Mining	Services	Total
1851	60.8	366.4	66.2	347.6	48.1	380.8	1269.9
1901	210.4	299.2	147.7	237.3	127.9	879.6	1902.1

Table 1.4   (Source: TC Smout *A Century of the Scottish People 1830-1950'* p87)

occupied the lives of one out of every nineteen people in Britain.

In Scotland, textiles and clothing had already overtaken agriculture by the middle of the nineteenth century. However, in Britain as a whole, agricultural and domestic work were still by far the most most important occupations judging by the numbers employed. Other traditional crafts continued to provide a living for many thousands eg. in 1851, there were more shoemakers than coalminers and more blacksmiths than iron mill workers. On the other hand, hand-made goods could no longer compete with the new power-driven machines which were putting thousands of handloom weavers out of work. In Scotland between 1840 and 1850, the number of handloom weavers dropped from 84, 500 to 25,000.

Although the Industrial Revolution caused much disruption and suffering, it is also true that many people prospered at this time. By the middle of the nineteenth century, Britain was the world's leading industrial nation and it was able to sell its finished products abroad unhindered by any serious competition. Factory, mill and mine owners generally were amassing great fortunes. Typically, these self-made entrepreneurs would build large country houses in an effort to imitate the lifestyle of the landed gentry. Most people looked up to the aristocracy as their social 'betters' and for leadership in the world of politics.

The government in mid-nineteenth century Britain was dominated by the upper class. Both the Conservatives and the Whigs drew their leaders from the same narrow social base. The new middle class, which had grown up with the industrial revolution, was still excluded from real political power. As table 1.5 shows, most of the key Cabinet positions were held by men with titles:

The historian W L Burn has described politics and society in mid- nineteenth century Britain as the "age of equipose". It was "... a generation in which the old and the new, the elements of growth, survival and decay, achieved a

balance which most contemporaries regarded as satisfactory". (WL Burn *The Age of Equipose* p17) We have already noted the balance between old and new when looking at the social and economic statistics, but what about the political forces at work? From one point of view, Britain was entering a period of stability. After all, it had satisfactorily weathered the storm over the repeal of the Corn Laws in 1846. The more serious threat from the working class Chartist movement seemed to have evaporated in 1848. Also in that year, Britain emerged untouched by the revolutionary fever which had swept across continental Europe.

There are several factors which seem to account for Britain's remarkable political stability at this time. First of all, there was no revolutionary tradition in this country. By contrast, the French revolutionaries in 1848 could refer back to the events of 1789. Secondly, the Chartists were divided over the use of violence in their campaign to achieve a more democratic political system. A third explanation for the relative docility of the working class is suggested by Seaman:

"The widespread popularity of...(the)..belief that by thrift and hard work any moral person could rise to eminence must be accounted one of the explanations of the social calm of the mid-century years. If, by a resolute acceptance of life as a competitive struggle, a man who braced himself for the effort might obtain the great prizes of prosperity and an assured competence, it was of little account if government remained in the hands of great ducal families."

(LCB Seaman *Victorian England 1837-1901* p95)

Governments anyway did not interfere in people's lives to any great extent. Laissez faire continued to be the fundamental belief of both major parties. In spite of massive social problems such as ill-health, poverty, poor housing and unemployment, governments expected people to look after themselves. The workhouse was deliberately designed to be a refuge of last resort and most people feared and hated the prospect of having to enter it. Governments were more concerned with keeping taxes down

British Cabinets 1846 - 1852				
	Prime Minister	Chancellor of the Exchequer	Home Secretary	Foreign Secretary
1846 (July)	Lord John Russell	Sir C Wood	Sir G Grey	Viscount Palmerston
1852 (Feb.)	Earl of Derby	B Disraeli	S H Walpole	Earl of Malmesbury
1852 (Dec.)	Earl of Aberdeen	WE Gladstone	Palmerston	Lord J Russell

Table 1.5

than with welfare measures. Nevertheless, the worst excesses of the Industrial Revolution had to be dealt with. Lord Russell's Government passed a *Public Health Act* (1848) to enable local authorities to set up Health Boards and two *Factory Acts* (1847 and 1850), both limiting the working hours of women.

Regulation of working conditions in the factory place had come about more from a paternalistic concern by the upper class rather than as a result of organised working class pressure. Trade unions in 1850 were confined mainly to skilled workers and even then, only a minority of the 'aristocracy of labour' were unionised. The Model Unions were very moderate. They wanted better conditions for their members rather than the overthrow of capitalism. Although Karl Marx had written the *Communist Manifesto* in 1848 and had come to live in London the following year, socialism was in its infancy in Britain.

Another potentially divisive political force, nationalism, was similarly at an early stage in its development. Mainland Britain in 1850 was not only stable and prosperous but also united. Most Scots seemed to believe that the Act of Union of 1707 had been to Scotland's economic advantage. On the other hand, Scotland continued to have its own political agenda. Whereas the repeal of the Corn Laws had caused splits in the Conservative Party in England, the major issue in Scotland was the Disruption of 1843, when the Free Church split away from the established Church of Scotland. The Tories were seen to be on the side of the established Church and consequently, they failed to make any headway north of the border, especially in the towns. No Conservative even bothered standing for election in Glasgow between 1852 and 1868 or in Edinburgh between 1852 and 1870.

Despite their marked hostility towards the Conservatives, most Scots were content to see their country assimilated into the general culture of Britain. However, in 1853 a National Association for the Vindication of Scottish Rights was set up. Despite the fact that this organisation was on the fringes of Scottish politics, it was perhaps an indication of the first stirrings of a nationalist movement north of the border. Within a few years, demands would be made for greater control over Scottish affairs.

Many of the issues which enliven politics in Britain today such as women's rights, trade unions and the Labour Party, Scottish nationalism and the devolution debate have their origins in mid-nineteenth century Britain. It is important, therfore, for us to study the history of changing Britain over the whole period from 1850 to 1979.

2 THE LABOUR MOVEMENT 1850-1979

This chapter will examine the development of the Labour Movement and its impact on the social, political and economic identity of Britain during this period. In order to do this, it is first of all necessary to arrive at a more precise understanding of the term the 'labour movement'.

It is generally accepted that the labour movement has two 'wings' – the *industrial* wing and the *political* wing. The industrial wing of the movement is represented by the trade unions while the political wing came to be represented in the Labour Party. Since the 1850s, the labour movement through growth, development and interaction between the wings has aimed to "negotiate a place for the working class within the framework of a capitalist democracy; the unions bargaining, the party reforming." (From *Labour and Socialism* by James Hinton p.13 Pub. Wheatsheaf.)

The development of the labour movement is thus a history of struggle which always aimed at changing the existing social order.

> "What constituted Labour as a *movement* was the belief that each struggle was, or could be linked into a larger social purpose. Embodied in the network of working-class institutions and practices was a sense of class identity and interest, of membership of an oppositional culture whose common objective was the creation bit by bit of a fairer and a more cooperative social order." (From *Labour and Socialism* by James Hinton p.13 Pub. Wheatsheaf.)

We will first of all examine the development of the Trade Union Movement up to 1900. Secondly, the forces, circumstances, and ideas which brought the Labour Party into being will be traced. Thirdly, we will study the development of the Labour Party and trade unions together up to 1979.

Background

The existence of organised groups of workers dates back to long before the Industrial Revolution. The fact that such bodies existed is emphasised by the amount of legislation which came into being in the 17th and 18th centuries to regulate the activities of such combinations of workers.

Industrialisation in the late 18th and early 19th centuries had the effect of bringing together large numbers of workers in a single place of employment. The emergent factory system gradually served to awaken some groups of workers to their common plight, thus bringing the need for workers to combine more sharply into focus. However, in the 1850s, trade union membership was confined to a minority of skilled workers.

At the turn of the century, trade unionism was affected by the passing of what some historians see as unusually repressive legislation in the form of the *Combination Acts* of 1799 and 1800. Despite these laws which prevented workers combining, there is good evidence of a growth in trade union activity, notably against the introduction of machinery in some trades, and in certain areas of the country, particularly London. When the Combination Acts were repealed in 1824, there followed an unprecedented explosion of industrial action across the country. Following a Committee of Investigation into trade unions in 1825, a further Combination Act was passed in the same year which confirmed the legal status of unions to work peacefully to improve wages, but curtailed their ability to use violence to interfere with the mode of production and made union members liable to prosecution under common law. Thus, while trade unions could now operate more openly, it was still easy for the employers to restrict their activities.

The 1830s marked a period of intense political and industrial activity for sections of the working class. The 1832 *Reform Act*, while granting democratic rights to the entrepreneurs, financiers and small businessmen of the Industrial Revolution, ignored the organised sections of the working class. The historian Henry Pelling describes the 1830s as a time when intelligent working men, in their disappointment and frustration at failing to get the vote in 1832, threw themselves into activities which attempted to raise and emphasise the status of the "work of the artisan or labourer" by setting up a "new system of cooperative production". Thus, the 1830s became the decade in which attempts were made to form general unions on a national basis, and also a time when industrialists such as Robert Owen began to articulate the ideas of workers' cooperation and socialism.

> "It is well known that during the last half century, Great Britain ... increased its powers of production; the natural effect of the aid thus obtained from science should be to add to the wealth and happiness of society ... and that all parties would thereby be substantially benefited ... On the contrary ... the working classes, which form so large a proportion of the population cannot obtain even the comforts which their labour formerly procured for them." (From *The Labour Party* by Peter Lane p.16/17 Pub. Batsford.)

While Owen's ideas offended both employers and some labourers, attempts were made to put Owenite principles into practice. In 1829, John Doherty organised the Grand General Union of Operative Spinners in the United Kingdom, and in 1830 set up the National Association for the Protection of Labour. Although short-lived, these organisations paved the way for the formation of the Grand National Consolidated Trades Union in 1834. However, the GNCTU collapsed in ruins within 12 months of its formation, despite achieving a membership of almost half a million at its peak. The GNCTU failed because:

- its leadership held differing views.
- poor communication made coordination of the union's activities difficult.
- Owen's vision of a shared community of interest amongst working men proved to be flawed. Local and sectional interests dominated.
- the intervention of authorities in bringing about the case of the 'Tolpuddle Martyrs' proved to be decisive in 'frightening off' working men from the GNCTU.

Trade unions did not, however, collapse with the demise

of the GNCTU. At a local level, most trades continued to have some form of workers' organisation, although these unions were usually small and confined to skilled workers. Far from being intimidated by the events of the mid-1830s, these unions continued to press for improved pay and conditions. In some trades however, the employers forced the workers to sign the so-called 'Odious Document', an agreement that individuals would cease to be union members.

In the 1840s, unions continued to operate in an environment where attention was drawn away from their activities and focused on Chartism and the Anti-Poor Law Movement. Thus, in Mid-Victorian Britain most unions, while operating satisfactorily, were small and were limited to skilled workers, although there were some larger unions, notably the Miners' Association of Great Britain.

TRADE UNIONISM 1850-1900

The historian James Hinton describes the economy of Britain in the 1850s as "an anarchic mixture of the old and the new". Some industries had embraced the new technology of the industrial revolution, whereas other areas of human endeavour, such as building and construction, were relatively unaffected. Thus the work force in mid-Victorian times was very diverse, encompassing the skilled craftsman down to the common labourer who relied on sheer muscle power to earn his living.

At this time, only a small minority of workers belonged to trade unions, these being the relatively skilled craftsmen. These so-called *Model Unions* saw their role as one of preserving the pay and conditions of their members while maintaining the division between their members and the rest of the unorganised and unskilled working class. These men are described by some historians as an 'élite' within the working class who, although they did not approve of the capitalist system, had made a temporary accommodation with it. They were suspicious of socialism, and concentrated their efforts in the 1850s and 60s on amalgamating their smaller local craft unions into large national craft unions, the most famous of which was the Amalgamated Society of Engineers.

These unions came into being when the economy was booming. Their members earned high wages and could therefore afford the relatively high dues, sometimes as much as 1/6 (7^1/2p) per week. In return the unions employed paid, full-time officials whose job it was to negotiate agreements on pay and conditions with the employers. In addition, they provided sickness, retirement, unemployment and injury benefits to their members.

Five of these Model Unions made their headquarters in London and their leaders met regularly, forming the London Trades Council. The leaders of this moderate group became known as the 'Junta', and during the 1870s it came to have a good deal of influence on national trade union development. Meanwhile, at a local level, craft unions set up trades councils across the country, some of which were a lot less moderate in their views than the London 'Junta'. Thus, in the sixties and seventies there were clashes at a local level between employers and groups of workers anxious to have trade union organisation at the

workplace. Occasionally, these clashes became violent, involving lock-outs and the use of 'blackleg' labour with the police and local magistrates usually siding with the employers.

In February 1867, the Government set up a Royal Commission of Inquiry into Trade Unions. This followed outbreaks of violence during a file-grinders' strike in 1866 in Sheffield, and the questioning of the legal status of trade unions raised a case involving the Boilermakers Union. The Commission heard evidence from the 'Junta' and also from representatives of the Manchester and Salford Trades Council who were keen to get all trade unions acting together rather than being dominated by the 'Junta'. In order to bring about this aim they arranged for a *Trade Union Congress* to be held in Manchester in 1868. The 'Junta' did not attend, perceiving the Congress as a rival to their own power base. Thus, the first historic meeting of the TUC went ahead without them.

The Royal Commission on Trade Unions published its report in 1869. It gave fulsome approval to the National Craft Unions for their organisation, benefits to members and absence of violence and strikes. As a result, Gladstone's Liberal Government passed two important pieces of legislation in 1871. (See p.71)

The Trade Unions Act – Trade Unions were given a status in law which they had not previously enjoyed. Their funds were also given legal protection from dishonest officials.

The Criminal Law Amendment Act – The practice of 'peaceful picketing', which had been legalised in 1859, was outlawed, with severe penalties proposed for the guilty.

> "The Junta's own moderation had betrayed them. They had presented their organisations as friendly societies rather than trade unions. Now Gladstone gave them what they had asked for more literally than they had anticipated." (From *Labour and Socialism* by James Hinton p.15 Pub. Wheatsheaf Books.)

The TUC meeting in 1871 demanded the total repeal of the Criminal Law Amendment Act and set up a Parliamentary Committee to pursue its demand. Meanwhile, the courts used the Criminal Law Amendment Act to pursue poorly organised workers. In one notorious case, seven women were sent to jail for saying "bah" to a blackleg.

This and other events merely served to strengthen the resolve of the TUC to campaign harder for the removal of the Act. In the ensuing 1874 General Election, the TUC ran a campaign to pressurise candidates to reveal where they stood on the matter. Trade union members were urged to vote only for those who supported the TUC's demands. The miners even put up independent candidates in some constituencies. Union support led to Conservative victory in 1874 and, in the following year, Disraeli's Government introduced two Bills which were important for trade unions. The first bill, which replaced the Master and Servant Act, meant that breach of contract was now a civil rather than a criminal matter, and was punishable by a fine rather than by imprisonment. The second repealed the Criminal Law Amendment Act, and so once again legalised 'peaceful picketing'. (See p.71)

Thus, by 1875, after a period of intense union activity in the early 1870s, it seemed that the Model Unions had achieved an accommodation with capitalism – but not without a struggle. Historians' opinions differ about the strategy of the 'Junta'. Some assess their approach of setting themselves limited but realistic aims and pursuing them in a statesmanlike manner as being the only viable strategy at the time, while others view them less charitably as "the servile generation".

In the early 1850s, it is estimated that the British Trade Union movement had about 100,000 members. By 1874 membership had shot up to over 1 million. However, from then until the mid-1880s membership declined due to economic recession, only to rise again by 1888 to about 750,000. These years saw hard times for the unions which had often to fight campaigns against wage reductions while facing dramatic membership losses. Some smaller unions went out of existence altogether.

The recession was merely a symptom of the beginning of Britain's relative economic decline in the last quarter of the 19th century. The rapid industrialisation in parts of the world (USA, Germany and Japan) which had previously imported British goods, cut Britain's share of world industrial production from 30% in 1870 to 15% in 1913. British businessmen reacted to the challenge of competition with the more advanced technological states like Germany and the USA by withdrawing and concentrating their efforts on markets within the Empire. While this policy served to maintain the viability of the economy in the short-term, it only served to store up problems for the future.

The New Unionism

Between the 1880s and the turn of the century is the period which historians describe as the decades of the *New Unionism*. During this period it is clear that trade unionism was gradually changing. Existing unions, such as the Amalgamated Society of Engineers, began to admit semi-skilled workers. New general unions were being formed, prepared to organise all who wished membership. Increasingly, trade unions began to associate themselves with the ideology of socialism and began to look outwith the established political parties as a means of winning demands for state intervention.

Case Study – The London Dock Strike
Duration – 12th August - 14th September 1889

Background – Dock labourers were unorganised, unskilled, casual workers whose job it was to load and unload the ships in Britain's ports. The chance of getting work was affected by the weather and the time of year. There were always more men than there was work available. In 1888, the socialist Ben Tillet founded the Tea Operatives and General Labourers Union. It was not very successful. In the same year Tillet led a strike at Tillbury Docks, which failed due to lack of interest from the dockers themselves. Tillet and his colleagues, however, took heart from the success of the match girls and gas workers strikes. (See p.••)

Immediate Cause – This centred around the unloading of a cargo vessel, 'The Lady Armstrong', at West India Dock. Once the ship's cargo was unloaded, there arose a dispute between the dockers and the Dock Superintendent over bonus payment. Will Thorne, leader of the Gas Workers, spoke to the dockers, urging them to refuse to work. This they did, and the strike had begun.

Tillet's union formulated demands for the strikers which included –

• Pay to be raised to 6d (2p) per hour (the 'Docker's Tanner').
• The minimum length of employment should be 4 hours.
• Overtime should be paid at 8d per hour.
• The contract system should be abolished.

Course of the Strike – With only seven shillings and sixpence (37p) in his union's funds, Tillet first of all set about persuading other dock workers to join the strike. Eventually, the strike spread throughout the London docks involving boilermakers, stevedores, coal heavers, ballastmen, lightermen, painters and carpenters. The problem of financial relief for the families of striking dockers was tackled through collections, and morale was maintained by organising daily marches with banners and bands. Money came in from a wide spectrum of the community, including a donation from fellow dockers in Australia. The strike committee, comprising Ben Tillet, Tom Mann, Eleanor Marx, John Burns, Harry Orbell and Henry Champion, organised what became a massive relief operation. Eight relief centres were established and it is estimated that at the height of the strike 25,000 people were being fed per day by the Lord Mayor of London, comprising the Lord Mayor and his deputy, the Bishop of London, Sidney Buxton MP, Sir John Lubbock (President of the London Chamber of Commerce) and Cardinal Manning.

After protracted negotiations, an agreement was signed on 14th September ending the strike. The dockers won their demand for 6d per hour, with 8d per hour for overtime.

Comment – The victory of the dock workers proved that unskilled and unorganised groups of workers could win concessions from their employers.

As the trade union movement grew in size, widening its membership, it also became more assertive. During this period, the state took union activity more seriously. The Labour Department of the Board of Trade began to record and measure levels of industrial unrest. In addition, a Royal Commission on Labour was established. Publishing 58 volumes of evidence between 1892 and 1894, the Commission was concerned that conciliation procedures be set up on a local basis, hoping that the new unions which had not adopted such practices would quickly do so.

The leaders of the New Unionism were often younger men with strong socialist principles such as Tom Mann and Ben Tillet.

"... we repeat that the real difference between the 'new' and the 'old' is that those who belong to the latter and delight in being distinct from the policy endorsed by the 'new', do so because they do not recognise, as we do, that it is the work of trade unionists to stamp out poverty from the land ... A new enthusiasm is required, a fervent zeal that will result in a sending forth of trade union organisers as missionaries through the length and breadth of the country. Clannishness in trade matters must be superseded by a cosmopolitan brotherhood, must not be talked of but practised ... We ... are prepared to work unceasingly for the economic emancipation of the workers." (Tom Mann & Ben Tillet, *The New Trade Unionism (1890)* p.15. Quoted in *British Trade Unionism 1770-1990* by Keith Laybourne p. 86 Pub. Alan Sutton)

The early victories of the 'new unions' led to a rapid growth in their numbers in the 1890s. Also at this time, clerical workers began to organise for the first time. Most historians agree that the success of New Unionism between 1884 and 1892 was based on low unemployment, good militant leadership, the strike weapon, police tolerance of vigorous picketing and the failure of the employers to unite in opposition.

Membership of Seven Largest New Unions	
Year	Number of Members
1890	320,000
1892	130,000
1906	80,000

Table 2.1

However, as the economic boom of the late eighties and early nineties came to an end, so did the growth of new unionism as the figures in Table 2.1 illustrate. However, this period is significant in the history of the labour movement because it allowed individual socialists and early socialist organisations to carry their message to the working class in a practical way by providing leadership and organisation where none had previously existed, thus allowing the political arm of the movement to come into being.

"The expansion of socialist influence in the working class movement represented by the formation of the ILP, was very largely a result of the activity of socialists in the trade union explosion. The subsequent development of the new socialist party however, owed as much to the limitations and failure of the New Unionism as to its successes." (From James Hinton *Labour and Socialism* p. 58.)

THE ORIGINS OF THE LABOUR PARTY

This section will examine the events which led to the formation of the Labour Party in the last quarter of the nineteenth century. In addition, we will look at the various ideological traditions and personalities which influenced the Party's development.

Although the nineteenth century saw a gradual move by governments away from laissez-faire policies in the area of social issues, the pace of change was slow and was limited in meeting the needs of the working classes. However, towards the end of the 19th century, various factors came together to bring about change in the established two-party system of government. Firstly, the Reform Acts of 1867 and 1884 together added about 8 million working-class voters to the electorate who, after the Ballot Act of 1872, were able to vote independently without fear of pressure from their employers. (See p.57 & 71) Secondly, radicals in both the Conservative and Liberal Parties perceived the need to capture this working-class vote, and in this area both Conservatives and Liberals were successful for a time. Thirdly, the leaders of the TUC, formed in 1868, adopted the strategy of campaigning to persuade Parliament to secure the rights of trade unions and their members. To this end the Labour Representation League was set up in 1869, and by 1874 had succeeded in getting two ex-miners elected to Parliament. These men sat with the Liberals in the House of Commons and took the Liberal whip. By 1885 there were eleven such working-class Lib-Lab MPs in the House of Commons. Fourthly, the development of unions for the unskilled, led by socialists who saw the role of unions as being wider and more political than just workers' welfare organisations, provided fresh impetus to the trade union arm of the labour movement. Finally, the decline of political radicalism towards the end of the 19th century left a void which came to be filled by socialism.

"The decline of the Radicals was not due to the misadventures or treacheries of a few leaders. It was in part due to the faults of the programme itself ... the levying of 'ransom' on capitalists is possible only so long as they are willing and able to pay it. But it was due also to the emergence of a new movement which demanded and promised a great deal more than the Radicals had ever done – the Socialist Movement." (From *The Common People* by Cole and Postgate p. 414/415 Pub. University Paperbacks.)

What were the major elements of this 'Socialist Movement' which gave birth to the Labour Party at the turn of the century? Clearly the unions, as has been shown, were a major element, but there were other organisations, groups of people and individuals who can legitimately claim a place in the history and traditions of the Party, notably the Social Democratic Federation, the Fabian Society and Keir Hardie.

The Social Democratic Federation (SDF) (See p. ••)

Founded – 1881 as the 'Democratic Federation'. It became the SDF in 1884.

Leaders

HM Hyndman - Old Etonian and London Stockbroker who wrote the classic *England for All* which tried to popularise the ideas of Karl Marx.

William Morris – Poet.

HH Champion – A former military man.

RB Cunninghame-Graham – Scottish laird and Liberal Crofters MP. (See p.106)

The SDF was the first socialist body in Britain since the phenomenon of Owenism in the 1830s. Its ideology was Marxist and its objective was to build a mass working-class political party. Hyndman and his colleagues in the SDF actually fixed the year of 1889, the centenary of the French Revolution, as the beginning of "the complete International Social Revolution".

The SDF was temporarily important in the labour movement during the 1880s, although it was dogged by internal disputes. Early in its career, Morris quarrelled with Hyndman. Morris left the SDF along with other prominent personalities to form the Socialist League. During the eighties and early nineties, the SDF attempted to organise the unemployed. Some SDF activists even went as far as drilling the unemployed. For many socialists in the labour movement the SDF's revolutionary line was far too extreme. The SDF, however, argued that socialists in the mainstream labour movement were weak and indecisive.

By the end of the decade, when trade revived, the SDF went into decline. Although it failed to gain any real electoral support, the SDF contributed much to the development of socialist thought.

The Fabian Society

Founded – 1884.

Leading Members – Sydney and Beatrice Webb, George Bernard Shaw, HG Wells, Frank Podmore.

This small socialist society, whose middle-class intellectual membership came from around the London area, played a key role in developing the ideology of British socialism. Originally the word 'Fabian' was used by Podmore when describing the strategy which he believed socialists should adopt. He said that

> "For the right moment you must wait, as Fabius did most patiently when warring against Hannibal, though many censured his delays: but when the time comes you must strike hard, as Fabius did, or your waiting will be in vain and fruitless." (Quoted in *The Origins of the Labour Party* by Henry Pelling p. 34 Pub. Oxford.)

In the early days the Fabians opposed the more revolutionary views of the SDF, choosing to concentrate on the production of tracts and essays, which have become a notable contribution to socialist thought.

In 1888, a series of lectures entitled 'The Basis and Prospects of Socialism' were given in London's Radical/Liberal clubs. These were published in 1889 as the *Fabian*

Sydney and Beartrice Webb

Essays in Socialism. Pelling, the historian, describes these essays as "the most important literary product of the Society, or for that matter the indigenous socialist movement as a whole".

The conclusions of these essays are as follows:

- Webb argued that the ideas of socialism were already winning, and that socialism meant that there should be public control of the means of production.
- William Clark argued that Britain would follow the USA in the creation of large industrial combines and the existence of these would make an easy transfer to state control.
- Graham Wallas and Annie Besant looked to a decentralised socialist Britain, stressing the implementation of a socialist programme through local government.
- George Bernard Shaw emphasised that the extension of democracy would advance the cause of socialism. He stressed a gradual approach towards the ending of private property with owners receiving compensation.

Like the SDF, the Fabians never had a large membership, numbers being in the hundreds rather than in the thousands. Nevertheless, the society had a profound influence on the history and development of the British labour movement.

> "...it was not for their immediate political tactics, but for their success in formulating a long-term evolutionary programme, that the Fabians were to be important in the eventual foundation of the Labour Party." (From *The Origins of the Labour Party* by Henry Pelling p. 77 Pub. Oxford.)

James Keir Hardie

Hardie was born at Legbrannock, near Holytown, in Lanarkshire in 1856, the illegitimate son of Mary Kerr who later married David Hardie, a ship's carpenter. As the eldest child in the family, he started work at the age of eight, first as a message boy then as a trapper down the mines. He received his education at night school.

James Keir Hardie

As a young man, he became a strong temperance supporter and joined the Evangelical Union, despite the fact that his family was not at all religious. Gradually he became involved in trade union activities, where, in common with most unionists, his political sympathies lay with the Liberal Party.

Hardie was sacked from his local pit for trying to organise trade union activities. Continuing with this work he earned a living for four years as a local correspondent with the *Cumnock Advertiser*. By 1887 he had succeeded in setting up the Ayrshire Miners Union and the Scottish Miners Federation.

During these years, Hardie read the works of Marx, William Morris, HH Hyndman and Henry George. He visited London in 1887 with a delegation of miners. Here he made contact with socialists and attended several SDF meetings. In the end, Hardie rejected the revolutionary class war analysis of the SDF.

> "His views had already developed by way of Henry George from Liberalism to Socialism; but these views were assimilated into the background of his own life and experience, which was something that the London Socialist could not share." (From *The Origins of the Labour Party* by Henry Pelling p. 64 Pub. Oxford.)

In the autumn of 1887 Hardie was adopted as the Parliamentary candidate for North Ayrshire on behalf of the miners, and in early 1888 when the mid-Lanark seat became vacant he stood at the by-election. Despite vigorous campaigning, and standing on a platform of representation for the working-man, he came bottom of the poll with 617 votes out of 7,000. In 1888 the power of the existing parties was still too strong, even for a local candidate.

Convinced of the need for a separate political party with a distinctive socialist identity, Hardie and others formed the Scottish Labour Party in 1889. At the same time he resigned from the Liberal Party.

In the 1892 General Election Hardie was elected as the independent MP for the constituency of West Ham, having been adopted as a candidate by a local Radical club. At the same time, John Burns was elected as MP for the constituency of Battersea. These two men were the first Labour MPs, marking a significant milestone in the history of the labour movement. In 1893, Hardie was instrumental in forming the Independent Labour Party which, in 1900, became part of the Labour Representation Committee which later became the Labour Party as we know it today.

By the early 1890s, it was becoming clear that there was a need to bring the various traditions and organisations of British socialism together. Keir Hardie called for such a meeting at the TUC in 1892. At what became the founding conference of the *Independent Labour Party* at Bradford in 1893, the delegates adopted a gradualist programme of social reform which sought to win the eight hour day, state benefits for old age and sickness, free education and the abolition of all indirect taxes.

> "Proclaiming a Socialist system as their objective, both the Fabian Society and the Independent Labour Party set out in practice to get not Socialism, but social changes pointing in a Socialist direction." (From *The Common People* by GDH Cole and Raymond Postgate p. 423 Pub. University Paperbacks.)

Neither the Fabians, representing the gradualist, nor the SDF, representing the revolutionary strands in British socialist thought were satisfied with the birth of the ILP. The Fabians tried and failed to persuade the TUC to set up its own Labour Party, and in the short-term saw the future of socialism in the Liberal Party. The SDF believed that the ILP would water down socialist principles in order to gain votes and funding from the unions.

Unlike the established political parties, the ILP did not have a centralised organisation, which was a major weakness. In addition, it was always short of funds as local branches regularly failed to pay their subscriptions to the national headquarters which employed one secretary and an assistant. The ILP appealed to the unions for financial support, but in the early 1890s the movement was still dominated by the skilled unions whose leaders supported the Lib-Lab perspective.

At the 1895 General Election, the ILP put up 28 candidates, none of whom were successful, Hardie himself losing his seat at West Ham. However, the ILP did have some success in the 1890s in local elections and by the turn of the century could claim 106 local councillors and a good representation on School Boards and Poor Law Boards of

Towards the turn of the century, changes in the trade union movement itself, added to economic uncertainty and a growing realisation that the Conservative and Liberal Parties had little to offer the poor, turned many skilled workers in the direction of socialism. In addition, the employers' 'counter attack' of the late 1890s persuaded the unions that a political defence through Parliament was needed. Accordingly, at the 1899 TUC, the Railways Servants Union proposed a conference of all "cooperative, socialistic, trade unions and other working organisations ... to devise ways and means for securing the return of an increased number of Labour Members to the next Parliament".

The historic Conference (now regarded as the birthplace of the Labour Party) took place on the 27th February 1900 in London. At the Conference the SDF called for the new organisation to have clearly defined socialist aims, whereas those of the Lib-Lab viewpoint supported more limited aims. The ILP took a middle course between the two opposing points of view.

The Conference accepted a resolution from Hardie which proposed that:

- A distinct Labour group in Parliament be set up.
- Such a group would have its own Whips and distinct policies.
- It would legislate "in the direct interests of labour".

Thus, the *Labour Representation Committee* was set up. It became simply the *Labour Party* in 1906.

The LRC had an Executive Committee of 12: 7 from the unions, 1 from the Fabian Society, and 2 each from the ILP and the SDF. From the outset the LRC was going to be dominated by the unions.

> "The foundation of the LRC was a triumph for the advocates of independent labour representation, but it did not overnight transform the character of working-class politics." (From *Labour and Socialism* by James Hinton p. 72 Pub. Wheatsheaf.)

The LRC was now, however, a distinctive political party. Each group put forward its own candidates at elections and was responsible for their expenses. The LRC had no national party organisation because it was a coalition of organisations which already existed. Individuals became LRC members by joining an organisation like the ILP or the SDF. Nevertheless, the LRC was the base from which a national Labour Party could be formed in the future.

THE LABOUR MOVEMENT 1900-1979

As we have seen, the year 1900 brought together many of the different strands within the labour movement in the formation of the LRC.

The years 1900-14 were difficult ones for the labour movement. Early in the new century the unions came under attack, and in 1901 the Taff Vale Railway Company of South Wales sued the Amalgamated Society of Railway Servants for damages caused by a strike. The case went to the House of Lords and, against expectations, the com-

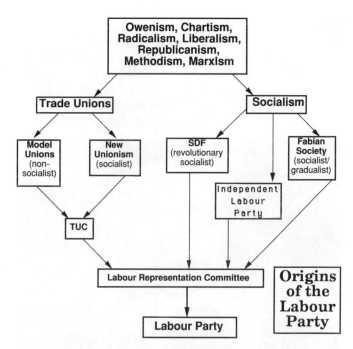

Figure 2.1 (Adapted from *A Social & Economic History of Britain* by SL Case & DJ Hall p.89 Pub. Edward Arnold)

pany won damages of £23,000 from the union. This was a crushing blow to all trade unions since it meant that strike action would be impractical if their funds were not protected by law. Nevertheless, while the Taff Vale case limited union freedom of action, it unexpectedly helped the LRC. Unions which had failed to affiliate in 1900 now rushed to do so. By 1903 individual membership had doubled, bringing in workers from the older skilled unions as well as the new general unions.

Politically, Labour made some notable gains. Victories at by-elections in 1902-3 increased Labour's representation in Parliament from 2 to 5. However, the LRC's candidates only did well in areas where the Liberals did badly or even withdrew their candidate. With a general election looming, both the LRC and the Liberals realised that it would be electoral suicide to fight each other in certain constituencies. In the light of this, the parties concluded an electoral pact by which the LRC was unopposed by the Liberals in 30 constituencies.

The LRC fielded 50 candidates in the 1906 General Election, 29 of whom were elected. Added to the 13 miners MPs, 4 unaffiliated trade union MPs and 7 Lib-Lab MPs, Labour's total representation in the House of Commons was 53. (See p.59 & 73) Although the Liberal Party had won a crushing victory, Labour was now in a stronger position than ever before to influence events. Thus, the years 1906-14 saw Labour cooperating with the Liberals to bring into being the social legislation which is generally regarded as having laid the foundations of the modern welfare state. (See p.59 & 73) In addition, Labour was able to persuade the Liberals to pass the *Trade Disputes Act of 1906*, which benefited the trade unions by setting aside the Taff Vale judgment.

Between 1906 and 1914, the Labour leadership concentrated the party's efforts on building up its strength across the country. This policy brought considerable success. In 1909 the Miners Federation affiliated to the Labour Party, immediately bringing in an additional 16 former Lib-Lab MPs.

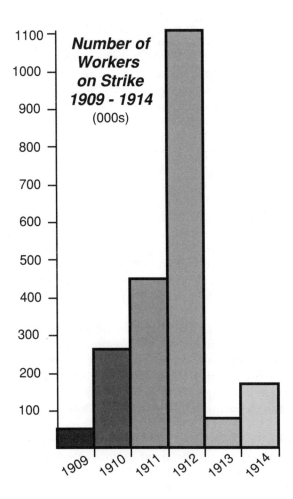

Figure 2.2

During this period finance was a problem for Labour as the Party's progress had been hindered for a time by the *Osborne Judgment* of 1909. When a union affiliated to the Labour Party, it used part of a member's weekly dues to help fund the Party. This was known as 'the political levy'. WV Osborne, a member of the Railman's Union and a Liberal, objecting to his union's support for Labour, took his complaint to court. In 1909 the case reached the House of Lords, where it was decided that, under the Trade Union Acts, unions could not use their funds for political purposes. As a result, the Labour Party was faced with financial disaster. It was partly saved by the *Parliament Act* of 1911 which made provision for the payment of MPs. The Osborne Judgment was finally reversed in 1913. The *Trade Union Act* of that year permitted a political levy to be charged by unions if a majority of members agreed and so long as those who objected were allowed to 'contract out'.

During this period, many socialists, both inside and outside Parliament, were far from happy with Labour's progress. The ILP tried to get the Party to incorporate into the constitution resolutions stating that socialism was the ultimate goal, but failed to achieve this before the war. Socialists were also sceptical of the Liberal welfare reforms which Labour had supported. (See p.60) These reforms, they asserted, did little for the poor, and the welfare bureaucracy which was set up served only to reward the 'deserving', while punishing the 'undeserving' poor.

Socialists wanted more rapid change. They pointed to the failure of Labour to win any of the 14 by-elections contested between 1910 and 1914 as evidence that a more radical approach was required. For people like Tom Mann and Ben Tillet, and Scottish socialists such as William Gallacher, the answer to the problems of the working class lay in *Syndicalism*, a brand of radical socialism which advocated workers' control of industry and direct action by the unions.

"... Syndicalism had come into Scotland with the formation in 1903 of the Socialist Labour Party, a breakaway from the SDF which took away the majority of the Scottish branches. Syndicalism was basically a plan for turning trade unions from organs of defence into organs to attack capitalism. The trade unions were to take over industry and run it themselves in the interests of the workers, bypassing orthodox political action which was regarded as worse than useless ... It was hostile to trade or craft unions, and wanted the workers to organise in industrial unions, ultimately to be joined in one big union which would be the instrument of social revolution." (From *In the Rapids of Revolution* by John McLean, p. 13 of biographical introduction by Nan Milton Pub. Allison & Busby)

The years 1910-14, as well as being years of general social unrest and economic uncertainty, were a time of trade union militancy and unprecedented industrial unrest, as figure 2.2 and table 2.2 demonstrate.

The syndicalists aimed at first of all creating large industrial unions. In 1910 Ben Tillet founded the Transport Workers Federation, which was unsuccessfully involved in strike action in 1912. In the same year 850,000 miners stayed out on strike for 5 weeks. Government intervention eventually guaranteed the miners a minimum wage. Also in 1912, three rail unions combined to form the National Union of Railwaymen, and the following year the 'Triple Alliance' of transport, mining and rail unions was formed. Unfortunately for the syndicalists, the 3 unions remained separate entities, but they did agree to act together in presenting their demands to employers simultaneously, and to go on strike together if necessary.

The coming of war in 1914 ended the unrest, but the period 1910-14 did demonstrate the impatience of many socialists in the trade union movement with the Labour Party in Parliament. In its own way, each arm of the labour movement had achieved significant advances for the working class. However, on the eve of war in 1914 Labour was still not a comprehensive working-class political movement. It had failed to organise two significant elements of the working class, women and the poor; it was

Number of Working Days Lost by Strike Action 1909-14	
Year	Days Lost
1909	660,000
1910	8,796,000
1911	4,974,000
1912	34,226,000
1913	3,937,000
1914	5,154,000

Table 2.2

still in a minority position in Parliament; and, more seriously, it believed that the working class was not yet strong enough to bring about radical change in society.

The Labour Movement and the War

When war broke out in August 1914, the labour movement as a whole generally supported it. There were, however, exceptions. (See p.45/6) Ramsay MacDonald, a member of the ILP and chairman of the Parliamentary Labour Party, took up an anti-war stance and was removed from his position, being replaced by Arthur Henderson.

Keir Hardie's anti-war sentiment stemmed from his Christianity and his Socialism. In the last years of his life he argued vigorously against the war fever which he saw gripping the country in 1914. His last article for the *Labour Leader*, shortly before his death, vividly portrayed his despair.

> "When a set of selfish and incompetent statesmen have plunged nations into shedding each other's blood, it is the worker who is called upon to line the trenches; to murder his fellow worker with whom he has not, and never had, any quarrel; it is the worker who is commanded, under the penalty of being branded a traitor, to carry woe and desolation into the hearts of womenfolk and children." (Quoted in *Keir Hardie and the Labour Party* by Hyman Shapiro p. 86 Pub. Longman.)

In Scotland, socialists such as Harry McShane and John McLean were active on Clydeside during the war. For them, the vital struggle was not for better conditions, or against dilution of labour as fought for by the Clyde Shop Stewards Committee, but the war itself. McLean was arrested in 1917 and sentenced to five years in jail. His colleague Harry McShane described McLean's trial in his book *No Mean Fighter*.

> "... John McLean turned his trial into a political forum. He conducted his own defence and spoke for over an hour in his final summing up. He said: 'I am not here to be accused. I am here as the accuser of capitalism, dripping with blood from head to foot.' He indicted international capitalism for what it had done in the war, and was preparing to do against the Russian Revolution. But he also attacked those workers who had been prepared to give record output for the war." (From *No Mean Fighter* by Harry McShane and Joan Smith p. 97 Pub. Pluto Press.)

Overall, the labour movement supported the war, some sections with 'jingoistic fervour', other sections giving just enough support to demonstrate their patriotism. During the war the TUC called an industrial truce with the employers, accepting that they would have to give up many hard won rights. Thus, the TUC accepted:

- Dilution of labour, that is the use of unskilled men and women in place of skilled workers.
- The provisions of the 1915 Munitions Act which effectively reduced the possibility of strike action.
- Compulsory arbitration of disputes.
- Direction of labour.

While most sections of the trade union movement followed the official line of cooperation, there was dissent in South Wales, Sheffield and Clydeside. In South Wales the miners came out on strike in 1915 and, refusing arbitration, they only went back to work when Lloyd George, at that time Minister of Munitions, gave in to their demands. On Clydeside and in Sheffield, socialists in the engineering unions saw the TUC's policy of cooperation as a betrayal of the working class. In both areas Shop Stewards' Committees were set up. On the Clyde, Committee leaders William Gallacher and David Kirkwood took a tough line on the issues of dilution, pay, and workers' control. The government reacted strongly, imprisoning some leaders, and the agitation slowly died down. In 1917 in Sheffield, the shop stewards, led by JT Murphy, brought the engineers out on strike to prevent the conscription of engineers into the forces. The strike succeeded in temporarily winning exemption for some skilled men.

Although socialists like Murphy, Gallacher and Kirkwood were always a minority in the labour movement, they are important because their views represent a continuing strand in socialist tradition. They saw the Workers Committees acting as the vanguard of socialism, gradually undermining and defeating capitalist control of industry.

In 1916 the Labour Party and Trade Unionists were brought into the coalition government. Arthur Henderson became Minister of Education, John Hodge (Secretary of the Steel Smelters Union) became Minister of Labour and George Barnes (Secretary of the Engineers Union) became Minister of Pensions. As part of the government, these men argued for nationalisation of key industries in the post war period.

Overall the war strengthened and changed the labour movement in the following ways:

1 Trade Union membership almost doubled between 1914 and 1920.
2 The percentage of unionised women workers increased from 9% to 24%.
3 Unemployment during the war years was low, and standards of living rose, although some historians would argue that union leaders were complacent in not gaining more at a time when they had the power to do so.
4 Employers' recognition of trade unions increased.
5 The experience of war served to draw the working class together as never before.
6 The achievement of a foothold in government served to enhance a general mood of assertiveness in the labour movement.
7 The ILP lost a lot of its influence within the Labour Party because of its opposition to the war.

During the war, the Labour Party produced two documents, which were of great importance to the future: the *Labour Party Constitution* and *Labour and the New Social Order*. From its inception the Labour Party had been at a disadvantage because it was a federation of local societies. Arthur Henderson and Sydney Webb changed the situation by writing a constitution for the whole party, to which all members would have to agree. It was accepted by the 1918 Party Conference. The socialist aims of the Party were outlined in *Clause 4* as being to "secure for the producers by hand and by brain the full fruits of their industry and the most equitable distribution thereof that may be possible, upon the basis of the common ownership of the means of production and the best obtainable system of popular administration and control of each industry and service." A new national party organisation was set up to recruit individual members who could identify with the constitution and programme of the Labour Party.

Labour and the New Social Order was the title of the Labour Party's programme published in 1918. It aimed to broaden Labour's appeal to the new electorate enfranchised by the 1918 Reform Act. Like the constitution, this historic document set Labour on the path of socialism, committing it to policies for:

- The nationalisation of land, and the fuel and transport industries.
- A planned economy.
- Full employment.
- The provision of adequate social welfare.

Following the armistice in November 1918, Labour withdrew from the coalition, in order to fight the ensuing election as an independent party.

THE INTERWAR YEARS

While the interwar years were a time of relative success for the Labour Party, in that it was elected to government, it was also an era of economic depression and real hardship for many of those the Party sought to represent. The effects of the First World War lasted far longer and were much more far-reaching in British society than initially thought, bringing about a readjustment in society, industry, industrial relations and politics between the wars.

In the industrial and political arena, the labour history of the twenties is dominated by the General Strike of 1926. However, the strike was merely part of the readjustment, mentioned above, which stemmed from the war. It also stemmed from the determination of governments, particularly Conservative, to deal with the problem of economic change by reducing wages and trade union power.

Initially, after the end of the war, the country enjoyed a brief period of economic prosperity. This lasted from 1918 until the spring of 1920. During this period, the Miners Federation made demands for a 6 hour day, nationalisation of the mines, and a 30% increase in pay. To avoid a strike, the Coalition Government appointed the *Sankey Commission* to investigate the industry. The Commission's report was rejected by the Government which at that time was dominated by the Conservatives. It had recommended pay increases for the miners and nationalisation of the pits. By 1920, the railwaymen and the miners had been on strike. In addition, the dockers had been awarded higher wages after a Commission of Inquiry. In Scotland, the so-called '40 hours strike' in 1919 had led to troops and armoured cars being deployed on the streets of Glasgow.

By the time the slump came in 1920 the Government, in anticipation of industrial conflict, had already made preparations. The *Police Act* of 1919 prevented the Police Federation from associating with other unions or the TUC, and

the *Emergency Powers Act* of 1920 gave the Government sweeping powers to deal with all-out strikes.

In early 1921, unemployment had increased to over 2,000,000 with some areas, notably South Wales, Lancashire, North East England and Clydeside, being particularly badly affected, due to their reliance on traditional industries which could not now compete with foreign goods. The coal industry, still run by the Government, was particularly badly hit by the recession. The Government saw a solution to the problem in returning the pits to their prewar private owners, a bitter blow to the miners who wanted nationalisation. While accepting the return of their assets, the owners stated that wage reductions would be necessary. Thus, when the leaders of the Miners Federation refused to accept pay cuts, a coal strike began on 1st April 1921. The miners called on other members of the Triple Alliance for support and a General Strike was set, originally for 12th April. The Government intervened at this point and the leaders of the Triple Alliance negotiated with Lloyd George. Hodge, the secretary of the Miners Union, accepted a deal by which the Government would subsidise the miners' wages at their old rate while negotiations continued with the mine owners, but it was rejected by his union executive. Meantime, the leaders of the rail and transport unions used Hodge's acceptance of Lloyd George's offer as an excuse to call off the threatened General Strike, only hours before it was due to start on the new date of 15th April. Thus the miners were left to fight alone and were eventually forced back to work on much less favourable terms than they were initially offered. On that occasion the power of the 'Triple Alliance' turned into a debacle. The date of 15th April 1921 became known as 'Black Friday', a day in trade union history now associated with betrayal, although in reality it was more a failure of the 3 leaders of the Triple Alliance properly to work out an effective mechanism for their alliance.

In order to prevent the same scenario repeating itself, the TUC took a hand in matters, and formed a General Council, whose aim was to coordinate the labour movement's 'industrial muscle', and thus prevent the future isolation of a single union in an industrial dispute.

On the political front, the Labour Party fought the 1918 General Election against the coalition on a socialist plat-

Labour's Performance at General Elections, 1918-1935				
Year	Votes	MPs Elected	Number of Candidates	% Share of Vote
1918	2,385,472	63	388	22.2
1922	4,241,383	142	411	29.5
1923	4,438,508	191	422	30.5
1924	5,489,077	151	512	33.0
1929	8,389,512	288	571	37.1
1931*	6,649,630	52	515	30.6
1935	8,325,491	154	552	37.9

Table 2.3

(*In the 1931 Election the Labour Party was split between those who were *National Labour*, ie. supporters of the Coalition, and *Labour* whose supporters were of the official Labour Party, and against the Coalition. National Labour in 1931 fielded 20 candidates of whom 13 were elected. It gained a total of 341,370 votes which was 1.6% of the total vote.)

form. It won 63 seats becoming, for the first time, the official Opposition in Parliament. One disappointing feature of the election was the failure of leading Party figures such as Arthur Henderson, Ramsay MacDonald and Sydney Webb to win seats. Nevertheless, Labour had, for the first time, contested an election without the cushion of a pact with the Liberals and had increased its representation in Parliament. As the reforms in national Party organisation, linked to the growth of active local constituency associations, began to take hold, so Labour was able to increase its share of the vote throughout the 1920s. In addition, the election of Ramsay MacDonald as Party Leader in 1922 automatically made him Leader of the Opposition in Parliament, gaining the Labour cause further exposure in the national media.

Chairmen and Leaders of the Parliamentary Labour Party in the Interwar Years

1922	JR MacDonald
1931	A Henderson
1932	G Landsbury
1935	C Attlee

Table 2.4

The 1922 General Election saw Labour massively increase its Parliamentary representation to 142 and increase its share of the vote to 29.2%. The following year, Baldwin became Conservative Prime Minister when Bonar Law resigned. Baldwin's strategy for dealing with unemployment was to introduce tariffs to protect British industry. Since this step meant abandoning Britain's traditional policy of free trade, he called a General Election on the issue. Labour emerged from the 1923 Election with 191 MPs, an increase of 49.

1923 General Election

Party	Number of MPs	% Share of Vote
Conservative	258	38.1
Liberal	159	29.6
Labour	191	30.5
Others	7	1.8

Table 2.5

Baldwin, as leader of the largest party, formed a Government, which lasted only a matter of weeks before the Labour and Liberal Parties combined to defeat it in the House of Commons. As only a minority of Conservatives could stomach an alliance with the Liberals to keep Labour out, Baldwin recommended to King George V that he ask MacDonald, as leader of the main opposition party, to form a Government.

MacDonald accepted the invitation and, with Liberal help, the first Labour Government took office on 22 January 1924. He insisted that his Party take office, believing that

Labour Government 1924

Prime Minister	JR MacDonald
Chancellor of the Exchequer	P Snowden
Foreign Secretary	JR MacDonald (PM)
Scottish Office	W Adamson
Minister of Health	J Wheatley
President of Board of Trade	S Webb

Table 2.6

it would only increase the credibility of Labour for the future by demonstrating that Labour could govern responsibly. His Government was, however, dependent on Liberal support which, in reality, ruled out the possibility of any real socialist legislation. As a result, little of any lasting socialist value was achieved. The Government tried to deal with unemployment by increasing benefits, and it planned to create jobs by road and rail construction projects. Labour's real domestic achievement was brought about by Wheatley, the only left-winger in the Cabinet, in the area of housing. Here, plans were set in motion to subsidise Local Councils which were prepared to build council houses at controlled rents for the poor.

During this period, relations with the TUC were soured when the Government responded to the threat of a sympathy strike by the underground workers by invoking the Emergency Powers Act.

MacDonald himself concentrated his efforts on foreign policy, acting as Foreign Secretary. He tried to reach a compromise on the reparations issue with Germany, which ran against Labour Party policy of opposing reparations altogether. However, MacDonald found favour with his party and the unions in his attempts to negotiate a trade agreement with the USSR. Nevertheless, it was over the question of the USSR that the Government fell from power in October 1924. While the ensuing election saw Labour increase its share of the vote, only 151 Labour MPs were elected. The issue of the forged 'Zinoviev Letter', leaked during the campaign, served to whip up anti-communist hysteria and paved the way for a landslide Conservative victory. For Labour, the reality and limitations of power during its first term in office had proved to be a salutary experience. Nevertheless, with the Liberals decimated in the House of Commons, being reduced to a rump of 40 MPs, Labour was now the major anti-Conservative Party in Britain.

Labour's first period in office put a huge strain on the relationship with the unions. In 1925, attempts were made by some trade unionists to persuade the Labour Party Conference to oppose future participation in minority governments. Although this failed, it was becoming clear that in the immediate future the unions were going to increasingly pursue their own political platform through direct industrial action. This strategy reached its climax in the General Strike of 1926 which, in the eyes of some observers, brought the country to the brink of revolution.

Background – In 1924 the mine owners, faced with foreign competition, falling profits and the need for investment, ended all national wage agreements and proposed that wage reductions would take place from July 1925. The Miners Federation, under AJ Cook, made arrangements to resist through strike action. It was supported by the TUC and the transport unions who agreed to an embargo on coal in the event of a strike. At the last moment the Government, fearing the effects of such action, intervened, promising a Royal Commission and a subsidy to the industry for 9 months. The unions saw this victory of 'Red Friday' (Friday 31 July 1925) as 'sweet revenge' for the defeat of 'Black Friday'.

The Samuel Commission (2 Liberals, a banker and a cotton industrialist) reported early in 1926. It proposed the reorganisation of the mining industry under private ownership and substantial wage cuts for the miners.

The Miners Federation refused to accept the findings of the Commission. As a result, the unions empowered the General Council of the TUC to negotiate directly with the Government on behalf of the miners. The policy of the Council during the negotiations was to get the Government to support reorganisation, in the hope that the miners might in return be prepared to accept the wage reductions. At the end of April 1926 the situation deteriorated quickly.

A bus being driven by a volunteer driver with a police escort

30 April   The miners refused to accept pay cuts, therefore the owners 'locked out' the miners. The TUC sent out General Strike notices to take effect from midnight on 3rd May. At the same time the Government activated the Emergency Powers Act.

1 May   The TUC took charge of negotiations. The dispute was now a direct conflict between workers and Government.

3 May   The Government terminated negotiations with the TUC on the pretext that printers had refused to print an article in a London newspaper. The strike began at midnight.

Course of the Strike – The TUC called 2.5 million workers in mining, transport, engineering, shipbuilding and steel, printing and the power industries out on strike. To some trade unionists, the strike foreshadowed a workers revolution. To TUC leaders like Bevin and Thomas, it was a last resort on behalf of workers trying to defend their living standards. In reality, trade unionists had made few preparations for the strike. During the strike, the Government recruited volunteers to keep essential services running. It also published its own newspaper, *The British Gazette*, in an attempt to manage the news. The Government presented its case as a challenge to Parliament by a minority trying to impose its will on the whole community.

In response to Government propaganda, the TUC produced *The British Worker*. Local strike committees also produced their own newssheets.

In Scotland, the STUC had waited for a lead from the London TUC before taking action. Consequently, few preparations were made. Nevertheless, the strike in Scotland was virtually solid.

"The News Bulletin issued by Head Office of the National Union of Railwaymen on the evening of 4th May indicated that, in a random list of almost 40 Scots branches, only Forres with 4 and Polmont with 3 had members who refused to strike. At Aberdeen the position was said to be, 'On strike, 1200 : Blacklegs – Nil'." (From *Some Aspects of the General Strike in Scotland* in *Essays in Scottish Labour History* by Ian MacDougall (Ed) p. 175 Pub John Donald.)

Although numerous clashes between miners and the army and police did take place, the strike was remarkably free of serious violence. Troops had to be called in to restore order in the docks in London, and a railway line was sabotaged in County Durham. In Scotland, there were some violent incidents, mainly associated with pickets and blacklegs.

"The running of trams in Glasgow prompted a march into the city on 6th May by some 500 miners from Cambuslang and Newton, intent on strengthening the pickets at the tramway depots at Ruby Street and Paton Street. A 'fierce struggle' with police ensued and sixty six people were arrested. At Tranent in East Lothian on 7th May, a road-picketing incident led to a serious melee during which police were forced to retreat to the police station. It was then besieged by a crowd of over 1,000 and all the windows smashed." (Ibid p. 184 .)

At Blantyre, near Glasgow, miners reacted angrily to the "importation of miners from other districts" under police guard.

"Shortly after three o'clock on Wednesday a serious

strikers came into conflict with the police who were ultimately compelled to draw their batons and charge the mob, which numbered about six or seven hundred. On the police making their charge, the crowd scattered in all directions, and in a few minutes the police were masters of the situation." (From *Hamilton Advertiser*, October 23, 1926. Quoted in *A History of the Scottish Miners* by R Page Arnot p. 177 Pub. Allen & Unwin.)

Seven men were arrested in connection with the incident.

The General Strike lasted for nine days, ending on 12 May. The more moderate TUC leaders had begun to waver at the end of the first week, fearing a move to extremism in some local areas. The ending of the strike came about when Sir Herbert Samuel suggested to JH Thomas of the NUR that a negotiating committee from the TUC meet him for discussions. The committee was formed with no miners' representation. It accepted a memorandum drawn up personally by Samuel. A deputation from the TUC then met with Baldwin and the strike ended. In effect, the TUC had surrendered unconditionally to the government.

In his memorandum Samuel had proposed that a national Wages Board for the coal industry be set up and that wages would be reduced only when the proposals of the original Samuel Commission had been carried out.

There was little change between these proposals and the government's original negotiating position prior to the strike. Further, the TUC secured no guarantee that strikers would not be victimised.

Initially workers believed that a victory had been won, but when the terms became known the initial euphoria gave way to bitterness and betrayal. The headlines in the *Daily Mail* of 'Surrender of the Revolutionaries', and in the *British Gazette* of 'Surrender Received by Premier' fuelled the resentment. Stunned by the TUC's desertion of their cause, the miners fought on, against the advice of many of their leaders, until November.

In the end they were forced back to work on terms which included longer hours, cuts in pay, and a return to the hated district agreements which, in effect, prevented the union from engaging in national wage bargaining. By the end of 1930, miners' wages had dropped to their pre-1914 level, and many had lost their jobs. One blacklisted miner only got his job back in 1939 when war broke out.

Was Britain on the verge of revolution during the strike? The evidence shows that, in fact, quite the reverse was true. The TUC was unprepared for the strike, whereas the Government had been preparing since 'Red Friday' of the previous year. Further, had the Government truly believed that revolution was imminent in 1926, it would have been irresponsible of it to provoke a strike. Indeed, it was the Government through its propaganda machine which raised the spectre of revolution rather than the unions. Trade union propaganda, such as it was, while emphasising class solidarity, also stressed order, discipline, and staying within the law. Finally, *the strike remained an industrial dispute.* The TUC's objectives were anything but revolutionary, and although Communists supported the strike, their power base was too small to have any influence.

In the wake of the strike, the Government hit back at the labour movement with the *Trade Disputes Act (1927)*. This piece of legislation symbolised the Conservative victory over the unions and its effect extended to the Labour Party itself. The main terms of the Act were:

- Sympathy strikes, and strikes designed to "coerce the government" or "inflict hardship on the community" were made illegal.
- Legal restrictions on picketing were extended.
- Closed shop arrangements in public sector employment became illegal.
- Civil Service unions were banned from affiliating to the TUC and the Labour Party.
- Trade Union members now had to 'contract in' if they wished to pay the political levy.
- Many of the clauses in this Act were deliberately vague in order to allow the government maximum scope in implementing the Act as it saw fit.

The General Strike and its aftermath had two important effects on the labour movement. Firstly, it drew the Labour Party and the unions closer together. Both groups saw the attack on the political levy in the Trade Disputes Act as a direct attack on the labour movement, and were determined to resist. Nevertheless, between 1927 and 1929 Labour lost 25 per cent of its funding due to the Act. Secondly, the attack on the political levy had a positive effect, in that it forced the Labour Party to develop its local organisation and recruit new individual members.

Labour in Power 1929-31

In the General Election of 1929, Labour emerged as the largest single party in the House of Commons.

1929 General Election	
Party	**MPs**
Conservative	260
Liberal	59
Labour	288
Others	8

Table 2.7

When Ramsay MacDonald accepted office for his minority Government, his aim was to ensure that, once in office, Labour would remain there. He was, however, faced with two problems. (See p. 85-88) Labour was in a minority position, dependent on Liberal support, and therefore it was going to be difficult to enact real socialist measures. In

The Second Labour Government 1929-31	
Prime Minister	JR MacDonald
Chancellor of the Exchequer	P Snowden
Foreign Secretary	A Henderson
Home Secretary	I Clynes
Minister of Health	A Greenwood
Minister of Labour	M Bondfield
President of Board of Trade	W Graham
Minister of Transport	H Morrison

Table 2.8

addition, the economic situation deteriorated rapidly between 1929 and 1931, which virtually ruled out plans for dealing with the unemployment problem by public works schemes and other measures.

While achieving some success in the area of foreign policy, Labour's domestic policy foundered on the rocks of a faltering economy. Three pieces of Labour legislation are worthy of note:

- *1929 Coal Prices Act*: Reduced the length of a mining 'shift' from 8 hours to 7.5 hours.

- *1930 Housing Act*: Provided grants for slum clearance programmes.

- *1931 Agriculture Marketing Act*: Protected farmers by allowing marketing boards to fix prices.

In other areas, Labour failed to repeal parts of the Trade Disputes Act, and Bills on Electoral Reform and Education were destroyed by amendments. One piece of socialist legislation, in transport, which set up a public corporation with a monopoly on public transport, was eventually passed by the National Government in 1933. (See p.88)

Labour's main concern was unemployment. When they took office, this had reached 1 million and was rising. Margaret Bondfield, the first woman Cabinet Minister, boasted that Labour would "cure unemployment in three weeks", but by the middle of 1931 the figure had almost reached the 3 million mark.

The Chancellor of the Exchequer, Philip Snowden, adopted *orthodox financial policies* to deal with the economic downturn. (See p.86) Income tax was increased to 4/6 (22.5p) in the pound and surtax was increased, both with the aim of achieving a balanced budget in order to maintain international confidence in the economy. Snowden believed that socialist policies of nationalisation and social reform could only be financed by a healthy economy. Thus, in the absence of prosperity socialism could not advance.

By the winter of 1930-31, the so-called policy of 'drift' had landed the Government in real trouble in the Commons. It was only able to prevent defeat by promising Commissions and Inquiries. In June 1931 the *Royal Commission on Unemployment Insurance* recommended a 30% cut in benefits, which infuriated the TUC. On 31 July, the *May Committee* (see p.87) on public expenditure warned of a £120 million budget deficit unless public spending was reduced. The report set off a run on the pound, and Government attempts to negotiate credits were made dependent on agreeing a package of spending cuts with the Opposition Parties. While the majority of the Cabinet favoured cuts, a minority refused to accept reductions in unemployment benefit. Deadlocked, the Cabinet resigned on 23 August. However, to the astonishment of the labour movement, MacDonald emerged the next day as leader of a *National Government*, made up of Liberals, Conservatives and three former Labour Cabinet Ministers, Snowden, Thomas and Lord Sankey. (See p.88)

In the history of the labour movement, MacDonald is often portrayed as a traitor who betrayed the working class by joining the coalition. He was expelled from the Party on 31 August 1931, Henderson taking over as leader of the Parliamentary Labour Party (PLP).

In the meantime, the National Government implemented the cuts. This policy led to such widespread opposition that foreign confidence in sterling slumped. As a result, the government abandoned the Gold Standard, the very principle MacDonald had formed the National Government to preserve. (See p.88-95)

The National Government went to the country in October 1931, seeking a fresh mandate. The election campaign was particularly bitter, with charge and counter-charge of betrayal coming from both Labour and National Labour (MacDonald's supporters). The National Government, dominated by the Conservatives, was returned to power with a massive majority. Labour, with 52 MPs, was back to its pre-1914 parliamentary strength, although its share of the vote still held up remarkably well. The Party made up some of its losses in the 1935 Election as well as its share of the vote, but was doomed to spend much of the next 14 years in opposition.

On the industrial front, the Depression of the early thirties decimated union membership. The figures recovered in the late thirties as the unions looked to the new industries for members.

Apart from the economy, the main issue for the labour movement in the 1930s was the advance of Fascism in Europe. The ideological conflict of the Spanish Civil War encouraged individuals such as Ernest Bevin and eventually the TUC to demand that the Labour Party take up a much more aggressive anti-fascist stance. Unions, such as the coalminers, also provided both moral and financial support as was witnessed by the presidential address of Andrew Clarke at the Scottish Miners' Annual Conference of 1937.

> "We as workers, cannot but be deeply concerned as to the ultimate fate of the Spanish Government when we realise the Sinister Forces that are behind the Insurgents, who are doing everything possible to discredit the *Democratically* elected Government of Spain. Every day brings forth fresh evidence of this and clearly reveals the issues involved in the fight that is being waged by the Spanish Workers. Theirs is a brave struggle indeed! One that has called forth the admiration of people in every country. While our members have already given financial assistance yet the need is still so urgent that I would again *appeal* to you for further generous assistance – not as a *Charitable Donation* but as a *Duty* to those who are fighting to preserve our present and future Democratic Rights and Liberties." (From the Scottish Miners' Annual General Meeting June 1937. Quoted in *A History of the Scottish Miners* by R Page Arnot p. 226 Pub. Allen & Unwin.)

In 1939 the TUC accepted what became known as the *Bridlington Agreement*. This agreement became a major symbol of the TUC's authority in the trade union movement. It set out principles designed to stop conflict between unions over members, and gave the TUC powers to intervene in disputes between unions.

19

The Labour Movement in World War II

World War II opened up new opportunities for the labour movement, laying the foundations for the Labour Party's landslide victory in the 1945 General Election.

Initially, the Labour Party declined an offer to serve in Chamberlain's Coalition Government. However, following the fall of France and the emergence of Churchill at the head of a new coalition in 1940, Labour joined the Government. Party Leader Clement Attlee and Anthony Greenwood represented Labour on the five man War Cabinet. Ernest Bevin, Secretary of the TGWU, was appointed Minister of Labour.

Gradually the Government built an integrated war economy, a major plank of which was manpower planning. This policy required good relations between government and unions. Accordingly, Churchill and his colleagues did not force the issue of statutory wage controls, opting instead for 'Order 1305'. This decree gave legal support to a no-strike agreement between unions and employers. It also set up a *National Arbitration Tribunal* to settle industrial disputes. Trade union leaders were expected to moderate wage demands, while the state provided food subsidies, controls on prices, and rationing to keep the cost of living down. In addition Bevin in 1940, by the *Essential Works Order*, got the power to enforce discipline on the labour force. Workers could be fined for absenteeism and indiscipline by this order.

Unemployment was reduced from 1 million at the beginning of 1940, to virtually zero for the duration of the war. Women were encouraged to enter the war effort, and increased welfare provision, in the form of cheap school meals and day nurseries, was provided to help meet the need.

While working-class people supported the war effort, industrial unrest increased. However, most strikes were short and on a small scale. Nevertheless, the average number of working days lost through strikes was higher during the war than in the 1930s. The mining industry was a focus for unrest with strikes in 1942 and 1944 over wages, the escalating accident rate and demands for outright nationalisation of the industry.

One interesting facet of the Labour history of the war is the advances made by the Communist Party. Founded in 1920, the Party made repeated attempts to affiliate to the Labour Party, all to no avail. When the USSR entered the war in 1941, the Communist Party, which had significant strength among trade union shop stewards, changed its policy to one of support for the war effort. Between May 1941 and the end of 1942, its membership increased by 50,000, a massive rise. This period of success was only temporary. Working-class support fell away with the onset of the Cold War.

Tension between left and right within the labour movement continued during the war. The debate over the *Beveridge Report (1942)* was a temporary issue which crystallised the ideological division in Labour's ranks. When the Cabinet only partially accepted Beveridge's proposals, 97 Labour MPs voted against the Government, frustrated at Labour Ministers' lack of fight against Churchill's nega-

tive attitude to the Report. The 1944 Party conference further exposed the impatience of the rank and file of the Movement towards the leadership's failure to 'stand up for Socialism'. While electing left-winger Aneurin Bevan to the National Executive Committee, the conference threw out the leadership's post war proposals because they did not contain any specific pledge for nationalisation. Instead, Ian Mikardo proposed that Labour should bring land, heavy industry, banking, transport and the fuel and power industries into public ownership. This resolution eventually became the basis of Labour's 1945 Election Manifesto.

Victory in the 1945 General Election, in the last two weeks of the war against Japan, may have come as a surprise to some elements of the Labour leadership. When Germany surrendered in May 1945, Churchill offered Attlee and Bevan the opportunity to continue the coalition. Although they wanted to accept, Labour's National Executive overruled their acceptance. Despite the trepidation of the Party leadership at contesting an election against a national war leader of Churchill's stature, Labour won a landslide victory and, securing 45% of the vote, it was able to form the first majority Labour Government.

LABOUR IN POWER 1945-51

Labour's clear mandate from the electorate enabled it to set about implementing a detailed programme of reforms in the areas of *welfare* (see p.100-104) and *nationalisation*. The measures taken in both areas were seen as a victory for socialist principle. To many in the labour movement it seemed that the foundations of a socialist society were being laid through the nationalisation programme (see box opposite). In retrospect, some historians interpret the situation differently.

1 Only 20% of industry was nationalised between 1945 and 1951.
2 Most of the nationalised industries were in a poor state, requiring reorganisation and massive injections of government money.
3 The main effect of Labour's nationalisation programme was to transfer responsibility for loss-making parts of the economy to the public sector.

In the early years of the post-1945 Labour Government,

Labour's Electoral Performance 1945-79

Date	Total Votes	MPs Elected	% Share of Vote
1945	11,995,152	393	47.8
1950	13,266,592	315	46.7
1951	13,948,605	295	48.8
1955	12,404,970	277	46.4
1959	12,215,538	258	43.8
1964	12,205,814	317	44.1
1966	13,064,951	363	47.9
1970	12,179,341	287	43.0
1974 (Feb.)	11,639,243	301	37.1
1974 (Oct.)	11,457,079	319	39.2
1979	11,509,000	268	36.9

Table 2.9

relations with the unions were generally good. About one-third of Labour MPs were sponsored by the unions and this fact, along with the socialist legislation being enacted, held the labour movement together. In 1946 the Government repealed the 1927 Trade Union and Trade Disputes Act, removing the last vestiges of the punitive anti-union legislation which followed the General Strike. In 1948 the unions agreed to a wage freeze in response to a request from the Chancellor, who wanted to keep industry's costs down to boost exports.

Within the trade unions, the issue of Communist influence came to the fore in the late 1940s. As has already been noted, the Communist Party was active in the trade unions in the 1930s and during the war. It supported the government until 1947 when, in response to Labour's anti-Soviet foreign policy, it reversed its stance. As a result, there followed a virtual 'witch-hunt' in the labour movement as 'crypto-communists' were expelled from both trade unions and the Labour Party.

Economically, the Labour Government faced enormous problems. Huge debts incurred during the war had to be paid, in addition to the cost of compensation payments for nationalisation and the cost of setting up the Welfare State. The situation was complicated by the ending of the 'American Lend-Lease Programme', which Lord Keynes described as "Britain's financial Dunkirk". As a short-term measure, the Government borrowed from the Americans and the Canadians, but the money was only used to finance essential imports for industry. The long-term solution was to boost exports, and this the Government attempted to do by maintaining rationing to control imports and by keeping a tight rein on industry to promote production for export. The so-called 'policies of austerity' adopted by Stafford Cripps, the Chancellor, had some success, but Britain's weak financial position led, in 1948, to a devaluation of the pound.

While Labour was undoubtedly successful in setting up the Welfare State and maintaining full employment, the Government failed to solve problems in other areas. In housing, Aneurin Bevan's target of dealing with the post war housing situation by building 200,000 houses per year was not met. In the areas of food and fuel, there were severe shortages in the winter of 1946-47, causing hardship for individuals and difficulties for industry. Taxes also remained high and, added to the continuation of rationing and shortages, began to overshadow the achievements of Attlee's Government.

In February 1950, Labour went to the country and, although returned to power, its Commons majority had dwindled to six. To many contemporary observers it seemed that Labour had simply run out of ideas, its leaders old and worn out by the burden of office.

In the Election, Labour had lost seats which it had previously won in the middle-class areas of the south of England. If the Election result showed anything, it was that those who had voted for Labour in 1945 now wanted an end to austerity, rationing and high taxation.

Nevertheless, Labour continued in office for a further 18 months amid growing disunity within the labour movement. Among rank and file trade unionists there was growing anger that union leaders had put support for the Labour Government before the interests of their members. The Government's handling of unofficial strikes by gas workers and port employees in early 1951 served only to worsen relations between Labour and the unions. The difficulty facing the labour movement is summed up by a letter to the Prime Minister from P Jordan, dated 6 October 1950.

"... It is argued that, under a Socialist Government the power of the Trade Unions to hold the loyalty of their members, must inevitably wither, because the unions are so completely connected with the Government, that they must attempt the impossible task of running with the hare and hunting with the hounds. The argument concludes that so long as wage restraint is necessary, unofficial strikes will become more numerous because men and women, who are mainly preoccupied with their living conditions will lose faith in a leadership that must now take account of interests far wider than those they were elected to serve." (From *British Trade Unionism 1770-1990* by Keith Laybourn p. 167 Pub. Alan Sutton Publishing.)

The outbreak of the Korean War in 1950 and the need for rearmament at the cost of £1,500 million per year further sharpened the tension between left and right in the labour movement. Increased defence spending meant cuts in welfare spending and when Hugh Gaitskell, Cripps' successor as Chancellor, proposed charges for prescriptions

---

POST-1945 NATIONALISATION

1946 – The Bank of England was nationalised.

1946 – The coal industry was nationalised by the Coal Industry Nationalisation Act 1946 which set up the National Coal Board.

1946 – Civil aviation was nationalised by the Civil Aviation Act 1946. It was privatised in the 1980s.

1947 – Public transport was nationalised by the Transport Act 1947. The Transport Act 1953 denationalised road haulage.

1947 – Electricity was nationalised by the Electricity Act 1947. It was privatised in the 1990s.

1948 – Gas was nationalised by the Gas Act 1948, setting up the Gas Council and twelve area Gas Boards. It was privatised in the 1980s.

1949 – The iron and steel industries were nationalised by the Iron and Steel Act 1949, by which the Iron and Steel Corporation of Great Britain was set up. They were denationalised in 1953, renationalised by Labour in 1967 only to be privatised again by the Conservatives in 1983 with another Iron and Steel Act.

1954 – The UK Atomic Energy Authority was set up to manage Britain's nuclear industry.

1968 – The Post Office became a public corporation.

and dental treatment, three left-wing ministers, Aneurin Bevan, Harold Wilson and John Freeman, resigned. As they saw it these measures were a betrayal of socialist principles.

In October 1951 Attlee again went to the country. On this occasion the Conservatives were returned to government with a majority of 17, despite Labour gaining a larger share of the vote. Division in the labour movement, changes in constituency boundaries and loss of political direction all contributed to Labour's defeat.

LABOUR IN OPPOSITION 1951 - 64
In the concluding chapter of his book *Labour and Socialism*, the historian James Hinton describes the post-1951 period as a time when the labour movement was in crisis. In the fifties and sixties Labour's share of votes at general elections fell (See Table 2.9) and Party membership declined dramatically. Trade union membership remained static, increasing in the 1970s but declining in the eighties.

Much of Labour's energy in its 13 years of opposition between 1951 and 1964 was spent in bitter conflict between the Party's left- and right-wing factions. The left continually tried to challenge what it considered to be the right's stranglehold on the Party. This conflict was about the future development of the ideology of Socialism in Britain. Two schools of thought emerged at this time. These were the *Fundamentalists* and the *Revisionists*.

In the conflict during the 1950s and early 60s, style, tone and individual personality were as important as the issues. Personal ambition occasionally came before political principle.

In the early years the conflict centred around Aneurin Bevan and the issue of nuclear disarmament. Official Party policy was to support the nuclear deterrent, but in 1955 Bevanites refused to support Labour Defence Policy in the House of Commons, causing further disagreement in the Party and weakening its public image. Gaitskell succeeded Attlee as Party Leader after the 1955 General Election. He brought Bevan into the Shadow Cabinet as spokesperson on foreign affairs, and in 1957 he reversed his position on the nuclear issue. Bevan remained a supporter of the leadership until his death in 1960.

Meanwhile, the ideas of the Revisionists were beginning to take hold in the labour movement. The left/right debate shifted to the amendment of *Clause 4* of the Party's constitution which laid down its socialist aim of the "common ownership of the means of production, distribution and exchange". Gaitskell, in particular, was keen to amend Clause 4 and in the wake of Labour's defeat in the 1959 General Election sought to do so. An alliance of trade union leaders and left-wingers prevented amendment at the 1960 Party Conference, where the nuclear issue again became a cause of division.

In the early 1960s the Labour Party's electoral prospects improved. The economic boom which won the Conservatives their third consecutive election victory in 1959 had become a slump by 1961. The 'Profumo Scandal' and the rejection of Britain's Common Market application also served to undermine popular confidence in the Conservatives.

Although he died suddenly in 1963, Gaitskell succeeded in reuniting the Labour Party on a platform of opposition to the Common Market. Harold Wilson, as the new Labour Party Leader, was then able to lead it to victory in the 1964 General Election.

LABOUR IN POWER 1964 - 70
Labour's election campaign had appealed to the middle class as well as to the working class. Wilson appealed directly to the products of the universities and colleges of technology to work with Labour in creating a society in which there would be equality of opportunity, social justice and economic planning. Clearly, Labour's message to the voters was different both in tone and in substance from any of its previous Manifestos.

Labour came to power with a small parliamentary majority of 13, later increased to 110 in 1966. Wilson said that Labour offered "professional Government" and he was determined to press ahead with its legislative programme in spite of the large balance of payments deficit inherited from the Conservatives. Thus, pensions and other welfare benefits were increased, health service charges were abolished and capital gains and corporation taxes were brought in. To deal with the balance of payments deficit, a 15% surcharge was placed on imports. However, as Labour

---

A Summary of the Left/Right Debate

Fundamentalists/Left
- Leading Figure – Aneurin Bevan.
- Believed in pure socialist doctrine.
- The maintenance of principle is more important than gaining political power.
- Politics is about class struggle.
- The mixed economy was a temporary step towards full socialism.
- In addition, Fundamentalists were in favour of
  - increased nationalisation.
  - the maintenance of Clause 4.
  - unilateral disarmament.
  - increased government spending.

Revisionists/Right
- Leading Figures – Hugh Gaitskell, Anthony Crosland.
- Believed in adapting and changing doctrine according to circumstances.
- Political power is vital in order to contain conflict.
- Politics is about achieving gradual social change.
- The mixed economy would be permanent.
- In addition, Revisionists were in favour of
  - improved economic management, rather than more nationalisation.
  - equality of opportunity.
  - maintenance of nuclear weapons.

pressed ahead with its programme, the City and foreign banks concluded that it was putting welfare spending before the strength of sterling. This perception caused a financial crisis which the Government temporarily resolved by borrowing 3,000 million dollars. Labour faced further crises of a similar nature in 1966, 1967 and 1968, which necessitated further borrowing, devaluation of the pound and massive cuts in public spending. Once again it seemed that a well-intentioned socialist government was to have its programme partially wrecked by external circumstances.

In the area of industrial relations, Labour's return to power led to the hope of a changed relationship between government and unions. Industry was to be managed through the *National Economic Development Council*, a new forum for government, employers and unions. In order to deal with inflation, Wilson put his faith in a 'Prices and Incomes Policy' which was to be implemented through a 'National Board for Prices and Incomes'. This policy relied on the principle of voluntarism and, accordingly, the Board had no legal powers to enforce any recommendations on prices and pay. Thus, as time went on and the Government staggered from crisis to crisis, the Prices and Incomes Policy fell by the wayside.

In the mid-60s the Government appointed the *Royal Commission on Trade Unions and Employers' Associations*. Its remit was to investigate the so-called 'British disease' of strikes which, it was alleged, had contributed to the nation's economic decline. The Commission reported its findings in 1968. It recommended that employers and unions improve their machinery for wage bargaining, which was accepted by most trade unionists. However, between 1965 and 1970, government-union relations deteriorated, particularly after 1966 when a pay and prices freeze was introduced. The situation worsened considerably when Barbara Castle, the Employment Secretary, published her draft White Paper *In Place of Strife* in early 1969.

The White Paper recommended that:
- a 28 day conciliation period be introduced before strikes were called.
- union members to be balloted before a strike called.

Labour 1964-70 – The Verdict

"... They had discovered no means of securing rapid and sustained economic growth without first confronting the power either of organised labour or capital." (From *Labour and Socialism* by James Hinton p. 192 Pub. Wheatsheaf.)

"The disillusion with Labour ... was bitterest of all on the Left. To the Left everything they had stood for seemed to be in ruins. They had seen mounting unemployment, curbs on trade unions and wage restraint – not even stopping short of the threat of prison ... All of these and a host of similar practices, which if carried out by a Conservative Government would have been denounced by every member of the labour movement, were being carried out by a supposedly Socialist Government." (From *Post War Britain* by Alan Sked and Chris Cook p. 250 Pub. Pelican.)

- legal sanctions would be taken against unions which did not comply with the law.

The unions and left-wing Labour MPs were outraged by the document. After protracted negotiations between the Government and the TUC, and a threatened back-bench revolt by Labour MPs, *In Place of Strife* was dropped in June 1969. Instead the TUC gave a "solemn and binding undertaking" that unions would abide by TUC guidelines for regulating unofficial strikes.

At the beginning of 1970, with the economy seeming to improve, with cuts in the bank rate taking it down to 7%, and local election results seeming to confirm that the tide of public opinion was in Labour's favour, Wilson chose to dissolve Parliament and run for a third consecutive term of office. It was a miscalculation. An electoral swing of 4.7% in favour of the Conservatives returned Labour not to Office, but to Opposition.

LABOUR IN CONFRONTATION 1970-74

Wilson's Government fell from power amid a new wave of trade union militancy and growth, which had its beginnings in 1968. Between 1968 and 1974, union membership grew by 15%, and union density expanded from 42.5% in 1968 to 54.9% in 1976. The increase in unionisation was particularly marked amongst women and white-collar workers. At the same time, industrial action escalated to a level unknown since the 1920s, with more frequent and longer strikes. The main reason behind this explosion was the effect of price rises and increased taxation on the real value of wages. Workers became increasingly militant in defence of their living standards, which Labour was accused of failing to defend.

Against this background, the period of Conservative Government between 1970 and 1974 became one of intense confrontation with the labour movement. In a situation of increasing inflation, Prime Minister Edward Heath attempted to manage the economy by cutting public expenditure, which meant allowing industrial 'lame ducks' to go to the wall, while at the same time undertaking a major reform of industrial relations.

By early 1972, the country was in the depths of an economic recession, with unemployment passing the 1 million mark. Until November of that year, the Government relied on voluntary agreements with the TUC and CBI to contain wage and price rises in the fight against inflation. The apparent failure of this policy led to the introduction of a Statutory Pay and Prices Standstill. This had the effect of provoking strike action by Gas Workers and Civil Servants early in 1973.

Heath's strategy for industrial relations centred around the *Industrial Relations Act* 1972. This piece of legislation, which was perceived by the entire labour movement as an attack on trade union rights, was vigorously opposed. Although the TUC refused to endorse strike action against the Act, it did refuse to cooperate with the new Industrial Relations Courts which had been set up.

In 1972 strikes by the miners, supported by the railwaymen and dockers, secured temporary victories. While industrial action declined in 1973, events in the second half of the year foreshadowed a return to union militancy. Conflict with the unions arose over Stage Three of Heath's counter inflation policy. This led to a second miners strike in 1974, the effects of which led to the declaration of a State of Emergency and a three day week for British industry. Despite numerous attempts by the TUC to avert the strike, the NUM called its members out on strike on 9th February.

Heath saw the miners' action as a direct challenge to Parliament, and went to the country seeking a fresh mandate for his policies. The election was a disaster for the Conservatives, their strategy of confrontation with the unions proving to be a decisive, if only temporary, failure.

LABOUR IN POWER 1974-79

Labour's minority position in February 1974 was converted to a majority in the Commons by a subsequent Election in October 1974. However, Prime Minister Harold Wilson was now in a position of having to govern when the decline in Britain's economic performance was rapidly accelerating.

The Party's response to the problems of rising inflation, coupled with falling industrial production and investment, was the *Social Contract*. Developed during its period in opposition, the Social Contract was a bargain between the two wings of the labour movement. In return for a freeze on rents, price controls and food subsidies, repeal of the Industrial Relations Act and capital investment in industry, the trade unions agreed to moderate wage claims. While the majority of the labour movement endorsed the Social Contract, some left-wingers opposed it. Arthur Scargill, the miners' leader, referred to it as the "social contrick".

Despite left-wing criticism, the Social Contract held up until the autumn of 1978. It persuaded workers to accept wage restraint which, in the circumstances, amounted to a real fall in their living standards.

On the political front, Harold Wilson resigned as Prime Minister and Party Leader in March 1976. The subsequent election of James Callaghan as Party Leader and PM served once more to highlight the tensions between left and right in the labour movement.

While Callaghan continued with the Social Contract,

Labour's small Parliamentary majority was being slowly eroded by the loss of by-elections. By 1978 the Government was in a minority position in the Commons, only staying in power through Liberal support in what became known as the *Lib-Lab Pact*. At the same time support was sought from the SNP which became vital when the Liberals later withdrew from the Pact.

The Social Contract came to an end in 1978 when the unions sought a return to free collective bargaining. The winter of 1978-79 became known as the 'Winter of Discontent', as the unions set about attempting to secure wage increases in the face of Government resistance.

Callaghan's Government eventually collapsed when the SNP withdrew its support, the devolution referendum having failed to secure a Scottish Assembly. (See p.127) The subsequent General Election on 3rd May 1979 led to Labour's worst election defeat since 1945. Its share of the vote was the lowest since 1931 and there was a massive swing of manual workers to the Conservatives.

Labour's fall from power in 1979 and the election of a right-wing Conservative Government under Margaret Thatcher was largely due to its failure to work effectively with the trade unions.

Within the labour movement as a whole, defeat led to anger and recrimination. Some blamed the unions for the 'winter of discontent', while others accused Callaghan of watering down the socialist content of Labour's Manifesto. Moderates concluded that the 'lunatic left' had driven voters away from Labour.

The 1980s saw the labour movement, as in the 1930s and 1950s, plunge into a period of renewed conflict between left and right. On the political front, defections by leading right-wing party figures, to form the new Social Democratic Party, were matched by attempts by the leadership to purge the Party of far-left supporters of the Militant Tendency. Industrially, the recession of the 1980s decimated trade union membership and along with Conservative anti-union legislation reduced trade union power and influence. At the same time, the 1980s saw the labour movement reassessing and reshaping its ideology, policies, strategy and tactics, to perhaps re-emerge in the 1990s with a much changed political and social identity.

3 WOMEN

"... the gradual transformation of the status of women has been one of the greatest social revolutions of modern times." (From *Out of the Doll's House* by Angela Holdsworth.)

n May 1979, Margaret Thatcher became Britain's first woman Prime Minister. It had taken 51 years from the legislation which granted all adult women equal voting rights with men for a woman to attain the highest political office in the land. In other spheres of social, political and economic life, women had made major advances, yet by 1979 women were still proportionately under-represented in many key sectors of British national life.

Nevertheless, the position of women has radically changed for the better since the 1850s. Two world wars and the effects of rapidly increasing social, economic and technological change have all played their part in enabling women to challenge deeply held assumptions about their status in society.

The Position of Women before 1850

The struggle for women's rights, and the development of a *feminist ideology* have a long history. The first published work on the subject was in 1792 by Mary Wollstonecraft. In her book, *Vindication of the Rights of Women*, she clearly challenged a society dominated by men by arguing that if women were endowed with the gift of reason, they should be treated equally with men. Such radical ideas did little to improve the position of women at the time. The social and economic effects of the Industrial Revolution proved to be a more potent force affecting the role and status of women.

Industrialisation fundamentally changed the importance of women and their economic worth. It meant the end of the home-based cottage system of manufacture, centred around the family unit, where women played a central role. Working-class women now had to go 'out' to work in the factory, while at the same time attending to their domestic duties of wife and mother after a long day of drudgery. Some married women remained at home to do paid work such as sewing or childminding. This work was entirely different from the family craft work before the Industrial Revolution. Payment was extremely poor, hours were long and the end result was mere subsistence for the family.

As the process of industrialisation accelerated into the 19th century, there emerged a new entrepreneurial middle class of businessmen, professionals and rich landowners. Their values were founded firmly on the rocks of hard work, thrift and the sanctity of the family. By the 1850s, the stereotyped image of the family in Britain was very much that of the middle-class family, with the male as breadwinner/decision maker/protector, and the wife as carer and provider for the husband and children. This image was reinforced by the religious and cultural values of the day.

Lack of education was a major handicap to the progress of women in the first half of the 19th century. For the majority of women who belonged to the working class, there was little chance of any education. The role of working-class women and girls was to work, either in the factory or at home. Education for them was seen as being unnecessary and by some as being dangerous. The conventional wisdom of the day was to encourage working-class women to be content and to behave themselves in the station of life in which providence had placed them.

Prior to 1850, there was little serious attempt to give middle- and upper-class girls any serious education. In most cases, girls were brought up at home and educated by a governess. They learned to read, knit, sew, play the piano, paint in water colours and speak a little elementary French. Serious educational study which might lead to future employment was very rare. The first duty of a well-to-do girl was to get married. Education served only as a means to that end. Nevertheless, there were notable exceptions to the norm in the first half of the 19th century. These women of ability and independence were all from the middle and upper classes and in various ways attempted to assert their independence. Notable examples are Elizabeth Fry who worked for prison reform, Mary Carpenter who founded the first reform school for girls, and distinguished novelists such as the Brontë sisters and George Eliot.

The position of women around 1850 is well described by the historian Angela Holdsworth who writes, "As many manual and professional jobs were closed to them it was a struggle for single women to support themselves. All they could hope for was marriage to a good man and a lifetime of keeping his house and rearing his children. Once married, women's property and income became their husband's by law. Circumstances forced them to depend on the goodwill of a father, husband or brother. Independence, a fulfilling career, even a decent job were not for them. Women were not allowed to vote, nor to stand for parliament, nor to hold any kind of public office. By necessity, their horizons were limited to their own private world at home."

Feminist Reform 1850-1918

'The Feminist Movement' or the 'Women's Movement' is the name used by many historians to refer to the efforts of women in the 19th century to improve their rights in law and society. Nineteenth century feminists had many aims: they wanted to train for work to enable them to take jobs outside the home; they wanted equal educational opportunities with men; they wanted equal rights with men in law; and they wanted equal voting rights with men.

The 'Feminist Movement' had no real organisation until the early 20th century, and had no real starting date. The leaders were from the upper and middle classes who had the material resources and sufficient leisure time to enable them to pursue their various causes. Their aims were wider than simply advancing the cause of women's rights. What they were attempting to do was to put right some of the many general social problems of the day.

It would be incorrect to attribute the success of the various feminist causes solely to outstanding female leaders, of whom there were so many. While people like Florence Nightingale, Josephine Butler and the Pankhursts played key roles in bringing about change, it is important to note that their efforts were undertaken against the backdrop of a society in which there were fundamental forces of social, economic and political change at work between the 1850s and 1918.

From the middle of the nineteenth century to the end of the Great War, the cause of women's rights made progress, despite the fact that Britain was a male dominated society with a woman on the throne (Queen Victoria) who was little disposed to the many feminist causes. The period to 1918 saw significant changes in the balance of power between men and women in the areas of employment and trade union membership, marriage and the family, education and working rights.

Employment and Trade Union Membership

As has already been stated, the idea that a woman's place is in the home is firmly rooted in Victorian middle- and upper-class society. This idealised picture of women in Victorian Britain is far from the truth, and is a measure of the hypocrisy which existed at the time. The first proper census, taken in 1851, revealed the extent of women's employment outside the home.

Women in Employment 1851	
Occupation	Number Employed
Domestic Service	1,135,000
Textiles	635,000
Clothing Manufacture	491,000
Agriculture	229,000
Professional	106,000
Food, Drink, Tobacco	53,000
Metalwork	36,000
Paper, Printing	16,000
Bricks, Pottery etc	15,000
Mining, Quarrying	11,000
Wood Furniture	8,000
Skins, Leather	5,000
Chemicals, Soap	4,000
Others	88,000

Table 3.1

Almost 29% of those of working age were in some form of paid employment. In addition, women made up 33% of the nation's total workforce. As Lindsay Mackie and Polly Pattullo state in their study of *Women at Work*,

> "during the period that the belief in the little woman being incompetent or unsuitable for outside employment was at its height ... these incompetents were in employment, admittedly appallingly paid for the most part, and only semi-skilled in the majority."
> (From *Women at Work* by Mackie and Pattullo Pub. Tavistock Publications Ltd. 1977.)

The figures in Table 3.1 further reveal that approximately 1.14 million women were engaged in domestic service, that is they worked in the homes of the middle and upper classes expending a vast amount of physical energy in order to maintain their employers in a life style which was alien to their own personal experience. Domestic service was therefore the main form of women's work. Most servants 'lived in', worked long hours, and had severe restrictions placed on their own social lives by their employers. Where families employed male servants (a sign of

great affluence), women were paid less than their male counterparts for doing the same work.

Annual Wages of Female Domestic Servants (1861)	
Housekeeper	£18 - £40
Cook	£12 - £26
Housemaid	£10 - £17
Maid	£7 10s - £11

Table 3.2

The wages recommended for female domestic servants in 1861 are shown in table 3.2. Low pay was a problem for most women in work. Women generally earned half or less than half of a man's wage for doing the same job and this picture was common to most areas of employment. Low wages were often the least of women's concerns in the industrial workplace. Throughout the nineteenth and into the twentieth century, they endured the worst ills of the factory system such as long hours, poor conditions in terms of light, heat, ventilation and protection from dangerous toxic substances and machinery, as well as running the risk of sexual assault from male foremen. Many women were even worse off than those in the factories. Pay and conditions in 'sweat shops' and in the 'sweated trades' were even worse than in regular factory work. Sweat shops were small workshops where women were employed in jobs such as making hats and jewel boxes for very low wages. The sweated industries were those where women worked from their own homes for a middleman. Those women were paid according to the amount of work they did or the goods produced. Woman in both areas of employment were ruthlessly exploited in Victorian times and beyond.

Wages Compared		
Occupation	Men (Average)	Women (Average)
Thimble Makers (Brass) 1851	15-21s per week	7-9s per week
Surface Workers in Tin Mines*	2s per day	1s per day
Tailoring Machinists*	22s 6d per week	11s per week
Office Work*	£2 per week	£1 per week
Domestic Service*	£35 per year	£10-£17 per year
Carpet Weavers, 1890s	£1 15s per week	£1 per week
Civil Service Typists 1914	£3 per week	£1 per week

Table 3.3 *1880s
(Source: *Votes for Women* by Diane Atkinson Pub.. Cambridge Educational 1988.)

Although the aforementioned patterns of work continued into late Victorian times, changes in the pattern of the nation's economic life meant new forms of employment for working-class women. Seebohm Rowntree in *Poverty, a Study of Town Life, 1901*, noted that in York, "The number of girls who enter domestic service, except as nurses, is small and decreasing. They prefer to become dressmakers, shop assistants or clerks, or find employment in the confectionery factories." (Quoted in *Human Documents of the Age of the Forsytes* by E Royston Pike, Pub. Allen & Unwin 1969, p142)

In the same work he also notes the importance of the skilled and semi-skilled working class to the national economy, and therefore, by implication, notes the economic worth of women.

> "Taken as a whole, Class D (the Working Class) is the section of our population upon which the social and industrial development of England largely depends."
> (Ibid p.144)

Towards the end of the nineteenth century, as Britain evolved into an advanced industrial society, the numbers of jobs available to nonmanual workers increased. The people to fill these jobs came mainly from those who had benefited from the increased educational opportunities after 1870. In the years between 1861 and 1911 there was a 307% increase in the employment of women in nonmanual work.

Technology opened up the way for women to make a career in office work. The development of shorthand and the invention of the typewriter transformed office work from a task to which young men were apprenticed for a number of years, to one in which much less training was required and which was therefore deemed to be suitable for women. As office technology developed, increasing numbers of women were sought to operate the new calculating and duplicating machines. Employers considered that women were more suitable than men for the new keyboard skills which the modern office demanded. In reality, the truth was that rather than being better at office work than men, women were preferred by employers because they could be paid less. In 1909, 97% of women in office work earned less than men. In addition, many areas of clerical work, and indeed other forms of nonmanual work for women, operated a marriage bar which meant that when a woman married she had to leave her job. In the civil service, the marriage bar was written into the law, underlining the legal and institutional discrimination against women in Victorian and Edwardian times. To get round the marriage bar, some women concealed their marriage from their employers for fear of losing their job.

Nevertheless, office work was a much sought after form of employment for women, being seen as more respectable than factory work and offering a better quality of life.

While the field of women's employment was undergoing change in the latter decades of the 19th century, it was also clear that the attitudes of women towards pay and conditions were also changing. These attitudes were in turn influenced by changes taking place in industry and society in general which were to affect the lives of working women.

Trade unions became legal in 1824 and were a vehicle through which women were able to work to improve their overall status, pay and conditions in the workplace. There was, however, no great influx of women into trade unions until the 1870s. This was due to the fact that women had the double burden of work and home to bear, the relatively unskilled nature of their employment, and, most importantly, the opposition of men to women union members.

Men opposed female union membership because, it was argued, the wages earned by a man were used to support an entire household. If women worked and became trade union members, it would destroy this argument and undermine efforts to secure higher wages for men. Female union membership was also opposed as men saw increased numbers of women on the labour market as a threat to their jobs. Yet in spite of these impediments, women's trade union membership increased dramatically between 1870 and 1914.

Date	Number of Women in Unions
1877	21,085
1886	36,900
1892	142,000
1913	433,000
1914	437,000

Table 3.4

It is not difficult to understand why female trade union membership increased during this period. As increasing numbers of women sought work, it was clear that opportunities for women were limited, and that in whatever job a woman chose to do, pay and conditions were usually worse than for men. Thus women had an equal if not greater need than men to join together and campaign for improved rights in the workplace. Although there was a strong tradition of female membership in the Lancashire Cotton Unions, overall, women were not being recruited into the individual male craft unions.

Thus, until mid-century women were excluded from most general trade union activity.

The formation of the Women's Trade Union League in 1874 was an early attempt to persuade women to join or organise their own trade unions. Although the League succeeded in setting up some small unions in London, many of these failed to survive for any length of time. Nevertheless, the League did serve to raise the awareness of women to their working conditions and particularly to issues of health and safety.

Although some success had been gained on the industrial front, trade unionism failed to make any impact on one of the largest sectors of female employment, domestic service.

The 1881 census revealed that more than 1.5 million women were in some form of domestic service. Attempts at forming unions for domestic service workers and those in other service industries (hotels, restaurants, etc) failed in the 19th century, although it is clear from the many accounts of 'life below stairs' that unionisation was needed. The main reasons for failure were rooted in the nature of domestic service.

- Women had little time off work.
- Women in service were isolated from each other, unlike those who worked together in factories sharing a common experience.
- Women in service were set against each other by the system of rank in the middle- and upper-class households. There was, therefore little chance of the domestic staff in a household uniting against their employers to secure improved pay and conditions.

Case Study - The Match Girls' Strike 1889

Towards the end of the 1880s, there was a considerable increase in industrial action by women. The reasons for these strikes varied. Some were undertaken to resist pay cuts, others for pay increases, while others still were about health, safety and discipline (the system of fines) in the workplace. The best known strike was that of 'The Match Girls' of the Bryant and May factory in London in 1889. This strike received a lot of publicity at the time and the successful outcome served as a milestone to encourage other women to organise and press their employers for improved conditions.

Many industries employing large numbers of working-class women put the health of their employees at considerable risk. In the white lead industry in the North of England, many women suffered illness and death from the lead poisoning contracted at the workplace.

The 'laissez-faire' attitude of the state to health and safety matters and the desire for profit meant that most industrialists paid little heed to such issues. Some employers in the white lead industry were considered to be 'enlightened' because they provided their girls with breakfast at the workplace. At this time, poisoning was thought to be caused through working with toxic materials on an empty stomach.

Members of the Match Makers Union, 1888

The Match Making industry inflicted equally hazardous conditions on its women workers. These were highlighted in a left-wing magazine called *The Link* which was edited by the socialist reformer Annie Besant. The *Link* article was the result of a campaign by a group of Fabian socialists, notably Sidney Webb, Bernard Shaw and Annie Besant, to publicise the horrifying conditions at Bryant and May's factory in the East End of London. Not only did the article emphasise the low pay and poor conditions which existed in the factory, it graphically brought public attention to the disease called necrosis of the jaw or 'phossy jaw' which workers in the factory risked contracting. Literally gangrene of the jaw, 'phossy jaw' was caused by exposure to the phosphorous used in the manufacture of matches.

The management of the factory responded to the article by asking their employees to sign a document stating that, contrary to the allegations in *The Link*, they were well treated. When one woman was sacked for refusing to sign the document, 1,400 of her colleagues came out on strike. Immediately, the strikers went to the offices of *The Link* in Fleet Street in search of advice and leadership. Through the magazine, help was sought from the Women's Trade Union League, which rapidly led to the formation of the Match Makers Union.

Media interest in the strike was strong, with the *Times* condemning strike leaders, particularly Annie Besant who had become the Secretary of the Union, as "socialist agitators". The publicity, however, won a good deal of support for the women, including funds of £400 which were sufficient to sustain their action. The strike lasted a fortnight, ending when the London Trades Council intervened and negotiated a settlement with the directors of Bryant and May. The resulting agreement was a victory for the women with all employees being reinstated, higher wages gained, fines abolished and the Match Makers Union being established and accepted.

The Match Makers strike was a famous victory for working-class women and it had widespread effects. Firstly, both male and female workers came to realise that only by joining together could they secure improvement in their pay and conditions. Secondly, and perhaps more importantly, the great new general unions of dock workers, gas workers and many other general labourers began to recruit women on an equal basis with men.

Within the trade union movement itself, women were beginning to assert themselves. In 1875 the first woman delegate attended the Trades Union Congress and by 1881 there were 10 women delegates. This was an important step for women, for by attending the TUC "they staked a claim for equality with men in Union policy making and leadership." (From *Women at Work* by Sarah Harris Pub. Batsford 1981.)

As in many other areas of life, women had to struggle for acceptance at the TUC. Some men reflected the prevailing attitudes of the day, ie. that women should not be working in factories but should be at home. The nineteenth century TUC tended to have a paternalistic attitude towards women. This can be seen in the debate over the issue of *protective legislation*, ie. the laws which governed the conditions under which women and children could work.

Women were overwhelmingly defeated in the TUC over the issue of protective legislation and the organisation stepped up its efforts to secure laws solely aimed at protecting women's working conditions. As a result, the Women's Trade Union League turned its attention to campaigning for the appointment of female factory inspectors who, it was hoped, would ensure that employers complied with existing legislation. The first woman factory inspector was appointed in 1893 and subsequent reports from female inspectors brought to public attention the conditions under which women worked.

In the early years of the twentieth century, women in the trade union movement turned their attention to lobbying for protective legislation for workers (mainly women) in the sweated trades. Low pay and extremely poor conditions were still the hallmarks of this type of work, and because most of the women worked from home, it was virtually impossible for them to be organised into unions. Their case was taken up by the National Federation for Women Workers, founded in 1906, whose secretary was Mary McArthur.

To publicise conditions in the sweated trades, an exhibition was staged which shocked Edwardian public opinion and led to the formation of the Anti-Sweating League. Through the activities of the League, the *Trade Boards Act* of 1909 was passed, setting up Wages Boards, whose job was to set minimum wage levels in trades where there was no effective union organisation. Like many other pieces of well-intentioned legislation, it took some time and a good deal of struggle by trade unionists, male and female, before it became effective.

From the setting up of the Women's Trade Union League until the end of World War I, there was a good deal of debate amongst women on the question of *separatism*. The debate centred around the wisdom of having separate unions or sections of unions for women. In the 1870s and 80s, when opposition to female union membership amongst men was still strong, it is understandable that separatism was an attractive argument for many activists. As the trade union movement grew, and with it the membership of women, separatism became less of an issue. By 1918 there were approximately one million women trade unionists in 383 unions, only 36 of which were all-female unions.

Although separatism still remains an issue for some women to this day, the real struggle in the early years of the twentieth century was pay, conditions and union membership. There is no doubt that between 1850 and the outbreak of World War I, women workers had achieved great improvements in their pay and conditions, but by comparison with men they still lagged far behind in those areas. For Mary McArthur, the crux of the matter centred around union membership when she said, "Women are unorganised because they are badly paid, and poorly paid because they are unorganised."

Marriage and the Family

In the middle of the nineteenth century, Queen Victoria and her family represented the ideal model of family life to the nation. Both Church and State emphasised the family as the cement which held society together in a rapidly changing and increasingly technological world. The family was particularly important to the middle and upper classes. The husband was head of the family and the wife was subject to her husband, just as in society women were subject to men. Thus, the aim of all respectable women was to marry an honest man of even temperament and have his children. Unmarried women were often viewed as having 'failed', becoming a source of pity and ridicule.

In order for a middle- or upper-class woman to acquire a husband, her education and upbringing had to be geared to fit her for the role of the dutiful wife.

> "The respectable woman must live up to an ideal created by man. She must be gentle, pure and ladylike and at least appear to be less intelligent than her husband. She must be perfectly mannered and very modest in her behaviour and speech. She must be talented in the drawing room ... despite her fashionable frailty she must manage her household efficiently, bear a large family willingly, and be utterly faithful to her husband." (From *Women in Society* by GM Cuddeford Pub. Hamish Hamilton 1976.)

Most working-class women in mid-Victorian Britain would have wished to aspire to the middle-class ideal of marriage, but were prevented from doing so because:-

1 Poverty and poor housing conditions condemned them to a life of drudgery, endless toil, and childbearing.
2 Cruelty towards working-class women was rife, many working-class men having a particularly brutal attitude towards their spouses. Two of the main causes of this were overcrowding and drink.
3 Lack of education and basic legal rights prevented working-class women from escaping from an unsatisfactory marriage.

On the surface, the Victorian middle-class family presented an image of stability, happiness and contentment.

However, there was a good deal of moral hypocrisy in Victorian Britain. Beneath the images of domestic bliss, lurked the evils of pornography and child prostitution which were popular with the men of the middle classes.

Marriage as an institution was popular with Victorian women of all social classes because they perceived that it would enhance their identity. This was another Victorian myth. Once the marriage bond was sealed, a woman literally became the 'goods and chattels' of her husband. In mid-century the legal position of married women left much to be desired.

"Legally, a married woman's status was that of an infant. She had no rights before the law and everything she owned was her husband's, even her own earnings and her children. For a woman, divorce was almost impossible. If she no longer wished to live with her husband she could apply to the Church courts, and might obtain a separation on the grounds of cruelty, adultery or unnatural practices. Her chances of getting a divorce were very slender, since that could only be granted by Act of Parliament. It was however, very much easier for her husband to obtain a divorce on for instance, the grounds of his wife's adultery, for the wife in a divorce suit could not be a defendant, a plaintiff, or a witness." (From *Marriage* by Jennifer Harris and Alistair Wisker Pub. Batsford 1976.)

Many of the changes brought about in the area of family law came from the efforts of middle-class feminists. These women were educated and had sufficient time, resources, and social connections to campaign for improved legal rights for women within marriage. Moreover, they were highly motivated by the sheer inequality of a woman's position before the law.

In the years around the middle of the century, the issues of divorce, custody of children and maintenance attracted a good deal of attention. The main changes made in family law are outlined below.

Matrimonial Causes Act (1857): This law gave mothers increased access to their children after divorce. In addition, wives could now keep any post-divorce earnings and keep or inherit property from the marriage.

Matrimonial Causes Act (1873): This law continued the unequal treatment of women over grounds for divorce. A husband could still sue for divorce on the grounds of the wife's adultery, whereas a wife had to be able to prove cruelty by the husband as well as adultery as grounds for divorce.

Additional legislation gradually, but not completely, improved the rights of married women.

Married Women's Property Act (1870): This law allowed married women to keep their own earnings up to a maximum of £200 per annum.

Married Women's Property Act (1882): By this law, husbands lost their automatic right to claim their wives' property as their own.

Although divorce had been obtainable by law from 1857 with the setting up of the Divorce Court, social convention in Victorian and Edwardian times was disapproving. Divorce was viewed as scandalous, ruining careers and bringing disgrace on those involved. For a woman, there was the added burden of supporting herself after the divorce. An Act of Parliament in 1866 gave divorced women the right to claim maintenance up to a level of £2 per week from their ex-husbands.

By 1895, women had the following additional rights in law:-

- The right to become the sole guardian of their children on the death of their husband.
- The right to claim maintenance from the husband even if it was the woman who sued for divorce.
- The right to obtain a separation order if the husband was consistently cruel or in prison.

In the early years of the twentieth century, a Royal Commission investigated the whole question of divorce, producing two reports in 1912.

1912 Royal Commission on Divorce

Report 1
- No major changes to be made in the law. Divorce should only be granted on grounds of adultery.
- Restricted press reporting of divorce cases.
- Equal rights for men and women seeking divorce.
- Divorce to be made possible for the poor.

Report 2
- Major changes recommended. Divorce should be granted on grounds of insanity, cruelty, adultery, drunkenness, desertion for three years.
- Restricted press reporting of divorce cases.
- Equal rights for men and women seeking divorce.
- Divorce to be made possible for the poor.

The fact that the Commission was forced to produce two reports illustrates the controversial nature of divorce at this time. Nevertheless, significant legal rights for women had been achieved by the outbreak of World War I. Marriage still remained popular, and although divorce was now easier for women, the notion that a woman had a duty to 'suffer in silence' in an unsatisfactory relationship still prevailed.

'Suffering in silence' was indeed the lot of many working-class women. Escape from a failed marriage was out of the question for them. Their duty was seen to be looking after the children of the marriage, for despite the wider use of birth control, working-class families remained large. In the 1890s, working-class girls married in their late teens and had at least ten pregnancies in their child bearing years. It is little wonder therefore that the life expectancy of working-class women was only 46 years.

By the beginning of the twentieth century, feminists were beginning to turn their attention to the roles of women within the family, and to the inequalities which existed there. Despite the extension in a woman's legal rights, the

Victorian and Edwardian marriage relationship was very much a one-sided affair.

Campaigning for change, feminists raised issues like:-

- The maternal responsibility of women for the upbringing of children.
- The duty of a wife to 'submit to her husband'.
- The question of large families and the burden they placed on a woman.
- Women's health issues.

Opposition to feminists who campaigned on these issues was fierce. Nevertheless, the picture of marriage which emerges prior to World War I, is one in which women are gradually beginning to work out an individual identity for themselves.

Education

England's education system in the middle of the nineteenth century lagged well behind that of some other European states, notably France, Prussia and Scotland. Education at this time remained the privilege of the middle and upper classes. Two religious societies almost wholly provided for the education of the working classes, the National Society and the British and Foreign Society. Few working-class parents were, however, in a position to enable their children to take advantage of what was available. Most working-class children, therefore, grew up unable to read or write. If the general state of education at this time was poor, opportunities for girls were extremely limited.

In mid-century, middle- and upper-class girls were educated to be good wives, mothers and homemakers. The curriculum offered to these girls emphasised 'accomplishments' such as social etiquette, music and dancing.

Male educationalists believed that the stress of a conventional education could damage the health of a girl in adolescence. They argued that adolescent girls needed rest, not an education which would tax the mind.

> "Women were thought to have smaller brains and, it followed, less intellectual potential than men. It was also a common belief that women were behind men in evolution, as their prime function, motherhood, kept them closer to nature. In short, they were inferior. An educated woman was a paradox, and if she showed she had brains, might frighten off potential husbands." (From *Out of the Doll's House* by Angela Holdsworth Pub. BBC 1989.)

Women were therefore educated for a life of subordination. Early feminists who questioned this view of women were criticised in the press and periodicals.

Much of the pioneering work in the field of women's education came in the second half of the nineteenth century. It began in 1848 with the founding of Queens College, London, as a training institution for women teachers. The early graduates from the college set new standards of education in girls' schools. However, good girls' schools were few and far between.

The scandal of middle-class girls' education was fully revealed in 1868 when the Taunton Commission on Education made its report. The Commission was set up by the government to enquire into the education of boys and only included girls' schools at the last moment due to the campaigning of Emily Davis, a feminist whose aim was to bring girls' education up to the standard available to boys.

The School Inspectors who reported to the Commission noted that in many cases they had great difficulty getting information due to "unrelenting hostility" from a number of schools. Overall, the Commission found that the "general deficiency of girls' education can be stated with absolute confidence". It found that almost everywhere the emphasis of the curriculum for girls was solely on domestic skills plus "accomplishments" like embroidery or playing the piano. The lack of academic achievement and the physical conditions in which many girls were taught also merited heavy criticism from the Inspectors.

Nevertheless, the picture was not entirely gloomy. There were some good girls' schools. The first academic schools for girls were set up in the 1850s when the North London Collegiate School for Ladies and Cheltenham Ladies College were founded by the early feminist pioneers, Dorothea Beale and Franchesca Buss. Such schools were, however, very much in the minority in offering girls subjects like mathematics, science, Latin and Greek.

There was universal agreement that girls' education needed to be reformed. A debate then arose among feminists over the nature of reform. One school of thought wanted the reforms to make education for girls *as good as but different* from that available to boys. The opposing group argued that equality was the only way forward: girls' education, it was said, should be *identical in all essentials* to that given to boys. Emily Davis argued that a *different* education for girls meant an *inferior* education. All were agreed that there should be an increase in the number of good schools for girls.

The logical conclusion to the extension of education for girls was that they would demand access to higher education at university level. Emily Davis campaigned to gain women the right of admission to university. In 1866, in her book *The Higher Education of Women*, she argued that women should have the opportunity to "find out what they could do". Educationalists of the day were less than charitable towards Miss Davis's attitude to the education of women. In the face of opposition, she opened a school for women students in Hitchin in 1869. In 1874, the school moved to Cambridge where it became Girton College, and was soon followed by the establishment, by Anne Jemima Clough, of a second women's college, which became known as Newnham Hall.

The aims of Emily Davis and Jemima Clough illustrate the difference in attitude to change which divided early feminists. Miss Clough adopted a gradualist approach over university recognition of women's colleges, being prepared to accept "lesser recognition" as a stepping stone to full and equal status with other colleges. Emily Davis on the other hand, aimed for full recognition of women's colleges which would have an identical curriculum and examinations to men's colleges. Miss Davis adopted an uncompromising attitude, arguing that the only way forward for women was to meet men on level terms. Partial or lesser recognition, she argued, would only serve to mark women's colleges as inferior institutions.

The opening up of higher education proceeded steadily as the twentieth century approached with women's colleges being founded at Oxford University in 1879 and increasing numbers of universities, including the four in Scotland, enrolling women as students on an equal footing with men.

By the turn of the century, small but increasing numbers of middle-class women were going on from school to higher education and thence to professions which had previously been male preserves. Some of these professions, such as nursing, teaching and social work, were areas where able women were extremely successful. In addition, the legal and medical professions, after a long and arduous struggle, had opened their doors to women practitioners.

Thus, by the end of the Victorian era there is no doubt that the cause of women's rights had made significant progress, yet in the key area of voting rights, and participation in the political process, women remained as outsiders, powerless with no rights. This lack of political rights simply served to underline the inferiority of women in spite of achievements in other areas.

WINNING THE VOTE

'The Cause' was the phrase used by many 19th century feminists for the whole movement for women's rights. By the close of the century, 'the cause' required an issue which would bring women of all shades of opinion together. The issue of the vote became the focus of women's struggle for equality.

The nineteenth century was the battleground for the extension of the franchise to the male population of the working classes. In the struggle, men who already had the vote took the lead in fighting for the rights of their peers. In their struggle for the vote, women had to fight for themselves, getting very little help from men. Yet the struggle itself provided women from many different social, cultural, political and religious backgrounds with a sense of solidarity which previous issues had failed to provide.

The issue of votes for women was taken up by the Chartists in the early years of their campaigning, but was subsequently rejected. It re-emerged in the debate which preceded the passing of the Second Reform Bill in 1867. It was raised by John Stuart Mill the economist who, in 1865, was elected to Parliament. He was in favour of widening the franchise to include women, and to that end introduced an amendment to the Reform Bill. Although it was defeated, seventy three MPs voted for it. In the years following from the Second Reform Act, women householders gained the right to vote in local elections.

The question of votes for women was again raised in the debate preceding the Third Reform Bill in 1884. Again an amendment to the Bill was moved, this time by a Mr Woodall (Liberal). The Prime Minister of the day, Gladstone, spoke against the amendment and again it was defeated, although this time 135 MPs voted for the amend-

ment to grant women's suffrage.

By the 1890s, as it became clear that women were playing a more important role in society, there was a steady majority in favour of Commons' resolutions declaring that women should have the right to vote. However, it was a far cry from giving support to a Bill which would enfranchise women. Indeed, it is more probable that at the turn of the century only a minority of the population wanted women's suffrage.

There are many reasons why people were opposed to women's suffrage at this time. Firstly, and most obviously, politicians were against the idea. The Conservatives were against it, although former Prime Minister Disraeli had argued in favour of women's suffrage. The main fear of the Conservatives was that women, once enfranchised, would vote for the Liberals, or even worse, the Labour Party.

The Liberals, although in favour of women's suffrage, voiced similar concerns to those of the Conservatives, ie. that women might vote for the opposition parties. The Leader of the Liberal Party and Prime Minister from 1908 to 1916, HH Asquith, was against votes for women. The disapproval and opposition of a Prime Minister proved to be a formidable hurdle for the cause of equal voting rights. The newly formed Labour Party gave qualified approval to women's suffrage. It wanted all adults to have the vote and argued that, if only property owning women gained the vote, the Conservatives and Liberals would be the sole beneficiaries.

Secondly, in society at large prevailing attitudes were against giving votes to women for the following reasons, many of which were spurious, but which were nevertheless taken seriously at the time:-
- If women became involved in politics it would threaten the family and therefore the stability of society.
- Politics would have a corrupting influence on women, making them less feminine.
- Women, being highly emotional, would be totally unsuited to making logical political decisions.
- Women were not educationally equipped to make proper use of the right to vote.

Those who accepted the above arguments came from all social classes and from all parts of the political spectrum.

Suffragists and Suffragettes

The movement to gain votes for women had two wings, the *suffragists* whose origin went well back into the 19th century, and the more militant *suffragettes* who came into being in 1903. The *suffragists* proudly traced their roots to the nineteenth century movement for social reform.

> "The early suffragists were a well-connected group of women who used their influence to try and persuade powerful men to take up their cause." (From *Out of the Doll's House* by Angela Holdsworth p 180 Pub. BBC Books.)

They became a national movement in 1887 when, under the leadership of Millicent Fawcett, various suffrage societies formed themselves into the National Union of Women's Suffrage Societies (NUWSS). The methods employed by the NUWSS were similar to those employed by the separate suffrage societies for the previous 30 years, ie. peaceful persuasion and education, always working within the law. Suffragists wrote pamphlets, held meetings, and sent out trained speakers, all with the aim of changing public opinion.

The leadership of the suffragists was exclusively middle-class, yet it was acknowledged early on that the movement needed to have the support of working-class women. Radical suffragists as they became known, led by the Gore-Booth sisters, worked in the mills of Lancashire to gain the support of working-class women for their cause.

Many of these mill workers who had involved themselves in trade union activities, but found themselves to be 'voices in the wilderness', turned to the suffragist movement as an outlet for their frustrations with the male dominated trade union movement. Diane Atkinson in *Votes for Women*, argues that the "NUWSS of all the women's suffrage societies, had the most to offer to working-class women". What is clear is that the issue of the vote was drawing women together as never before, and giving them an identity which they hitherto lacked.

The Suffragettes were born out of the suffragist movement in 1903. Mrs Emmeline Pankhurst, who had been a member of the Manchester suffragist group and who had been involved in the campaign to seek support from working-class women in Cheshire, decided to break with the NUWSS and form a separate society. She had grown impatient with the middle-class, respectable, gradualist tactics of the NUWSS. The new suffragette organisation was called the Women's Social and Political Union (WSPU). Its motto was "Deeds, not Words".

Strategy and Tactics 1903-1914

Both suffragists and suffragettes wanted votes for women. Where they differed was over strategy and tactics. The suffragists always kept their efforts *within the law* while the suffragettes were prepared to *break the law*.

In 1906, a deputation of suffragettes, suffragists and politicians met the new Liberal Prime Minister, Campbell Bannerman. He assured the group that, although he was personally in favour of women's suffrage, his Cabinet colleagues were divided. NUWSS members were disappointed in his attitude as many were Liberal supporters. Their response to the Prime Minister was to mount a campaign of petitions, leaflets and meetings targeted at Liberal politicians to try to persuade them to change their minds on the issue of women's suffrage. Later in the same year, the NUWSS adopted a new and more aggressive tone by threatening to put up independent candidates to run against Liberal politicians who were against votes for women.

Meanwhile, the WSPU campaigned in a much more robust manner. HH Asquith, the new Chancellor of the Exchequer and a leading opponent of women's suffrage, was heckled in the House of Commons. Marches and demonstrations were organised with women being arrested when they tried to demonstrate at the Commons. In 1907 the WSPU split into two groups following conflict between Mrs Pankhurst, her daughter, and other members of the WSPU's executive. Those who left formed the Women's Freedom League (WFL), while the Pankhursts and their supporters established an even firmer grip on the WSPU, foreshadowing even more aggressive tactics in the future.

In spite of internal bickering over strategy and tactics, the three women's groups continued to work together most of the time. Certainly their message was beginning to have some influence on the 'anti's'. In 1906 Beatrice Webb, the Fabian Socialist, explained to Millicent Fawcett how she had become a convert to women's suffrage.

> Women "... in my opinion are rapidly losing their consciousness of consent in the work of government and are even feeling a positive obligation to take part in directing this new activity. This is in my view, not a claim to rights nor an abandonment of women's particular obligations (bearing children and the advancement of learning), but a desire to fulfil their functions by sharing the control of State Actions in those directions."
> (Adapted from *Woman and the Welfare State* by Elizabeth Wilson, p.40-41 Pub. Tavistock Publications Limited, 1977.)

As time went on, demonstrations grew bigger and better. In London, Mrs Pankhurst and her daughter were arrested for trying to "rush the House of Commons". The WFL founded the Women's Tax Resistance League in 1909, and some of its members chained themselves to a ventilation grille in the House of Commons, shouting "votes for women" through it, until it was removed. All of these efforts gained the cause publicity. As a result, people began to think more seriously about the issue of women's suffrage.

By 1909 tactics had become more militant: politicians opposing women's suffrage were frequently interrupted; Winston Churchill was attacked by a woman with a dog whip; the new Prime Minister HH Asquith, the 'bête noire' of the suffragettes, had his windows broken. Increasingly he and other 'anti' politicians were relentlessly pursued the length and breadth of the country by women prepared to disrupt political meetings.

As the suffragette campaign intensified, the opposition from press and public also increased. In 1908, the leader writer in the *Daily Express* warned that "the time for dealing gently with idle mischievous women who called themselves militant suffragists has gone by", and demanded that "these women who unite to disorder and riot, shall be punished with the utmost severity". The popular press cruelly lampooned both suffragists and suffragettes in cartoons, describing the women as unfeminine, masculine, frustrated spinsters.

Despite the opposition from politicians, press and public, the organisation for women's suffrage seemed to be prospering. By 1909 the WSPU had branches all over the country, 75 paid office staff, and a newspaper, *Votes for Women*, which sold 20,000 copies per week but was read by many more. The NUWSS was also doing well. Its membership was 13,000 in 1909 and it had an efficient and well-run organisation nationwide. Increasingly, however, the two organisations were growing apart, with the NUWSS becoming particularly concerned that the growing militancy of the WSPU was losing the movement support from both MPs and public.

Emmeline Pankhurst being arrested outside Buckingham Palace, May 1914

In 1911 another Conciliation Bill, which proposed to give voting rights to women whose husbands were already voters, got no further than a Second Reading. The Bill was presented to the House again in 1912, but failed to get a majority at the Second Reading. Asquith later brought in a Bill in the same year to widen the franchise to all men, and proposed that the Commons could introduce an amendment to it in order to add votes for women.

As in 1867 and 1844, when the amendment was proposed, the Speaker ruled it out of order on the grounds that it would change the nature of the Bill.

Mrs Pankhurst returned from the USA in 1912 and immediately committed the WSPU to a new phase of violence and outrage which went far beyond the lawbreaking which had taken place since the beginning of the campaign. Suffragettes felt that they had been tricked and outwitted by Asquith, and now aimed "to create an intolerable situation for the Government, and if need be, for the public as a whole". Thus, the eighteen months prior to World War I are rightly described by historians as the 'wild period' of suffragette actions. Paintings were slashed, houses and business premises were firebombed and telegraph wires were cut. During this period the suffragettes gained a martyr in Emily Davison who, on 4th June 1913, threw herself in front of the King's horse 'Anmer' at the Derby. Suffragettes turned her funeral into an immense propaganda exercise for their cause. However, there is a great deal of evidence to show that the campaign of violence did the cause more harm than good. Churchill was of the opinion that "their cause had marched backwards".

In the summer of 1909 there was an outbreak of window smashing by suffragettes. This usually meant a jail sentence, the women being classed by the authorities as common criminals. The WSPU consistently claimed that since its members were involved in a political struggle, offences committed by them should be judged as political acts, and those who were imprisoned should have the special status of political prisoners. In July 1909, Miss Wallace-Dunlop went on hunger strike to gain political status. She was soon followed by others. At first the government released hunger strikers, fearing the adverse publicity that the starvation of imprisoned women would bring, but after a few months the decision was taken to feed them by force. However, force-feeding backfired on the government in that the militant suffragettes began to win back support which their tactics had previously lost them.

The Conciliation Bill and Its Failure

During the General Election of January 1910, Asquith promised that MPs would have the opportunity for a *free vote* in Parliament on a Bill for Women's Suffrage. A Conciliation Bill was drafted by an all-party Commons Committee in response to the Prime Minister's undertaking and was introduced in the House after the election.

It was given its Second Reading in July 1910, and in the debate 39 speeches were made for and against. Winston Churchill and Lloyd George both spoke against the Bill, on the grounds that, since it was designed only to give the vote to female property owners, it would automatically favour the Conservatives. The Bill passed its Second Reading with a majority of 100 votes, whereupon Asquith curtailed further discussion by suspending Parliament until November. There was initial violence by members of the WSPU after Asquith's announcement, but once this had died down, both the NUWSS and the suffragettes resumed peaceful campaigning in the hope that the Conciliation Bill would eventually become law in 1911. In the meantime, Mrs Pankhurst went on a speaking tour of North America. The NUWSS continued its attacks on the militants of the WSPU while defending its own constitutional approach.

Suffragettes sentenced to prison continued to go on hunger strike in pursuit of the demand for political status. In 1913 the Government passed legislation which, it was hoped, would strengthen the hand of the prison authorities in dealing with hunger strikers. The so-called 'Cat and Mouse Act' enabled the authorities to release hunger strikers on licence, then rearrest them once they had recovered their health. The aim of the Act was to demoralise the suffragettes, but it only succeeded in strengthening their resolve. Some women simply resorted to further lawbreaking while on licence, and in the end force-feeding was reintroduced.

In the early summer of 1914, amid impending civil war in Ireland and the possibility of large-scale industrial unrest, Asquith agreed to receive a deputation from the East London Federation of Suffragettes. This group was led by Mrs Pankhurst's other daughter Sylvia, who had been expelled from the WSPU earlier in 1914, due to the disapproval of her work with working-class women by her mother and sister Christabel. Asquith seems to have recognised that these women had genuine social grievances which could have been more effectively tackled if they had the vote. Although the Prime Minister was not going to change his mind on the question of women's suffrage overnight, there is a good deal of evidence that in time he would have brought in a Bill to provide for universal adult suffrage. War, however, intervened and the whole movement immediately scaled down its activities in the face of a greater threat to the nation.

World War I - Women and the Vote

There was a varied response within the women's suffrage movement to the outbreak of war. Angela Holdsworth writes that "the movement lost its impetus and its leaders went their separate ways. Christabel and her mother became super-patriots vigorously supporting the war effort, while Sylvia Pankhurst sided with the pacifists. Millicent Fawcett and the suffragists on the other hand, continued to lobby politicians while making themselves useful to the war effort by funding ambulances for women to drive to France, and organising women's voluntary work."

What the war did was to highlight the economic and strategic value of women to the State. This, however, did not happen immediately.

In the first year of the war women were, by and large, unaffected, although in certain areas of women's work, notably the cotton and clothing industries, the unemployment amongst women actually increased as imports fell and people bought fewer clothes. The first propaganda slogan of the war was "business as usual", and as far as everyone was concerned, war was a man's business. Professor Arthur Marwick notes in *The Deluge* that in the first year of the war, "the overall picture was one of willing women finding no outlet for their desire to serve".

Eventually economic necessity, rather than the demands of Mrs Pankhurst and other feminists for the "right to serve", drove the government to recruit women, first of all into the munitions industry, then into many other sectors of the economy.

Women Employed in the Munitions Industry	
Year	Number Employed
1914	212,000
1915	256,000
1916	520,000
1917	819,000
1918	919,000

Table 3.5

The figures show a dramatic increase in 1916 with the introduction of compulsory military service for men, and again in 1917 when National Service was introduced. The nation was involved in total war, and the nation as a whole had to be mobilised.

Thus, many other areas of employment show significant increases in the numbers of women employed. Although mainly from the working class, the war brought increasing numbers of women from all social classes into employment.

Marwick maintains that the war served to *accelerate* a process which had started well before 1914.

"The growth of large-scale industry and bureaucracy would undoubtedly have brought this development eventually, but it was the war, in creating simultaneously a proliferation of government committees and departments and a shortage of men, which brought a sudden and irreversible advance in the economic and social power of a category of women employees which extended from sprigs of the aristocracy to daughters of the proletariat."
(From *The Deluge* by Arthur Marwick Pub. Penguin, p 97-98.)

The Employment of Women 1914-1918		
	Number of Women Employed	
	1914	1918
Transport	18,000	117,000
Commerce	505,000	934,000
National and Local Government	262,000	460,000

Table 3.6

In addition, women in the medical services served with distinction during the war, bringing *credibility* to the cause. This was further magnified in 1917 when the government formed the various women's paramilitary organisations into the Women's Auxiliary Army Corps and later the WRENS and the WRAFS.

Marwick makes the point that the war heightened women's own self-image and their individual identity.

"Above all, in their awareness that they were performing arduous and worthwhile tasks and were living through experiences once confined only to the most adventurous males, they gained a new self-consciousness and a new sense of status."

During the war, the government made positive moves towards the introduction of votes for women. Britain's war propaganda, much of which was directed at the USA, stressed the fact that the Allies were fighting for democracy, which implied universal suffrage. The government, therefore, had to be seen to be acting in this direction.

The establishment of a Coalition Government during the war helped the cause. There were no longer the rigid party divisions which in the past had hindered the cause of women's suffrage, and as the war proceeded more men came into government who were well disposed to the cause. The questions was eventually referred to an all-party committee of the House of Commons which was chaired by the Speaker. This so-called Speaker's Conference made its report on 30th January 1917. Its recommendation was not unanimous, but by a majority decided that "some measure of women's suffrage should be conferred ...Any woman on the Local Government Register who has attained a specified age, and the wife of any man who is on that register, if she has attained that age, shall be entitled to be registered and to vote as a parliamentary elector." Eventually the "specified age" was agreed to be 30 and ironically H H Asquith, the former Prime Minister, moved that the recommendations be drafted into a Bill. This was passed in the Commons on its third reading by 385 - 55 and became law in June 1918.

As a result, about eight and a half million women who were over 30, who were householders or the wives of householders, or occupiers of property with a rent of £5.00, or who were graduates or 'qualified', were entitled to vote in the 1918 General Election.

Campaigners for women's suffrage were disappointed by the age bar. They wanted complete equality with men. Nevertheless, most activists were prepared to wait. The extent to which the war was a contributory factor to this winning of women's new found rights is a matter for *debate* amongst historians. Some argue that the government could not refuse to grant voting rights to women because they had contributed so much to the war effort. John Ray, in *Britain between the Wars*, contends that "women proved by their work that they deserved the vote equally with men. Thus their war efforts succeeded where the suffragette campaign had failed."

Other historians argue that the picture is much more complicated. Women were already campaigning for and winning new rights before the 1850s. Stevenson, in *British Society*, argues that "although the First World War has usually been taken as marking a turning point both in the acquisition of the right to vote and in wider opportunities for women, it is clear that the war was as much the occasion as the cause of growing female emancipation. AJP Taylor in *English History 1914-1945* simply argues, "War smoothed the way for democracy – it is one of the few things to be said in its favour."

FEMINIST REFORM 1918-1979

The years 1918-1979 again saw rapid advances in women's rights. During this period, women gained equal political rights, and equal opportunities in education and employment. The development of labour-saving devices gave women the opportunity to pursue careers and interests outside the home, and lack of a man in a woman's life no longer curtailed her rights to fulfil her potential in society. In addition, developments in medicine and birth control gave women more control over their own bodies. Many of the changes in the twentieth century have resulted from the efforts of women themselves, although many of the legal and welfare advances affecting women came about as a result of the changed role of the state in society to one of greater intervention in the lives of its citizens.

The identity of women grew stronger during this period, particularly in the post-1945 era; this saw the development of the Women's Liberation Movement, which highlighted women's issues as never before and led to renewed emphasis on the development of feminist ideology. However, while the identity of women was changing, becoming clearer and stronger, there were still those who argued that the changes affecting women's lives continued to conceal a great deal of inequality.

It would be wrong to analyse the changes affecting women in a vacuum. Women are part and parcel of British society and the changes affecting women to this day and beyond reflect and reinforce all the other changes taking place in society.

Women Between the Wars
The interwar period was a time of advance for women in some areas and a time of stagnation in others. While some women seemed to assert themselves more in the peripheral areas of their lives, notably in the social sphere, in other areas it seemed that with the winning of the vote in 1918 feminists assumed that all that remained was a "tidying up process ... of completing women's equality before the law." Elizabeth Wilson in *Women and the Welfare State* further argues that "despite the appearance of emancipation (confined in any case to the bourgeoisie), discrimination against women everywhere continued and particularly in the two vital fields of employment and welfare."

Angela Holdsworth describes the 1930s as "not a good time for feminists ... a growing consensus kept women tied to the home and rising poverty and international affairs tended to eclipse other issues." Both of the aforementioned historians paint a rather gloomy picture of women's progress in the interwar years. The reality is that the position of women did improve, but rather unevenly during a period of great social tension and upheaval.

Legal Reforms Affecting Woman
After the war, the Government brought in a number of new laws which positively affected the position of women in politics, employment and the family.

1919 - Sex Disqualification (Removal) Act: This law removed legal restrictions on women entering the professions, especially law. By 1923, there were about 4,000 women magistrates, Mayors and councillors in Britain.
1923 - Matrimonial Causes Act: This law removed from the wife the need to prove cruelty or desertion in addition to adultery as grounds for divorce.
1924 - Guardianship of Infants Act: This gave guardianship of infant children jointly to both parents. If they disagreed the courts would decide who got custody.
1926 - New English Law of Property: Women now had the right to dispose of their own property on the same terms as men.
1928 - Equal Franchise Act: This act finally gave all women aged 21 and over the vote, making them equal with men.
1935 - Law Reform Act: This law gave a married woman the right to dispose of her property as if she were single.

Although these laws gave women more rights, progress was still hindered by the very powerful force of prevailing attitudes. In the interwar period, many women still had a restricted view of their own place in society and were not willing to assert themselves. In such an atmosphere, making improvements effective was not easy.

Women in Politics
With the extension of the franchise to women over 30 in 1918 came measures which, for the first time, enabled women to become Members of Parliament. Opponents of female suffrage had sounded dire warnings of the creation of a women's party, and of Parliament being 'swamped' by women. In reality, quite the reverse has been the case.

Seventeen women were Parliamentary candidates in the election of 1918 and all were defeated except Constance Markiewicz who, although elected, never took up her seat as she was against Irish representation in Parliament. Thus, the first woman to take her seat in the Commons was Nancy Astor who was elected for the Conservatives at a by-election in 1919.

Mrs Astor was an American by birth, and at the time of taking her seat in Parliament to the cheers of veteran suffragettes, she had never campaigned for women's rights. This situation was soon rectified as she became an effective voice on behalf of women.

When women achieved equal voting rights with men in 1928, it was again expected that there would be a large influx of women into Parliament. This did not happen, although in 1929 the first female Cabinet Minister, Margaret Bondfield, was appointed by Labour. During the interwar period, women MPs reached their maximum of 15 after the 1931 election.

Between the wars, the very small number of female MPs were virtually forced into confining themselves to speak-

Women MPs Elected between the Wars

General Elections	Con.	Lab.	Lib.	Other	Total	(%)
1918	-	-	-	1	1	0.1
1922	1	-	1	-	2	0.3
1923	3	3	2	-	8	1.3
1924	3	1	-	-	4	0.7
1929	3	9	1	1	14	2.3
1931	13	-	1	1	15	2.4
1935	6	1	1	1	9	1.5

Table 3.7
Source: Adapted from Factsheet No. 5, House of Commons Library.

ing for women and women's problems, which were perceived to centre around prices, social policy and domestic matters.

Were women effective in politics during this period? Angela Holdsworth, in *Out of the Doll's House*, argues that although women made little impact, "sixteen acts protecting women's interests were passed in the early 1920s ... these changes in the law may well have had more to do with politicians' awareness of women's voting power than the lady MPs".

Women and Employment Between the Wars
The First World War did a great deal to help change attitudes, particularly in the area of the employment of women. Before the war, certain jobs were seen as male preserves, but this could no longer be sustained during the war. This change in attitude can be seen in the *Haldane Report (1918)* on recruitment into the Civil Service:

"The practical question whether women can be found suitable to perform duties comparable with those assigned to men in the Administrative Class (ie. the top grade in the Civil Service), has to a large extent found an answer in the experience of the last four years, which has gone far to resolve any doubts upon this point. We therefore think that it is no longer expedient in the public interest to exclude women on the grounds of sex from situations usually entered by competition." (From *Britain between the Wars* by John Ray.)

However, the true value of women in society post-1918 is well illustrated by the speed with which they were ejected from the employment market. For many women, the newfound prosperity which they enjoyed through employment came to an abrupt end as they were dismissed from their jobs with little hope of future employment. The authorities assumed that women would return to their previous roles as wives and mothers, but this was no longer possible owing to the effects of the war. Writing in his book about the Women's Movement in 1928, Ray Strachey graphically described the predicament of women after the war.

"The war had enormously increased the number of surplus women so that nearly one in three had to be self-supporting; it had broken up innumerable homes and brought into existence a great class of new poor ... public opinion assumed that all women could still be supported by men, and that if they went on working it was from a sort of deliberate wickedness. The tone of the press swung, all in a moment from extravagant praise to the opposite extreme and the very same people who had become heroines and saviours of their country a few months before, were now parasites, blacklegs, and limpets ... the women themselves acquiesced to the situation." (Adapted from *The Cause* by Ray Strachey, quoted in *Women and the Welfare State* by Elizabeth Wilson Pub. Tavistock Publications Limited, 1977)

Despite this initial setback, the number of women in work increased after 1918. For example, there were 250,000 more women working in 1921 than ten years before and 500,000 more working in 1931 than in 1921.

The changing technology of modern industry helped to involve more women. The new light industries were ideal areas for women as opposed to the male-dominated heavy industries. The new industries valued women employees, not so much for their skills, but because they were still cheaper to employ than men. Typically, women were in low-paid, unskilled jobs with no trade union to back them up. Pay was usually half that of men and promotion prospects were very limited. Many able women became frustrated at the lack of opportunity to pursue a career beyond a certain level.

Some of the most powerful opponents to greater employment opportunities for women were male trade unionists. As the Depression began to bite deep in the early 1930s and unemployment rose sharply, hostility to working women increased. All unemployed workers suffered during the Depression, women more than most. Unemployment benefit for women was well below that payable for men, but very often when a business laid people off, women were the first to go.

"One of the tragic consequences of the depression and discrimination against working women was the enormous rise in the number of babies who died at birth. Many women were afraid to leave work for a minute, knowing that they would never get the job back. Some babies were born in factories. Other women, who could find a sympathetic doctor, took a day off with 'lumbago' and were back at their work benches often within hours of birth. It was hardly surprising that many of these babies died, but the possession of a job, however badly paid, was the key

to the whole family's survival."
(From *Women at Work* by Sarah Harris p.56. Pub. Batsford)

Clearly, despite remarkable progress in the employment field, women were still regarded in many quarters with suspicion and prejudice.

Greater Freedom in the Social Sphere

During the interwar period, there was a noticeable tendency for women to take a more independent line in social affairs. This was reflected in their dress, a more confident manner outside the home, and in the new organisations and magazines being set up for women only.

Women demonstrated their newfound freedom after the war in their dress and appearance. Partly influenced by wartime work in the factories, shorter hair became fashionable with the 'Eton Crop' and 'bobbed' hair becoming popular. Clothes became more functional in appearance, designed to emphasise the 'juvenile shape' of the body. Undergarments such as corsets were replaced by lighter underwear, manufactured from synthetic materials, and as leisure and sport became popular, women began to wear shorts when taking part in activities such as tennis.

A further indication that women were becoming more independent was the growth of self-help women's organisations. For some working-class women, the Cooperative Guilds and Labour Party Women's Sections provided a new and wider perspective on the world. Lectures ranged from birth control to international affairs. In the country, Women's Institutes grew rapidly, and between the wars branches were being opened at a rate of five per week. As well as learning new recipes for making jam, the Institutes provided a structure where women could meet together and discuss issues, listen to invited speakers and go on outings.

In 1930, the Women's League of Health and Beauty was started, coinciding with the new 'keep fit' fad. Women met in gym halls across the land to perform graceful rhythmic movements to contemporary music.

Magazines geared exclusively to women's interests became hugely popular in the twenties and thirties. The most successful of all was *Woman*, which had acquired a readership of 750,000 by 1939. *Woman* dealt with issues of beauty, fashion, furnishing, cookery and child care. Whether magazines such as *Woman* have helped the cause of women is still a matter of debate today.

Women were therefore taking a much more confident and independent role in social affairs during the interwar period. They were, however, still being hindered by a pervasive prejudice, both from within their own ranks and from all sectors of society.

Birth Control

A major factor in limiting women's potential to pursue life outside the home was the fact of high birth rates, especially in working-class families. With 5 or 6 children to look after, there was little scope for personal fulfilment for many women. However, in the twenties and thirties there was a clear trend towards smaller families and fewer births. During this period, the number of families with 5 or more children fell from 27.5% to 10.4%.

The most important factor accounting for this fall was the increasing awareness about and practise of birth control. For most couples, this consisted of simply abstaining from sexual intercourse, the use of coitus interruptus – the withdrawal method – and induced abortion. Since abortion was illegal until 1960, all manner of self-induced methods were used. Ted Willis, for example, has written about his mother's attempts to prevent his own birth:

> "She bought gin she could ill afford and drank it neat. She carried the tin bath in from the back yard, filled it to near boiling with water and then lowered herself into it, scalding her flesh so painfully that she was in agony for days. She ran up and down the stairs until she was exhausted. And when all this failed to check my progress, she procured some gunpowder – enough to cover sixpence – mixed it with a pat of margarine, and swallowed it. This was reckoned in those days to be almost infallible, but it succeeded only in making her violently ill. In the end, she reconciled herself to the inevitable, and I emerged, none the worse for those adventures, to add another dimension to her problems." (From, *British Society 1914-1945*, by J Stevenson p.152)

Backstreet remedies like this were based on ignorance and folklore, but indicated the lengths to which some women would go in order to limit family size. Few mothers of large families had not at some time attempted self-induced abortion.

The most prominent advocate of birth control at this time was Dr Marie Stopes. She hit the headlines with her book *Married Love*, which was a guide to sex and marriage. Published in 1918, the book had sold 400,000 copies by 1923. Family planning was the central theme and Stopes carried this message on through public meetings. In 1921, she opened her first birth control clinic in London. By 1939, there were 60 such clinics throughout the country.

Although the ethics of birth control are still an issue today, it had gained a good deal of respectability and acceptance between the wars. Also, with rising living standards many people realised that raising a family need not be a time of severe financial hardship. By limiting the number of children, it was possible to enjoy a reasonable lifestyle, as well as giving the children a better start in life. Children, it could be argued, were becoming regarded as a 'consumer durable', competing with other household items for a share in the family budget.

Women, then, were beginning to gain more control over their own bodies as they acquired knowledge about birth control methods. Contrary to traditional assumptions, many women did not want to remain housewives all of their lives. The average age when women were having their last child dropped from 33 in 1890 to 28 in 1930, leaving more time for them to start paid work.

Women's Advance Between the Wars

Women continued to make steady progress in the interwar period, although the advances made were less spectacular than those made between 1850 and 1918. In the employment field, women had managed to gain a foothold in areas formerly reserved for men. However, in terms of pay and promotion they still lagged well behind their male colleagues. They were typically employed in unskilled, nonunionised jobs in the distributive, clerical and service industries.

In the area of voting rights, women eventually gained equality with men in 1928. In terms of political power, only a tiny minority were beginning to play an active role in public life and politics remained largely a male preserve between the wars.

Socially, women began to establish an identity of their own, by breaking free from the conventions of the past. The trend towards smaller families, better education, and increased employment opportunities, all provided more scope for women to break away from their conventional 'kitchen sink' image. Nevertheless, prejudice still remained deep within the social and cultural fabric of British society.

WORLD WAR II AND ITS AFTERMATH

At the outbreak of war in September 1939, the Government had made few plans to include women in the war effort. Early propaganda emphasised women's role in the family and in helping maintain morale. However, the fall of France, the blitz, and the growing realisation that Britain was fighting a total war led the Government to reassess its position.

In 1941 the Manpower Requirements Committee concluded that over and above the 5 million women already in work, an extra 1.5 million women would be required, while the war lasted, to take the place of men conscripted into the armed forces.

In December 1941 the *National Service (No 2) Act* conscripted all single women between the ages of 18 and 30 into the armed forces or industrial war work. Britain was the only country to take this step, and although some MPs, including Churchill, were against the measure, most women (ninety seven per cent according to a Mass Observation Survey) were for it.

In 1943 ninety per cent of single women were working in industry or carrying out non-combat support work in the armed forces. In the same year it was estimated that 3 million married women and widows were working, which was double the 1939 figure. Indeed, as the war continued it was increasingly difficult for women to avoid war work, unless they could prove that they had above-normal family responsibilities, or had war workers or evacuees living with them.

It is clear that, like the Great War, World War II temporarily changed the way in which women saw themselves and also their role in society. However, many of the old attitudes prevailed.

During the war many married women badly needed work to augment the wages of their poorly paid husbands in the armed forces. Yet for many who wanted to take on war work, the task was virtually impossible due to the low wages being offered, lack of day nursery facilities, long hours, shopping problems and poor transport. For those who had families and who did volunteer, life became a constant struggle of maintaining two jobs, as housewife and war worker.

Women's membership of trade unions grew during the war, with some of the skilled workers' unions having to admit women to their ranks for the first time. During the war the number of female trade union members doubled. Women were also able to enter areas of work in which they previously had little involvement, such as engineering, chemicals and local government. Male workers in the trade unions became concerned about this trend, fearing that in peacetime men would be replaced by women on lower wage rates. Thus the unions sought agreements with the government on women's wages in the traditional male sectors of employment. However, they seem to have been more concerned about the long-term employment prospects of male members than the wartime wage rates of their female members. In the shipbuilding, metalwork and printing sectors, the employment of women was seen as a temporary measure, and at the end of the war most women members in these industries lost their jobs.

Most working women during the war continued to be treated as second-class employees in terms of pay. Although trade unions took up the case of equal pay for some groups of women, they were, on the whole, more concerned with the problem of 'dilution', that is men losing their jobs to women on lower wage rates. Thus, throughout the war inequalities in wage rates continued.

While most women continued to be treated unequally in the area of pay during the war, a significant victory was gained in 1943 over the question of equal compensation for injuries. Until that time, women received about two-thirds the compensation of men for injuries received as a result of war service, industrial accident or bombing. Pressure from female MPs eventually led to equal rates being granted by the government.

Generally, the war brought hard times to the lives of all women in Britain. They had to cope with rationing, shortages, evacuation and the blackout, as well as the inevitable separation from loved ones who were serving in the armed forces. In the workplace, despite continued inequality, the influx of women into industry brought benefits to all workers which continued long after the war. Many larger companies were forced to employ personnel officers and improve conditions by providing restrooms, canteens and improved sanitary conditions.

The ending of the war saw a change in attitude from the state and industry towards women. Propaganda which, during the war, had encouraged women to go out and work for the war effort, changed overnight to persuading women to stay at home in order to win the peace.

"The Directors and the Management wish to take the opportunity of thanking all employees for the manner in which they have cheerfully carried on ... during the last five and a half years ... Our first duty is to find jobs for those who are returning to us from the forces. In many cases a returning man must displace someone, man or girl, who has been holding down the job during the war." (Letter, 1944, issued to employees of Tate & Lyle's sugar factory in London, quoted in *Keep Smiling Through* by Caroline Lang Pub. Cambridge.)

The emphasis on women's role at home and in the family was written into the Beveridge Report of 1942, which laid the basis of the Welfare State. The introduction of family allowance, a weekly, non means tested benefit, payable to mothers (although not initially) for the second and subsequent children, seemed to underline the image of women's role in the home rather than at work.

The post war Labour Government encouraged women to stay at home for two main reasons. Firstly, jobs were required for men after demobilisation. Women were only encouraged to remain in industries such as textiles which were essential to the post war export drive. Secondly, Britain's prewar population had been falling, thus the 'baby boom' post-1945 would benefit the country.

In the late forties and early fifties women's role was portrayed by experts and the media as being in the home. Some experts even claimed that children of working mothers were more likely to become juvenile delinquents. However, as prosperity returned to Britain in the 1950s and unemployment fell, more women began to return to work.

Attitudes to working women, even in the early 1940s however, remained, at best, patronising. The prevailing attitude was one of women working to buy 'luxuries' for the family (items which today we consider to be necessities) or that they were working for 'pin money'. This attitude helped to support the view that it was acceptable to pay women less than men for equal work.

By the end of the sixties, women still only accounted for twenty per cent of trade union membership. The TUC took on the cause of inequality in the workplace in 1963 with the launching of its *Women's Charter*. It proposed the following:

- Equal pay based on the value of the job and not the sex of the worker.
- Opportunities for promotion for women.
- Apprenticeship schemes for girls in industries.

Feminism – The Development of an Ideology

One definition of 'Feminism' is a set of beliefs or a movement which advocates equal rights for women.

"The word 'feminism' was first used in France and denoted 'qualities of woman'. In the early and mid nineteenth century, feminism was not used to describe any of all the various emerging movements for a fairer position in society for women. The terms used were Woman's Rights, especially in America, and Equal Rights and even the Woman Movement. It was not until the 1890s that the word 'feminism' started to appear and quickly came to mean simply anything to do with trying to advance the position of women. It has become a blanket word covering a multitude of meanings, some of them contradictory."
(From *Significant Sisters* by Margaret Forster Pub. Penguin, 1986)

"Nineteenth century feminism ... was a call for the rights of women analogous to the claim for the rights of men. It expressed the liberation of the age, and JS Mill (1869) for example, based his arguments for women's suffrage on those used by the men of the bourgeoisie to obtain their rights, and he saw that the subjection of women was out of line with the rest of bourgeois society." (From *Woman and the Welfare State* by Elizabeth Wilson p.56, Pub. Tavistock Publications Limited, 1977)

"The thrust of feminism wavered between the wars, partly because it was believed that with the vote women had achieved emancipation. The feminist organisations continued to be orientated towards Parliamentary reform, although now of a rather piecemeal kind ... others paid a good deal of attention to the inadequacies of welfare provision for women, especially mothers, there was little analysis of women's Motherhood role." (From *Women and the Welfare State* by Elizabeth Wilson Pub. Tavistock Publications Limited, 1977)

After the war, "a new generation was growing up, unclear what it stood for, other than general dissatisfaction with their parents' way of life". (From *Out of the Doll's House* by Angela Holdsworth Pub. BBC 1988)

"Into the void came the intellectual gurus with a feminist analysis of what was wrong. First Simone de Beauvoir with *The Second Sex* ... In 1963 Betty Friedan's *The Feminine Mystique*, and later Germaine Greer's *The Female Eunuch*." (From *Out of the Doll's House* by Angela Holdsworth Pub. BBC 1988)

"Mary Stott calls the 1960s 'the do-it-yourself decade' with British groups being born to a large extent by women contacting each other through *The Guardian* women's page ... By 1969 many British towns had women's groups. Some of them catapulted into being after headline hitting events such as the Ford women's strike in 1968, which looked as if it might be the beginning of a new era of women using their industrial power to better their position." (From *Out of the Doll's House* by Angela Holdsworth Pub. BBC 1988)

"We wanted to change everything, absolutely everything ... Every cultural value with which we had been brought up, we wanted to change. We thought we could change the world and not just the relationships between men and women, but everything that flowed from that – the way we brought up our children, the kinds of people that we would raise ... At that time there was no vocabulary to describe what women were about. They had to invent a jargon to explain their analysis. Identifying with the national liberation movements of the 1960s, they borrowed some of their vocabulary, using such words as male 'chauvinist', women's 'liberation' ... Liberation seemed to open up possibilities of an entirely new and different relationship between the sexes." (From *Out of the Doll's House* by Angela Holdsworth Pub. BBC 1988)

- Improved opportunities for training young women in skilled work.
- Retraining facilities for older women who return to industry.
- Special care for Health and Welfare of women workers.

In 1968, a landmark strike at Ford's Dagenham Plant by women demanding equal pay rates led to women delegates to the TUC in that year demanding that equal rights should be one of the main goals of the TUC.

At the 1968 STUC in Aberdeen, Scottish women pressed the trade unionists to give a lead and support women who were fighting for equal pay for work of equal value.

> "Of the 22 women present amongst the 471 delegates two came to the rostrum. Mrs VD Donald of the General and Municipal said that 'in all of the fifty or so statements issued by the Prices and Incomes Board, the subject of equal pay had scarcely been mentioned'. It was up to the women themselves to organise strongly in their unions and seek legislation. Agnes McLean of Glasgow Trades Council asked, 'did Congress really know what was happening in the electronics industry? Hundreds of women were entering it at the women's rate of wage.' She added she was 'totally fed up with the mood of pessimism and gloom which had overtaken so many trade unionists on this issue'. She added that in her many visits to factories in the West of Scotland she had 'seen women coming out and fighting for equal pay whenever a proper lead was given them'. Later that day Congress elected to the new General Council of 17 members the first woman since 1943; this was Betty McIntyre of Hosiery and Knitwear, and six years later she was to occupy the Presidential chair."
>
> (From *The Scottish Trade Union Congress – The First 80 Years* by Angela Tuckett Pub. Mainstream Publishing.)

The following year the Labour Government promised that by 1975 equal pay for equal work would be a reality. Thus by the late 1960s, although women had made some gains in the field of employment, there were still major similarities with the employment pattern of previous decades:

- Women were still concentrated in low paid work.
- Women were still concentrated in caring or serving jobs.
- There were more women than men in education and medicine, but men still had the top jobs.
- Women still faced prejudice and discrimination in pay, promotion prospects, education and training.

Changes in Women's Occupations 1931-61
(As a percentage of Women Employed)

	1931	1951	1961
Domestic Service	20	5.5	3.6
Textiles	11	5.5	3.3
Typists	10.2	20	25
Electrical & Electronics	2.7	5.8	5.2
Nurses	2.2	2.7	3.8
Teachers	2.7	3.0	3.6
Others	50	56	54

Table 3.8

Struggling for Equal Rights

During the 1960s and 70s the wider question of women's rights came into prominence in Scotland and the rest of Britain. This was due in no small measure to an upsurge in feminist writers who, in the sixties, began to analyse and question the traditional roles of women in western society. Three examples of such writers are given below.

Betty Frieden (USA) – Published *The Feminine Mystique* in 1963. In it, she argued that women were forced by education and the media to accept traditional roles of motherhood and marriage which left many dissatisfied with their lives.

Germaine Greer (Australia) – Published *The Female Eunuch* in 1971 which dealt with the question of sexuality.

Kate Millet (USA) – Published *Sexual Politics* in 1977 which argued that political action was necessary for the liberation of women.

Books by feminist writers were widely read during the sixties and by the end of the decade many areas had women's groups which were mainly made up of the young and educated. In February 1970, the first national meeting of women's groups was held at Ruskin College, Oxford. The meeting had originally been arranged as a small women's history conference. Eventually, 600 women attended, and resolutions were passed demanding equal pay for equal work; equal job opportunities; equal education; contraception and abortion on demand; free child care; and financial and legal independence for women.

As the Women's Movement grew in the 1970s, there came an almost inevitable backlash from the popular media. Activists were variously described as 'man-haters' and 'bra-burners'. However, as the Movement grew and its initial idealism and optimism began to wane, it took on a more serious slogan, 'The personal is the Political'. Feminist ideology rejected the idea that women's personal lives and domestic existences were mere 'emotional experiences'. Instead, feminists insisted that areas such as childbearing, childrearing and family matters were political issues. Thus women had to become involved in politics by campaigning and by forming pressure groups.

The seventies, therefore, saw a proliferation of campaigns related to women's issues, such as contraception, abortion and childbirth, rape, violence in the home and general women's health issues such as breast cancer screening.

As the seventies progressed, divisions appeared in the Women's Movement, owing to the diversity of opinions it contained. At the 1977 Conference of the Movement, debate centred around the need for more revolutionary feminism as opposed to the liberal school of thought.

> "... the umbrella organisation had outgrown its usefulness ... The movement had served a lot of women who are now in strategic positions in the media and places like that, and a lot of working-class women were left standing there, you know, hands on hips, wanting to know where do we go from here?"
>
> (From *Out of the Doll's House* by Angela Holdsworth.)

The Feminist Debate

Radical School

- Women should separate themselves from men.
- Men assert their power over women through sex.
- Men abuse women and pornography degrades women.
- The only answer is feminist revolution – wholesale changes in sex roles.
- Women are victims.

Liberal School

- Men and women should work together to bring about sex equality.
- Men assert their power over women in a whole variety of ways.
- Some men abuse women and some women allow themselves to be degraded by pornography.
- The 'Feminist Revolution' is illiberal – a gradual approach to equality of sex roles is necessary.
- The debate within the Movement grew so heated that after 1978 there were no more national conferences. As a result, the Women's Movement split into a collection of smaller pressure groups.

Despite the eventual demise of the Women's Movement, the 1970s was a decade of significant progress for women's issues. Action in the political arena brought legislation in a wide area from equal pay to sex discrimination.

The Equal Pay Act, 1970 – Employers were given until 1975 to 'phase in' 'equal pay' for a job which was deemed to be of 'equal value', in terms of skills, to that of a man's job.

The Social Security, Pensions Act, 1975 – This tried to increase women's pensions. It introduced a new state pension scheme and proposed changes to private and company pension schemes. Until the Act women had been unfairly treated in this area because most were unable to contribute for the stipulated amount of time towards their pension because they had to stop working to have children, or to care for elderly relatives. In the area of private pensions the Act put an end to practices which excluded women from pension schemes because they earned too little, worked part-time or because of the existence of different entry requirements for men and women.

The Employment Protection Act, 1975 – This Act recognised that a woman should have the right to give birth to a child during her working life without her employment being penalised. Under the Act women gained 3 new rights:
– Not to lose their job through pregnancy.
– To receive 6 weeks paid maternity leave.
– To be able to return to the same or a similar job up to 29 weeks after the birth of the child.

This Act was restricted in 1980 when the Conservative Government passed the *Employment Act*. Under this piece of legislation, the provisions did not apply to firms with less than 6 employees. Thus, some women who gained important rights in 1975 lost them in 1980.

The Sex Discrimination Act, 1975 – This Act made it illegal to discriminate on the grounds of sex. It covered discrimination in the areas of employment, education, training, housing and the provision to the public of goods, services and facilities. The Act allowed positive discrimination in favour of the sex which had been left out in the past.

The Government also set up the Equal Opportunities Commission (EOC) to supervise the working of both the Sex Discrimination Act and the Equal Pay Act. The job of the EOC is to enforce, promote and maintain the working of these pieces of legislation.

In the area of politics women failed to make a real breakthrough in the 1970s, with the exception of Margaret Thatcher who became Prime Minister in 1979. After the 1979 General Election, there were fewer women MPs than at any time since the war, only 20 out of 635. Despite the fact that women formed 51 per cent of the population in 1979, they were represented by 3.7 per cent of MPs. Discrimination, family responsibilities, rejection of politics, and social attitudes all seem to have continued to work towards giving Britain in the early eighties the lowest percentage of women in Parliament in Western Europe. Although the '300 Group', set up in 1980, aimed to get that number of women elected to the House of Commons, it recognised that far-reaching changes, both in attitudes and in the way Britain conducted its political business at Westminster, would be necessary.

Thus, despite the advances which women had made in the latter decades of the 20th century, Britain of the 1980s still remained largely a man's world. Women were still more likely than men to be poor; they still shouldered the burden of family responsibilities; they were still more likely to be in low paid work and to suffer harassment at their place of employment. As a class, women were still grossly underrepresented in politics and in the top jobs in industry and the professions. According to Angela Holdsworth in *Out of the Doll's House*, "emancipation is not a once and for all achievement, but has to be re-examined and fought for in each succeeding generation." The following statistics, from a 1984 survey of public attitudes, would seem to support that point of view.

	Agree %	Disagree %
A wife should avoid earning more than her husband does	14	57
More women should enter politics	52	8
Children are essential for a happy marriage	29	41
Women generally handle positions of responsibility better than men do	22	25
It is wrong for mothers of young children to go out to work	42	32
It should be the woman who decides how many children a couple has	27	42

(From *Women & Power* by Sue Mayfield p. 54 Pub. Dryad Press.)

4 PEACE MOVEMENTS

"19th century Peace Movements set out to improve the world; 20th century ones struggle to save it." (From Protests & Visions by J Hinton)

Peace activism in Britain has a long history which dates back to the post-1815 era. However, a single unified 'Peace Movement' with a continuous institutional structure has never existed. Rather, the twentieth century movement for peace has developed from many different *peace traditions* of a moral, religious, ethical and political nature.

The tradition most commonly associated with peace activism is that of *pacifism*. In the early 20th century, pacifism had a general meaning. Until the 1930s a pacifist was someone who "rejected the doctrine that the best way to preserve peace was to prepare for war (the basic philosophy which always underpinned government defence policy), and looked for the ultimate removal of force from international relations".

During the 1930s, pacifism took on a much narrower meaning associated with the ideas of the minority 'absolutist' conscientious objectors of World War I.

Peace activism in the 20th century has ebbed and flowed according to the nation's circumstances. From time to time, it has surfaced in a series of 'shortlived outbursts' which have coincided with war, the threat of war, or economic crisis. During each upsurge, the various peace traditions provided the philosophical basis for peace activity.

The Nineteenth Century Background

Twentieth century peace activism is built on a wide variety of traditions. Throughout the 19th century, various peace societies, associations, and individuals struggled against a background of growing British imperialism to bring their theories to the attention of the public and politicians. This in itself was no easy task at a time when 'Pax Britannica', supported by economic and military power, was widely accepted as the best method of preventing major conflict in the world.

The first stirrings for peace came in 1816 with the formation of the *British Peace Society*. Led by Quakers and other Christians, its aim was to bring together all religious pacifists to cooperate with wider pacifist opinion. In the 1840s, the society took heart from the ideas of the *Free Trade Movement*. The radical intellectual, Richard Cobden, a leader of the movement, argued that free trade was the best way of achieving peace in the world.

"Cobden rejected nationalist economics. It was an archaic delusion to believe that one country's gain was another country's loss. The free exchange of goods across national boundaries worked to the advantage of all involved ... Through peaceful commercial intercourse the virtues of Victorian bourgeois culture would be diffused across the globe."
(Adapted from *Protests and Visions* by James Hinton p3.)

By the middle of the 19th century, religious and moral pacifism and middle-class anti-protectionism formed the basis of peace campaigning. However, these theories had little effect on the Foreign Office which was still controlled by the landed aristocracy.

"The heights scaled by Cobden and Bright were not exactly commanding, and the popularity of Palmerston's foreign policy grieved the Peace Society. The Crimean War demonstrated that the power of the peacemakers was very limited." (From *The Abolition of War* by Keith Robbins p.2.)

The 1860s and 70s saw a revival of interest in peace and pacifism with the founding of 3 organisations. *The International Law Association*, though American, was supported by some British lawyers. Its aim was to further the cause of *arbitration* as a way of keeping the peace between nations. In 1871, the *Workmen's Peace Association* was founded by Randall Cremer. Under Cremer's energetic leadership the WPA tried to encourage regular international meetings of Parliamentarians with a view to fostering greater understanding. Cremer, who became an MP in 1885, was particularly keen on arbitration as a means of settling disputes, and constantly urged peace societies to keep the issue at the top of their agendas. In 1880, the *International Arbitration and Peace Association of Great Britain and Ireland* was formed under the leadership of Hodgson Pratt. This organisation tried to avoid the overtones of religious morality which, he believed, had prevented peace issues capturing the popular imagination. Thus, the IAPA confined its efforts to working out practical procedures for arbitration.

Although the aforementioned groups could, by the turn of the century, claim endorsement from well-known middle-class radical intellectuals, it is clear that they had little popular impact. Indeed, popular enthusiasm for the Boer War only served to depress the peace organisations.

There were however a small number of positive signs:
- Some Liberal MPs were critical of the Government, but failed to bring their own party to an anti-war stance.
- Certain areas of the country, notably Wales, were critical of government policy.
- The Nonconformist churches were divided over the war, but the Church of England clergy supported the war, almost to a man.
- Keir Hardie condemned the war but, in the 1900 General Election, ILP candidates fared poorly. Although the Government came under pressure during the war, the reason was for failure to secure victory, rather than the war itself.

Thus, at the turn of the century, while peace movements in the rest of Europe were beginning to enjoy a new lease of life, the position in Britain was not encouraging. Nevertheless, the period to 1914 became a time of intense peace activity as the international situation began to deteriorate. Individuals, the Liberal and Independent Labour parties and the churches all played a role in giving substance and publicity to the wider developing peace movement.

Peace Campaigning to 1914

The new century saw British workers for peace more determined than ever to demonstrate that international solidarity for peace was becoming a reality. To this end, they organised a series of international peace congresses, the first of which met in Glasgow in 1901. The first congress is noteworthy because the word 'pacifist' was first used.

> "It was agreed that a pacifist was anyone who in the general sense was working to create or perpetuate peace." (From *The Abolition of War* by Keith Robbins p.10.)

In 1904, the *British National Peace Council* was formed. Its aim was to bring together the various *religious, radical* and *socialist* traditions which, although working for peace, did so in isolation.

Pacifists welcomed the Liberal victory in the 1906 General Election. They believed that the Liberals would take a strong stand against the arms race. The various Peace Societies were determined to force the new Government publicly to maintain a pro-disarmament stance. They were, however, disappointed when the Second Hague Conference of 1907 failed to achieve a lasting peace with Germany. The peace activist WT Stead strongly condemned the Government, accusing the Foreign Secretary, Sir Edward Grey, of being dominated by the 'reactionary' permanent officials at the Foreign Office and the Admiralty, who were against arms reductions.

The 1908 Peace Congress was held in London, and pacifists took heart when it resolved that all states should submit disputes to the Court of Arbitration at the The Hague. Following the Congress, the British National Peace Council decided to embark on an ambitious publicity and information campaign. The organisers were soon dismayed when they found that the member peace societies were more interested in promoting their own distinctive features rather than the cause of peace.

It is now clear that in the years before 1914, the wider British peace movement was undergoing change. New ideas were coming to the fore which often conflicted with the style and ideologies of the more traditional peace societies. The leadership of the Peace Society, for example, came to be increasingly out of touch with its supporters by emphasising the Society's liberal and nonconformist roots. By stressing arbitration rather than disarmament, the Society alienated itself from popular opinion. To rescue the Society from stagnation, a campaign against militarism and the possibility of conscription was organised. However, this had little effect. Thus, if the movement for peace was to have any effect on the course of events, it had to appeal to the opinion makers, ie. the labour movement, the parliamentary parties and the churches.

The Labour Movement and the Peace Issue

In the years preceding the outbreak of World War I, pacifists increasingly looked to the labour movement as a political platform for their ideas. Many ILP members were pacifists who had a strong nonconformist upbringing, and its leaders believed that the struggle for social reform was inextricably linked to the struggle for peace.

As a socialist party, the ILP was influenced in its development of a policy on war and peace issues by the Second Socialist International. The 1907 Congress of the Second Socialist International declared that:

> "If war threatens to break out, it is the duty of the working class ... and their parliamentary representatives ... to do all they can to prevent the outbreak of war by whatever means seem to them most appropriate. Should war nevertheless break out it is their duty to intercede for its speedy end, and to make use with all their power, of the economic and political crisis caused by the war to rouse all strata of the people and to hasten the fall of capitalist domination."

The ILP held a special conference in 1911 to consider how Labour could prevent war. The conference condemned the arms race and the strong links which existed between the armaments industry and the Admiralty, favouring as a solution the nationalisation of the industry. Hardie argued for a general strike if war took place and for cooperation with European trade unions.

Labour's main problem in the years prior to World War I was the fact that, while it argued for disarmament, an estimated 1.5 million workers had a vested interest in the arms race, as employees in the defence industries. The Party tried to overcome its dilemma by trying to link plans for disarmament with legislative proposals which would guarantee the right to work. When war broke out, it became clear that the leaders of the labour movement had underestimated the indifference of the working classes to foreign affairs and to the part which they played in the arms race.

The Liberals and the Peace Issue

The main strategy of peace activists prior to World War I was to attempt to sway public opinion, via pamphlets, journals and public meetings, and to work through the existing political structure in order to bring about changes in defence and foreign policy. They looked particularly to those Liberal MPs who wrote articles for their journals and generally were sympathetic to their cause.

The Liberal Party was recognised by many pacifists as their natural political home. However, the years 1906–1914 called this assumption into question. Britain's stance in the Moroccan Crisis of 1911, and the attitude of the Foreign Secretary, Sir Edward Grey, towards Germany worried pacifists within the Party. They feared that Britain would get drawn into a war with Germany. In 1912, Liberal dissidents formed a Parliamentary Foreign Affairs Committee.

The Committee concentrated its efforts on 2 issues: the 'balance of power' and 'secret diplomacy'. Leading pacifist members mounted a popular campaign against secrecy, advocating popular control over foreign policy. The committee had some success. A Cabinet Committee on Foreign Affairs was set up, and in the last months of peace, a Royal Commission began to investigate the structure of the Foreign, Diplomatic and Consular Services.

Other issues were taken up by Liberal pacifists. In 1913, when Churchill announced large increases in defence spending, 40 Liberal MPs protested to the Prime Minister. They were supported by ILP MPs and the Peace Societies, but failed to prevent the increases from taking place. The result was that, increasingly, pacifists outside Parliament looked to the labour movement for a political lead.

The Churches and the Peace Issue

Churches took an increasing interest in the peace issue before 1914. Anglican and Nonconformist clergy were anxious to seek good relations with Germany through the churches. To this end, the *British Council of Associated Churches for Fostering Friendly Relations between the British and German Peoples* was set up. This organisation held discussions with church and lay people in Germany, and advocated Christian methods for settling disputes between states. Its views were publicised through a journal called *The Peacemaker*, which by 1914 had a circulation of 67,000.

However, the British Council was never able to claim that it spoke for all Christians, and there were differences between the churches over the peace issue. The Anglican Church, as the Established Church, was in a difficult position as it had a unique relationship with the State which made outright opposition to the government difficult. The Nonconformist churches emphasised that Christians should participate in politics in order to preserve peace. Thus, the mainstream churches, while emphasising the concept of peace, were vague about what Christians should do if war broke out, and even more non-committal if that war happened to be a 'just war'.

The only Christian group to be clear on the peace issue before 1914 was the Society of Friends, or Quakers. This group, though few in number, had been associated with peace issues for 200 years. It stressed that *individual conscience* and the '*light within*' should guide people in their response to issues of war and peace.

The Society had many members who were active in the Peace Societies. There was also a Quaker Peace Committee which monitored the international situation and advocated policies such as arbitration.

Overall, the churches, collectively and individually, gave important support to the movement for peace, but failed to form a powerful united lobby for peace.

Pacifists and the War

The years immediately before the outbreak of war in 1914 saw some of the most intensive peace activity in British history. The coming of war in August of that year did not bring the various active peace traditions into one unified movement. Rather, war served to highlight the divisions which had been papered over in peacetime. In August 1914, pacifists divided as follows:

- A large majority of the churches supported the war, or at least did not actively oppose it. Some Quakers even served in the armed forces.
- Those who were against conscription continued with their opposition, but supported the war effort while it was based on voluntary enlistment.
- A large majority of Liberals supported the war effort as a crusade for democracy and justice. A minority continued to criticise the Government.
- In the labour movement as a whole, nationalist patriotism rather than socialist pacifism was the overriding sentiment. Although a majority of ILP members supported Hardie in his opposition to the war, a significant minority backed the war effort, as did a large majority of trade unionists.
- The Women's Suffrage Movement split into 2 groups. A minority opposing the war was made up of pacifists, socialists and liberals, including Sylvia Pankhurst, while the pro-war majority included such figures as Mrs Pankhurst and her other daughter, Christabel.

The Union of Democratic Control

As the war progressed, new peace groups arose to take up issues which were directly linked to the conflict and its aftermath. *The Union of Democratic Control*, founded in September 1914 by ED Morel, Norman Angell and Ramsay MacDonald, became Britain's major wartime peace organisation.

> ### The UDC's Four Points:
> 1 No annexation of territory without the prior consent of the people involved.
> 2 The abolition of secret diplomacy and Parliamentary control over foreign policy.
> 3 Balance of Power politics to be replaced by a Permanent International Council which would deliberate in public. All disputes to be settled by arbitration.
> 4 Armaments firms to be nationalised and international armaments to be limited by agreement.
> (Adapted from *The Morrow of War* by ED Morel.)

The UDC was not a 'Stop the War' organisation, rather it was concerned with the construction of a new international order after the war. Morel, the leading figure in the UDC, persuaded an impressive list of intellectuals, Peace Societies and other organisations to affiliate. At the height of its popularity in 1947, the UDC could boast a collective membership of 650,000.

During the war the UDC maintained a campaign for pacifism within the labour movement at a time when the ILP was concentrating its efforts on all party recruiting platforms. However, it failed to take up the issue of compulsory recruitment. It also debated the draft Covenant of the League of Nations, coming out against the League, describing it as "lacking moral validity" and a "betrayal of democracy".

The main achievement of the UDC during the war was that of keeping the cause of pacifism alive, particularly within the labour movement. When Labour eventually published its own war aims memorandum based on the principles of 'no annexations' and 'no indemnities', it was broadly in line with UDC principles.

The Labour Movement and the War

The labour movement was divided by the war. The ILP was overwhelmingly anti-war, and with pacifists and revolutionaries in its ranks, was in a difficult position. Eventually, the ILP leadership resolved its dilemma and joined the Coalition Government in May 1915.

The revolutionary Marxist banner within the labour movement was carried by the small British Socialist Party, and in Scotland by the tiny Socialist Labour Party. Individuals from both of these groups played a part in the disruption on 'Red Clydeside'.

Before the war, it was believed that the workers in South Wales and Clydeside would actively oppose any conflict when it arose. However, when war came, opposition was confined, in all but a few cases, to the effects of the war on workers, rather than the war itself. On Clydeside, socialist activists, disillusioned with the ILP, came to dominate the unofficial Clyde Workers Committee. Some members of the Committee, notably John Maclean and William Gallacher, were Marxists who wanted to stop the war. Others such as David Kirkwood were more concerned about defending the position of skilled workers. Most of the industrial unrest took place in the years 1915 and 1916. During this period, the government became sufficiently alarmed about the situation on Clydeside to arrest some members of the Clyde Workers Committee and to suppress its literature. However, the expected war resistance on the Clyde did not become a reality.

"The Clyde workers' movement, and the Shop Stewards' movement in England even more so, were about resistance to the effects of war (dilution, wages, rents), not to the war itself." (From *War and Peace and British Marxism* by Martin Shaw, in *Campaigns for Peace* by Richard Taylor and Nigel Young.)

"The most militant workers were often also the most patriotic – South Wales and Clydeside, the 2 centres of industrial discontent, also provided the highest proportion in the country of recruits to the army." (From *English History 1914-1945* by AJP Taylor, p.70 Pub. Pelican)

Conscientious Objectors

In order to avoid compulsory military service, conscripts had to prove that they were conscientious objectors according to the military regulations. During the war there

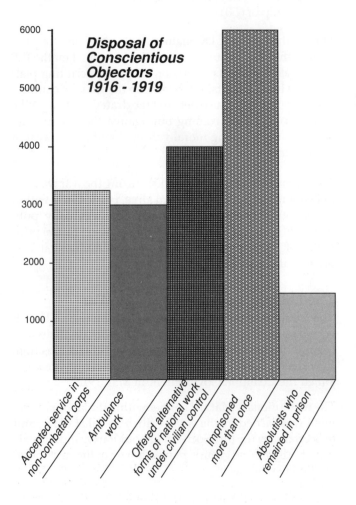

Disposal of Conscientious Objectors 1916 - 1919

Figure 4.1

were 16,000 official Conscientious Objectors, of whom 1 in 5 refused to come under military control.

All 'absolutists' were pacifists. Many were also socialists, anarchists and non-registrants. The treatment meted out to this group of 1500 in prison was extreme. Over 30 were sentenced to death, 73 died as a result of their treatment in prison and 40 were driven insane.

Opposition to Conscription

- "Compulsory military service is a negation of democracy." (Keir Hardie, ILP)

- "The claim of the state to dispose of a man's life against his will is the most insidious danger that can confront a free people." (Clifford Allen, NCF)

- "It is wrong to delegate one's private judgment by agreeing to obey orders without question." (David Garnett)

The 'No Conscription' Fellowship
A Case Study of War Resistance

From the mid-nineteenth century, compulsory military service was a concept which had always met with opposition from pacifists. However, from the turn of the century, the influence of the pro-conscription lobby, comprising Conservative politicians, military men and some newspaper men, grew.

Although 2,700,000 men had volunteered for military service by 1916, in 1915 the Government had been moving gradually towards conscription. The forces opposed to conscription – pacifists, socialists, trade unionists, liberals and Christians – also organised, forming the 'No Conscription Fellowship' in 1915. Initially the NCF acted as a pressure group against the Government, but gradually moved towards more radical tactics when the *Military Service Act* became law in 1916.

The 'No Conscription Fellowship' Statement of Faith
The 'No Conscription Fellowship' is an organisation of men likely to be called upon to undertake military service in the event of conscription, who will refuse from conscientious motives to bear arms, because they consider human life to be sacred, and cannot therefore assume the responsibility of inflicting death.

The NCF always denied the right of the government to force anyone to bear arms and its main objective was to frustrate its plans. At times forced to work underground, the NCF built up local networks of people who were trained to act independently in order to counteract government harassment or the arrest of its leaders.

The aims and work of the NCF was part of a wider war resistance movement which developed during the war. Clifford Allen at the NCF National Convention in 1916 argued that the alternative to conscription should not be a return to voluntarism. Instead the country should immediately enter into peace negotiations.

Two Evaluations of War Resistance

"Part of the failure of war resistance can be ascribed to the state's monopoly of repression; whilst organised war resistance eventually became a prerogative of other groups, the NCF was so harassed and persecuted under the Defence of the Realm Acts that ... the whole system of English liberty was on trial."

(From *War Resistance since 1914* by Nigel Young in *Campaigns for Peace* by Richard Taylor and Nigel Young.)

"The critics were right to the extent that the original policy of the NCF had failed. The Military Service Act was still on the statute book. The cause of peace had not been further advanced. Partly as a result of support received from non-pacifists, the issue had been presented as simply one concerning 'rights of conscience' ... to its dismay the NCF found that a large number of conscientious objectors were often quite a-political in outlook."

(From *The Abolition of War* by Keith Robbins p. 91.)

PEACE ACTIVISM 1918-1945

Pacifist feeling in Britain during the interwar period reached its height in the early 1930s. There were three main reasons for this.

Firstly, the experience of the First World War conditioned the British to fear war and ensured that, in contrast to the nineteenth century, foreign policy would have a higher profile in politics.

CONSCIENTIOUS OBJECTORS IN WORLD WAR I
The Case of Howard C Marten

Conscientious objectors were often portrayed as being cowards during the war. The evidence of the following case puts paid to the myth.

Howard C Marten, a Quaker by conviction, was conscripted into the army. He and three others were charged with military disobedience for refusing to obey the commands of their superiors, a crime for which a Court Martial could invoke the death sentence.

Marten's case was taken up by the Quakers, the NCF and anti-war MPs including Philip Snowden, the future Labour Chancellor of the Exchequer. His supporters in England went to great lengths to canvas prominent personalities concerning his plight, even securing an interview with Lord Kitchener.

Marten had to undergo the trauma of two Court Martials in France. The first, held on Friday 2 June 1916, at which legal aid was denied, was aborted by the authorities because of a legal technicality. At the second trial, held five days later, Marten based his defence on his Christian principles: that his crimes had been forced on him by the State, due to his beliefs in the wrongfulness of war.

He was initially found guilty and sentenced to be shot. His punishment was later commuted to ten years penal servitude. Witnesses said that Marten "never flinched" when he heard the sentence. Letters written to his family at the time of the trial are evidence of his courage.

He was later shipped back to Winchester prison, then taken to a work centre at Dyce Granite Quarry near Aberdeen where he served his sentence.

(Adapted from *Conscientious Objection* by Peter Lane, p. 38-40. Pub. Longman 1977)

Secondly, technological advance and its application to warfare, particularly the development of the bomber, brought the possibility of mass civilian casualties nearer. The notion that 'the bomber will always get through' coloured the thinking of both the public and politicians in the thirties.

Thirdly, the international situation in the 1920s seemed to offer hope that a positive change towards peace was taking place. Perhaps naively, many believed that the League of Nations, the Locarno Treaties of 1925, and the Kellogg-Briand Pact of 1928 were evidence of that change.

The post-1918 movement for peace developed in this environment and by the late twenties had consolidated its position. Liberal pacifism dominated during this period, the other main traditions of pacifism, socialist pacifism and radicalism having lost ground. This tradition was embodied in the *League of Nations Union* (see p.48) which, along with the *Peace Pledge Union* (see p.49) , became the standard bearer of peace activism in the interwar period.

By the end of the twenties, the LNU was pinning its hopes for peace on the World Disarmament Conference planned by the League for 1931. Lord Cecil, speaking to the League of Nations Assembly in September 1931, declared that "there has scarcely ever been a period in the world's history when war seems less likely than at present".

Cecil and his colleagues in the LNU were overoptimistic about the international situation. Nine days later Japan invaded Manchuria, foreshadowing the aggressive policies which were to be pursued by the European Fascist states. These acts led to a remarkable realignment in British politics in the thirties, with the anti-war Left campaigning for collective security through the League of Nations, while the Conservative Right supported a policy of appeasement towards the dictators. With all these changes occurring, the movement for peace gradually lost its way and its support.

The Manchurian Crisis 1931
The Japanese invasion of Manchuria led to disagreement within the LNU. Supporters of the LNU wanted sanctions against Japan, but its leadership refused to criticise either the Government or the League of Nations for their weak stance against Japanese aggression. However, the sanctions issue refused to go away. In 1932, the question was linked with disarmament when the *New Commonwealth Society* called for the League of Nations to be equipped with an international police force. This question divided the LNU between those who believed that disarmament would bring increased security, and those who argued

Profile of the League of Nations Union

The LNU was founded in 1918 and grew to be a peace society of unprecedented size and influence in the interwar period. It was granted a Royal Charter in 1925.

Dominant Ideology – Liberal pacifism.

Aims and Methods – Educational work to foster the League of Nations ideals of disarmament, conciliation and collective security. Campaigning for peace, acting as a pressure group, and organising the 'Peace Ballot'.

"The LNU had a faith in British public opinion as a force capable of moulding a new world order. A large and influential Union could sway the Government which in turn could lead the League and the world." (From *The League of Nations Union 1918-1945* by D Birn p. 198.)

Membership – All shades of political opinion, although in the 1930s mainly liberals and socialists.

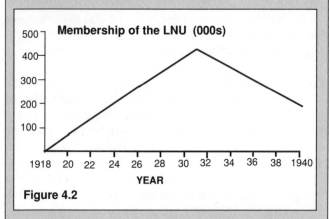

Figure 4.2

Leading Figures – Lord Robert Cecil, Gilbert Murray.

Successes – Organisation of the 1935 'Peace Ballot'. The aim of the ballot was to rescue the LNU from decline, and to demonstrate support for the League. From autumn 1934 to May 1935, 11.6 million people were polled in their own homes by 500,000 canvassers. Five questions were asked. The first three, concerning British membership of the League, disarmament and arms manufacture, received ninety per cent support. The fourth question on the abolition of air forces got eighty per cent support. The fifth question concerned the problem of aggression.

Should aggressor states be stopped:
(a) *by economic and nonmilitary measures?*
(b) *if necessary by military means?*

Ninety per cent supported economic sanctions, but less than sixty per cent supported military measures.

The LNU considered the ballot to be a success. The Government, for a short time, seemed to recognise public support for the League and talked cynically about collective security during the 1935 election campaign. When the Hoare-Laval agreement over the Abyssinia crisis was made public, the Government had no option but to sack Hoare. The LNU saw this as proof of the effectiveness of its stance.

Reasons for Decline
Internal policy differences.and problems of organisation. Supporters said that the European situation in the late thirties made the League of Nations irrelevant.

---

that security was an essential prerequisite for disarmament. Unfortunately this debate dominated the LNU until the mid-1930s and was a contributory factor in its decline.

Hitler in Power
Hitler's rise to power in Germany increased international tension. In Britain it led to an upsurge in pacifism and sentiment for war resistance. Examples of this are given below.

In 1933 the Oxford Union debated the motion 'This house will in no circumstances fight for King and country'. The motion was carried, amid much publicity.

"The resolution became and remained a potent source of myth. There is ... no documentary evidence that foreign governments noticed it or drew from it the moral that Great Britain had ceased to count in the world." (From *English History 1914-45* by AJP Taylor p. 448.)

At its 1933 conference, the Labour Party committed itself to a resolution that it would "take no part in war".

Within days of Germany's withdrawal from the Disarmament Conference, Labour won the Fulham by-election. This was regarded at the time as a great victory for pacifism, although historians such as AJP Taylor have since pointed out that the main issue in the by-election was, in fact, not peace but the 'means test'.

In mid-1934, the Government began the gradual process of rearmament as the pacifist euphoria of the previous year began to subside. Increasingly, two policy choices towards Germany were becoming apparent: containment or accommodation. The Labour Party and the LNU began to move towards containment. Dropping its war resistance policy of the previous year, Labour threw itself behind collective security through the League of Nations, while the LNU set in motion its 'Peace Ballot', hoping to bolster support for the League.

The Abyssinian Crisis, 1935
Italy's invasion of Abyssinia brought the issue of containment versus accommodation to the fore. Labour accepted the need for sanctions against Italy, and the Government, in its November General Election campaign, came out in support of the League of Nations position in response to public opinion.

The Year of Crisis – 1936
The 3 crises of 1936 – the final defeat of Abyssinia, the reoccupation of the Rhineland and the outbreak of the Spanish Civil War – constituted the 'watershed of the decade' in the eyes of many commentators. As a result, public concern for peace reached new heights. New peace groups, many affiliated to the *National Peace Council* which had a coordinating role in their activities, were started.

Fear of modern warfare came to dominate discussions of peace issues. This was fuelled by the publication in 1936 of Lionel Charlton's book *War Over England*. Charlton vividly described the potential destructiveness of modern air power against defenceless cities. His book was popular with both politicians and public.

The LNU began to face the possibility that collective security through the League of Nations was becoming less acceptable to the public. Its membership was beginning to decline, and so in November it began to move towards the notion of *appeasement* by adopting as its official policy a "manifesto which urged the League to study *territorial revision* and economic co-operation – a move which its annual report for 1937 noted to have been 'an influential factor in preventing further defections'."

(From *Peace Movements between the Wars* by Martin Caedel p. 91 in *Campaigns for Peace* by Richard Taylor and Nigel Young.)

The last hope for pacifists seemed to lie with Dick Shephard's *Peace Pledge Union*, which grew rapidly in the years preceding the war. This organisation campaigned for disarmament by means of 'Gandhi-style' nonviolence. By the end of 1937, however, even the PPU had started to move towards a position of 'peaceful change' rather than its former policies.

When Neville Chamberlain became Prime Minister in 1937, 'peaceful change' became Government policy in the form of appeasement.

From Munich to War
The events of 1938, the Anschluss of Austria and the cession of the Sudetenland after the Munich Conference, raised doubts within the broader movement for peace about the wisdom of the policy of 'accommodation'. The German occupation of what remained of Czechoslovakia in March 1939 finally dispelled any doubts in the minds of all but a minority of peace activists that Hitler was an aggressor who would not be satisfied by accommodation. Thus, support for the appeasement of Germany evaporated almost overnight. Peace activists felt that they had no choice but to give 'reluctant approval' to outright rearmament and attempts to build military alliances with eastern Europe and the USSR. When war broke out in 1939, activists for peace could only endorse the LNU executive statement from the previous year:

"positive peace represents a spiritual ideal which

however paradoxical it may seem, men will defend, if need be, with their lives." (From *The Peace Movement between the Wars: Problems of Definition* by Martin Caedel, in *Campaigns for Peace* by Richard Taylor and Nigel Young.)

Peace Activity during the Second World War

"The First World War produced not only a mass peace movement, while it lasted, but also a postwar current of public pacifism ... The second great European bloodletting produced no such peace movement, and the lessons it taught were those of militarism not pacifism." (From *Protests and Visions* by James Hinton. p. 118.)

Early opposition to the war came from the Communist Party which, after initially supporting the war, followed the line of the Communist Party of the Soviet Union (CPSU) in condemning the war as "imperialist" and calling for a "people's peace". However, following Hitler's invasion of the USSR in 1941, the party changed its policy to one of enthusiastic support for the war effort. The only other real voices of dissent came from certain Scottish Nationalists, the PPU which organised a Women's Peace Campaign, and pacifists who argued against the saturation bombing of Germany in the war.

The SNP and the War Issue (See p.112)
From 1937, the SNP was bedevilled with the issue of whether to take part in the forthcoming war. Three different strands of thought emerged within the party.

1 Moderates who were in favour of Home Rule, not separation, were willing to fight, feeling that an anti-war stance would only damage the Party at the polls.
2 Hardline nationalists argued that the Act of Union did not entitle a British government to commit Scotland to war. As early as 1934, a nationalist Anti-Conscription League was set up to promote this position.
3 Pacifists such as RE Muirhead were opposed to war per se.

Profile of the Peace Pledge Union

The PPU was founded in 1936 and became the largest absolute pacifist organisation in history.

•*Dominant Ideology* - Pacifism involving Gandhian nonviolence.

•*Aims and Methods* - The organisation encouraged people to *pledge* themselves to the statement "We renounce war and never again, directly or indirectly will we support or sanction another." The PPU then trained its members to be war resisters.

•*Membership* - By 1939, the PPU had 130,000 members, 30 full-time officials and over 1,000 branches nationwide. It is, however, difficult to estimate the true strength of the PPU because many people signed the pledge but did not become active in the organisation.

•*Leading Figures* - Formed by the Reverend Dick Shephard, the well known 'radio parson', the PPU attracted support from a wide spectrum of opinion. Members included George Lansbury, the ex-Labour leader, Siegfried Sassoon, Aldous Huxley and Bertrand Russell. Dick Shephard died in 1937 and was succeeded by Canon Stuart Morris.

•*Successes* - Very few concrete successes. The PPU provided a comfortable 'niche' for committed pacifists who were uncomfortable in other organisations. The PPU set out to be 'politically effective', but by the outbreak of war, most of its members had accepted the view that "pacifism was a faith rather than a policy".

•*Reasons for Decline* - The active membership was probably never more than 10,000. The PPU damaged itself by becoming involved with the British Union of Fascists. According to George Orwell, this led to the PPU's "moral collapse". It also failed to develop a consistent policy and became increasingly linked with appeasement. Finally the cause of war against Fascism was increasingly perceived as a 'just war'.

With such divergent views within the SNP, party policy chopped and changed in a vain attempt to accommodate everyone. eg. The 1937 Conference passed a resolution whereby male members would refuse to serve in the army until the SNP's aims were fulfilled. However, the 1938 Manifesto stated that "Scotland would fight with England and the rest of the Commonwealth for ideals appealing to our people". (From *The National Movement in Scotland* by J Brand.)

Working outside the SNP was a future Chairman of the party, Arthur Donaldson. He had set up a nationalist organisation called the *Scots Neutrality League*, whose aim was to keep Scotland neutral in the coming war. For his work, Donaldson was kept under police surveillance, arrested and sentenced to 6 weeks in jail. Donaldson claimed that, "One inspector said Norway and Holland had given Quisling and company too much rope and paid for it when the Germans invaded. England wasn't going to make that mistake". (From *Scottish News and Comment* No 49, Second Quarter, 1944.)

Germany, it should be noted, did set up a 'Radio Caledonia' to exploit disaffection north of the border.

Contrary to expectations, the anti-war stance of the SNP leadership did not harm the SNP's electoral fortunes. Just before the war ended, they returned their first MP to Parliament, despite the election of Douglas Young as Party Chairman while he was facing a one year prison sentence for refusing to be conscripted. (See p.112)

Conscientious Objectors in World War Two - Some Facts -	
Total number of COs	60,000
Percentage of conscripts claiming CO status in 1940	2.2%
Percentage of conscripts claiming CO status in 1945	0.2%
Percentage of conscripts having CO claim dismissed outright by tribunal	30%
Percentage of COs imprisoned during World War I	30%
Percentage of COs imprisoned during World War II	3%

Conscientious objectors fared better in the Second World War than in the First. The Government resolved to avoid confrontation with pacifists, and therefore treated the objectors relatively well. Despite the fact that there were almost four times as many conscientious objectors in World War II, a comparable organisation to the World War I 'No Conscription Fellowship' was never established.

PEACE ACTIVISM 1945 - 1979

The ending of the Second World War did not usher in a 'golden era' of peace. Soviet expansion into Eastern Europe, American possession of the atomic bomb and the post war weakness of Western Europe all combined to plunge the world into the years of the 'Cold War'.

In Britain, the post war Labour Government, while embarking on an ambitious programme of nationalisation and social reform at home, pursued a foreign policy largely dictated by fear of Soviet expansionism and the desire to maintain Britain's independence and status as a world power. Under these circumstances, the late 40s and early 50s were lean times for peace activism. Unlike the 1930s, the overwhelming ideological emphasis of the Labour Party was that of *socialist nationalism* which culminated, in the late 1940s, with:

1 A secret decision taken by the Attlee Government to go ahead with the independent production of nuclear weapons. The decision was justified on the grounds that "it would make for an easier, more equal, more even relationship with the Americans".(From *The Making of British Foreign Policy* by David Vital p. 37.)
2 British membership of the North Atlantic Treaty Organisation in 1949. NATO became a collective defence organisation, pledged to the deterrence of Soviet expansion in Europe with conventional and nuclear weapons.

By the mid-1950s, the implications of nuclear weaponry and the rapid advance of military technology began to be widely debated. For pacifists, "man ... now possessed the means to annihilate not only his civilisation, but the very existence of human life on the planet", while on the other hand, "... strategists calculated the potential casualties of an atomic clash in millions of deaths, or 'megadeaths', and evaluated the effects of deterrents and counter-deterrents, of 'first strikes' and 'second strikes', on a nation's ability to wage atomic war and survive. The balance of power was spoken of as a balance of terror." (From *A History of the Modern World* by Palmer and Colton p. 887 and 901.)

As the full implications of the 'nuclear age' began to unfold, the policy of a national defence, based on the possession and possible use of nuclear weapons, became the central issue for peace activism in post war Britain. In the period to 1979, 'anti-nuclear' peace activism reached its height in the late 1950s and early 60s in the activities of the Direct Action Committee Against Nuclear War (founded in 1957), the Campaign for Nuclear Disarmament (founded in 1958), and the Committee of 100 (founded in 1961).

CND and Nonviolent Direct Action 1957-1964

Britain began testing its own atomic weapons in 1952 at Christmas Island in the Pacific. Yet until 1956, when testing of the much more powerful hydrogen bomb began, protest had been limited, focussing on the broad concept of nuclear weapons rather than on the government's nuclear weapons policy.

In February 1957, the *National Campaign Against Nuclear Weapons Tests* was founded. Its aim was to persuade the government to halt unilaterally weapons testing to give a 'moral lead' to the Americans and Russians. The Campaign had some success when the United Nations Association and the British Council of Churches (against the advice of the Archbishop of Canterbury) came out in opposition to H-bomb testing.

Campaigners hoped that the Labour Party would support their stance against testing, a not unreasonable expectation given that Labour left-wingers were beginning to call for Britain to disarm unilaterally. Labour debated the issue at its 1957 Party conference, but left-wingers were stunned and angered when Aneurin Bevan, a previous advocate of

1959 Aldermaston March - Mrs JB Priestley, Benn Levy and Michael Foot

ported by letters from other well-known figures such as Bertrand Russell, Trevor Huddlestone, and Stephen King-Hall. As a result, the editor, Kingsley Martin, brought together a small group to form, eventually, the *Campaign for Nuclear Disarmament* which was officially inaugurated on 17th February 1958.

As CND grew rapidly, the leadership put its faith in a political strategy of winning the Labour Party to unilateralism. This, it hoped, could be achieved through the Labour left wing, and by the pressure of a public campaign. Once in power, Labour would implement unilateral nuclear disarmament. This strategy, however, failed. The issue of unilateralism in the late 1950s became increasingly tied up with the Party's internal struggle between left and right. The key figure in the debate over Labour's future defence policy in the years 1958-61 was the party leader, Hugh Gaitskell, a fervent advocate of Britain's nuclear deterrent.

unilateral disarmament, reversed his position. Bevan's so-called defection convinced left-wing Labour MPs that extra-parliamentary action against nuclear weapons was now the only logical step left.

Meanwhile, in the same year, a small group of pacifists, supported by well-known figures like Bertrand Russell, found the the *Direct Action Committee*. Its initial aim was physically to disrupt the H-bomb tests on Christmas Island. Although the disruption failed to take place, the DAC went on to play an important role in the movement for peace.

Following the 1957 Labour Party conference, peace activism gained in momentum. In November of that year, JB Priestly published an article in the *New Statesman* in favour of unilateral nuclear disarmament. His article was sup-

Gaitskell's beliefs formed the basis of Labour's 1958 policy document *Disarmament and Nuclear War*. However, there were clear signs that a growing element on the left of the labour movement had been moving towards unilateralism since the Suez Crisis of 1956. Gaitskell's belief in the independent British nuclear deterrent received a severe setback in the spring of 1960, when the Government was forced to abandon 'Blue Streak', a programme designed to give Britain its own missile to deliver a nuclear weapon. Cancellation of 'Blue Streak' meant, in effect, that Britain no longer had an 'independent' deterrent, and could not, therefore, maintain itself as an independent nuclear power.

Defence became the battleground for the struggle between

Profile of the Campaign for Nuclear Disarmament

Founded 17 February 1958.

Leading Members: Bertrand Russell - *President*; Canon Collins - *Chairperson*; Peggy Duff - *Organising Secretary*
Michael Foot; Jacquetta Hawkes

Aims

1 To persuade the British people that Britain must renounce unconditionally the use or production of nuclear weapons and refuse to allow their use by others in her defence.

2 To remove US nuclear weapons from British soil.

3 To end British membership of NATO.

Methods: Marches (CND became famous for the Aldermaston Marches in the early 60s), demonstrations, meetings, petitions, letters, pamphlets.

The main CND tactic in the late 50s to early 60s was to convert the Labour Party to a unilateralist stance. Once in government, Labour would implement a policy of unilateral nuclear disarmament.

"I know of no other way of obtaining a non nuclear Britain except converting the Labour Party. Unless they work through the Labour Movement, nuclear disarmers are simply marching to satisfy their own

consciences and expressing their sense of horror of nuclear war." (Kingsley Martin 1960. From *Protests and Visions* by James Hinton p.162.)

Reasons for Failure

• Failure to bring the Labour Party to a unilateralist stance in the early 1960s.

• Disagreement within the leadership about tactics causing the defection of leading figures like Bertrand Russell to more radical organisations like the Committee of 100.

• Improvement of the international situation from the mid-60s to the late 70s.

Postscript: CND returned to prominence in the late 70s and early 80s with the siting in Britain of American medium-range Cruise missiles. Leading figures were the historian EP Thompson, Mgr Bruce Kent and Joan Ruddock. Strategy and methods were similar to those used in the 60s.

Profile of the Committee of 100

Leader Bertrand Russell   *Founded* October 1960.   *Motto* 'Act or Perish'.

Aims

Mass, nonviolent, civil disobedience to awaken support for unilateral nuclear disarmament. "For twelve months it became 'the cutting edge' of the peace movement." (From *Protests and Visions* by James Hinton.)

Actions

1 *February 1961* - Sit-down protest by 5,000 outside the Ministry of Defence in Whitehall, led by Russell. No arrests.
2 *April 1961* - Sit-down protest by 2,500 outside the Ministry of Defence in Whitehall. 1,000 arrests.
3 *August 1961* - Dignified sit-down protest at the Cenotaph in Whitehall. No arrests.
4 *August 1961* - About 50 members of the Committee of 100 arrested and imprisoned for one month, including Russell who was eighty-nine years old.
5 *September 1961* - Trafalgar Square sit-down involving between 12,000 and 17,000 people. 1,300 arrested. The previous day the Scottish Committee of 100 organised a demonstration at the Polaris base at the Holy Loch involving 500.
6 *December 1961* - 5,000 people protested at seven US air bases. 850 arrested and given heavy jail sentences. National organisers of the Committee of 100 arrested and charged under the Official Secrets Act. Sentenced to 18 months in jail.

Reasons for Failure

1 The Cuban Missile Crisis demoralised the entire peace movement.
2 The authorities always managed to deal with the demonstrators.
3 Repressive action by the authorities in 1961 discouraged people from taking part in further demonstrations.
4 Moving the demonstrations away from London to military bases was a tactical error. Demonstrations got much less media coverage.
5 The Committee could not sustain such a high level of activity after 1961.

---

left and right at the 1960 Labour Party conference. Gaitskell vigorously defended his position on the issue, emphasising Britain's nuclear deterrent as part of the nation's contribution to NATO. Although the left, and therefore CND, won the Labour Party over to the cause of unilateralism at the 1960 Party conference, victory was short-lived. During the next 12 months, the right wing of the party fought back, and the 1961 conference reversed the unilateralist decision of the previous year by a substantial majority.

Richard Taylor, a historian of British peace activism, argues that the failure of CND to win the Labour Party was a turning point in its fortunes.

> "The CND leadership had based its whole strategy on winning over the Labour Party to a unilateralist policy ... and having lost the vote so decisively in 1961, what alternative strategy could now be adopted? ... as the 'Labour tactic' appeared less and less viable, and the leadership floundered, so the Movement began to splinter into its various constituent parts and subsequently to disintegrate."
> (From *The Labour Party and CND* by Richard Taylor, in *Campaigns for Peace* by Richard Taylor and Nigel Young.)

Meanwhile, the Direct Action Committee rejected the CND strategy of trying to 'win the Labour Party'. Instead, it opted for a more radical campaign involving nonviolent, sit-down protests and occupations. The most dramatic DAC protest took place in the summer of 1961 when demonstrators in small boats attempted to board a US supply ship for the Polaris submarine fleet based at the Holy Loch. Preceded by a 6 week protest march from London to Glasgow, the DAC actions gained national publicity.

The work of the DAC was, however, superseded in the second half of 1961 by the campaign of 'mass civil disobedience' organised by the *Committee of 100*. Led by Bertrand Russell, who had resigned as the President of CND, and young radicals who had grown impatient with the tactics of the other peace organisations, the Committee persuaded 100 well-known writers, artists and actors to 'put themselves at risk of arrest' in order to awaken the public to the need for nuclear disarmament. Until it was wound up in 1968, the Committee of 100 organised nonviolent action, mainly in the form of sit-down protests, at military bases across the country.

Anti-nuclear peace activism had passed its peak by the end of 1963 and from then on, organisations like CND and the Committee of 100 went into decline. Commentators have offered many explanations for this decline, eg. the Cuban Missile Crisis led activists to believe that their efforts had been in vain; the Test Ban Treaty of 1963 led activists to believe that the arms race was under control; the movement for peace had exhausted itself after five years of intense activity; peace activists simply moved on to other issues as a focus for their activities, for example the Anti-Vietnam War Movement, the Anti-Apartheid Movement and the growing Green Movement; peace activists expressing 'moral outrage' cannot compete for influence with the professional politicians of the 'secretive nuclear state'. Clearly the reasons for decline are complex and involve many factors.

The decline of anti-nuclear peace activism in the 1960s and 70s did not lead to its extinction. The return to 'Cold War' politics in the late 70s was accompanied by renewed efforts from peace activists in CND and other organisations to keep the issue of nuclear disarmament at the top of the political agenda as the arms race once again threatened to escalate out of control.

5 THE GROWTH OF DEMOCRACY

The system of government which exists in Britain today is known as *Representative Liberal Democracy*. The main components of this system are adult suffrage; the secret ballot; the right of citizens to participate in the political process; government which rests on majority support in the House of Commons; a free press and media with the right to criticise; and regular free elections.

The years 1850 to 1979 were a time of major political change in terms of *Authority* and of Britain's *Political Identity*. In the nineteenth century, the traditional authority of the Monarch and the landed aristocracy was eroded in favour of a limited form of democracy. The twentieth century brought in further change in the form of universal adult suffrage at the age of eighteen.

In this chapter we will explore the process by which these changes came about, the legislative detail of the changes which took place, and the effect which change has had on Britain's political identity.

Background

Prior to the First Reform Act of 1832, the system of Parliamentary representation had remained largely unchanged since the 16th century. At the beginning of the 19th century, both Houses of Parliament were wholly dominated by the landowning class. The House of Commons was elected at this time by 4.16 per cent of the population.

The Industrial Revolution, in a relatively short space of time, changed the social and economic structure which underpinned the existing system of representation. In addition, the outbreak of the French Revolution led to an upsurge of interest in reform. During this period, Reform Societies were set up which discussed and wrote about some of the radical political ideas being popularised by writers such as Thomas Paine in his *Rights of Man*.

However, the violence, disorder and war which the French Revolution brought led to the introduction of repressive government in Britain. This state of affairs continued after the war until the early 1820s, as the government sought to deal with the problems of post war economic readjustment, coupled with the increasing demands of the radical reformers for an extension of the franchise.

The first real political reform came in 1829, when Roman Catholics gained the right to become MPs. Reform organisations such as the Birmingham Political Union, formed in 1830, worked for much wider reform than had been gained by the Irish Catholics.

Of the two political parties of the day, the Whigs and Tories (later to become the Liberal and Conservative Parties), the Whigs were more sympathetic to the idea of very limited political reform. Thus, concerned by support for groups like the Birmingham Political Union, and alarmed by the so-called 'Labourers' Riots' in 1830, the Whig Government, under the leadership of Lord Grey, introduced a Reform Bill to the House of Commons in March 1831.

There was fierce Tory opposition as the Bill was debated in the House. Defeat at the Committee Stage led to the Government's resignation. At the subsequent General Election, the Whigs were returned to power with a majority of 136. A second Reform Bill then passed all of the stages in the Commons, but was rejected by the House of Lords.

The action of the Lords provoked popular discontent in parts of the country with riots, disturbances and damage to property. A third Reform Bill passed all stages in the House of Commons, but at the Committee Stage in the House of Lords, it stalled due to Tory opposition. The Whigs resigned from government when the King refused Grey's request for the creation of 50 Whig peers to allow the Bill to become law. Once again, the reformers outside Parliament mounted a popular campaign in favour of the the Bill.

At this stage the King was forced to ask the Duke of Wellington, leader of the Tories, to form a government. However, Wellington's efforts failed due to disunity within his own party and, once again, Grey and the Whigs returned to office. As a result, the Reform Bill became law in June 1832 due, in the end, to the deliberate absence of Wellington and other Tory peers from the Lords at crucial stages of the Bill's passage.

THE 1832 REFORM ACT

The Act covered two areas – the *Electors* and the *Constituencies*.

The Electors: Before the Reform Act the electorate was small, about 435,000 voters, under 5,000 in Scotland. There were no uniform rules determining who could vote, resulting in many variations across the country: eg. in some boroughs, every freeman could vote; in others only resident freemen had the vote; in other areas ratepayers could vote, while in some parts of the country, local custom dating back to the Middle Ages determined the franchise; in yet other parts of the country, the local landowner nominated the voters. Naturally these voters always returned the candidate favoured by their nominee. In some country areas, the landowner chose the MP – there was no election.

After the Reform Act the electorate was marginally increased to 652,000 voters; over 60,000 in Scotland. On the surface there seemed to be a more uniform franchise, eg. in the boroughs every man owning or renting property worth more than £10 per year in rateable value got the vote. All of the ancient local customs were abolished. In the counties owners of land worth £2 or more per year in rent got the vote. In addition, the vote was given to tenants who either rented land, paying more than £50 per year, or held land on a long lease of more than £10 per year. The limitations of the Act are demonstrated by the fact that:

- five out of six males still had no vote;
- in the English counties there was one voter for every 24 citizens;
- in Scotland there was one voter for every 5 citizens.

The Constituencies: Before the Reform Act the total number of MPs was 658 (Scotland had 45). There were 2 kinds of constituency: boroughs and counties. Most boroughs and all of the English counties sent two MPs to Parliament. Most Welsh and Scottish counties had only one MP. Large towns like Leeds, Manchester and Bradford had no MPs. Some constituencies had no voters or had ceased to exist, but still sent MPs to the Commons, eg. Old Sarum was one of the so-called 'rotten boroughs'. Other constituencies were known as 'pocket boroughs', as the local landowner nominated the MP. Pocket boroughs were bought and sold as financial investments. Before 1832 it is estimated that 160 landlords nominated almost half the MPs in the Commons.

After the Reform Act the total number of MPs was 658 (Scotland had 53). Fifty six towns with a population of less than two thousand lost both their MPs. Thirty towns with a population of between two and four thousand lost one of their two MPs. In addition, twenty two new two member boroughs were created; twenty new one member boroughs were created; six additional MPs were given to the larger counties; and Scotland gained eight new members. Thus, while some of the anomalies of the old system were corrected and the trend of urbanisation was recognised, the Commons still came largely from the south and south west of England, and continued to be dominated by the landed interest.

Clearly the First Reform Act did nothing for the vast majority of people, who remained powerless. Thus, demands for reform by the radicals continued in the 1830s and 1840s. The most spectacular of the movements demanding further reform at this time was the Chartists. Originating in London, with the formation of the London Working Men's Association for Benefiting Politically Socially and Morally and Useful Classes, the ideas embodied in Chartism became the focus for many democrats who had been disappointed by the 1832 Reform Act.

The Six Points of the People's Charter
- Universal adult manhood suffrage.
- Secret ballot.
- Equal constituencies.
- Abolition of the property qualification for MPs.
- Payment of MPs.
- Annual general elections.

The Chartists campaigned in the 1830s and 40s for an extension of democracy to working people. They believed that this was the only means by which working and living conditions could be improved. Their strategy was to present petitions to Parliament demanding that the six points of the 'People's Charter' be enacted into law. Chartism attracted a large amount of support, particularly in the north of England, at times of economic recession.

Petitions were presented to Parliament in 1837, 1839, 1842 and 1848, all to no immediate effect. The Chartists organisation died out after the 1848 petition. Violence associated with the 1842 and 1848 petitions, a divided leadership, the lure of other causes such as trade unionism and the Anti-Corn Law League, and a general improvement in economic conditions all contributed to the failure of Chartism to achieve its aims.

However, the necessity for political reform and the movement towards democracy was not extinguished with the failure of Chartism. While many upper- and middle-class citizens saw Chartism as a dangerous menace to the stability of the country, gradual social and economic change combined to make further political reform not only desirable but inevitable.

THE POLITICS OF REFORM IN MID-VICTORIAN BRITAIN

Although the electoral system put in place by the 1832 Reform Act still remained intact in mid-Victorian Britain, it came increasingly under pressure in the 1850s. The passing of a quarter century had brought increased urbanisation, industrialisation and general social change, yet the government of the country was still carried out by the middle and upper classes and was elected by a small minority of the population.

In Parliament, the two main parties, the Whigs and the Tories, had also changed during this period. The Tories, who were traditionally supported by the landed gentry, had split in 1846 over the repeal of the Corn Laws. Increasingly therefore, the party moved towards the ideology of Conservatism. The Whigs, on the other hand, were turning to the ideology of Liberalism and, as a result, the property owning middle class came to identify with it. Thus, by the 1850s a number of leading Liberals, as the Whigs had become known, came to accept that further Parliamentary reform to take account of social change was necessary.

Between 1852 and 1860, four Reform Bills were presented to the House of Commons. Three of these Bills came from Lord John Russell, whose belief that the 1832 Reform Act was "final", had earned him the nickname of 'Finality Jack'. Abandoning his position in 1852, Russell put forward proposals to lower and widen the property qualification in order to increase the electorate by giving the vote to working people of property and education. By 1860, all four Bills had failed to become law. However, by this time it had become clear that further measures of reform would be necessary, if only to take into account factors such as growth and movement of the population. In Parliament, Radical and Liberal MPs argued for limited reform.

Leading figures who supported reform became popular heroes, as public enthusiasm for political change grew in the early 1860s. Gladstone, the future Prime Minister, became a focus for attention in 1864 when he declared that "Every man who is not presumably incapacitated by some consideration of personal fitness or of political danger is morally entitled to come within the pale of the Constitution, provided this does not lead to sudden or violent or excessive, or intoxicating political change." (From *Democracy and Reform 1815-1885* by DG Wright p. 64 Pub. Longman.)

Gladstone's argument was based on the idea of moral right, which caught the public imagination. Outside the Parliamentary arena, the writings of JS Mill in his books *On Liberty* (1860) and *Representative Government* (1861) served to underline the principles of democracy with the educated classes. At the same time, popular enthusiasm for democratic sentiment grew with support for the Northern cause in the American Civil War and the struggle for Italian liberty.

However, within the Liberal Party there was still a debate over the question of reform, and here it must be remembered that even the pro-reformers only wanted safe measures of limited reform.

Outside Parliament, public pressure in favour of reform mounted. In 1864, the National Reform Union was founded to promote the idea of a community of interest between the working and middle classes. It argued that the political aims of the two classes were similar and that they could work together in the political arena. Also founded in 1864, the Reform League was much more radical, working for manhood suffrage and a secret ballot. The League was numerically strong, attracting support from trade unionists, socialists and former adherents of the Chartists' cause. By 1866, the London Trades Council began to campaign actively for manhood suffrage.

While the 1865 General Election returned the Liberals to power under the leadership of Lord Palmerston, the issue of reform had remained dormant during the election campaign. However, the death of Palmerston, who had consistently opposed political reform, brought the question back to life. Russell succeeded Palmerston as Prime Minister and Gladstone became Chancellor of the Exchequer. Both men now felt able to tackle the reform question, albeit in a cautious manner which they hoped would avoid dividing their party. Russell's strategy was therefore to play for time by proposing a Commission of Inquiry into the electoral system. This was to report in two years. Radical pressure from his own party forced Russell to drop the idea of the Commission and set about drafting a Reform Bill.

Britain in 1865 – Some Political Facts

- 116 MPs were sons of Peers and their relations.
- 109 MPs were sons of Baronets and their relations.
- 50% of MPs in the House of Commons (ie. 328MPs) were elected by 20% of the voters in England and Wales.
- Many towns in the North and Midlands were like Leeds, which had a population of 200,000 but had only 7,000 voters.
- In Britain the total population was 30 million, of whom 1,430,000 could vote.

The 1866 Reform Bill

This bill aimed to add significant numbers of the working class to the electorate without threatening the establishment. It made the following proposals:
- Men owning or renting a property of £7 per year rateable value would get the vote in the boroughs.
- £10 lodgers in the boroughs would get the vote.
- County tenants who rented land and who paid more than £14 per year would get the vote.
- £50 bank depositors would get the vote.

- In all, an additional 400,000 would have got the vote. Thus the electorate would have been increased by 5%.

Russell's fears of party disunity were confirmed when the Bill was published. The radicals were disappointed because the Bill had not gone far enough, while the anti-reformers, led by Lowe, vigorously opposed it. Lowe's supporters were nicknamed the 'Adullamites' by John Bright the reformer, after the Old Testament Bible story where David and his friends escaped from his enemies to the cave of Adullum. Working with the Tories in opposition to the Bill, the Adullamites forced the Government to accept an amendment to its proposals. With his party split, Russell resigned on 26 June 1866.

"Thus in June 1866 the Adullamite-Tory alliance succeeded. Disraeli had triumphed. Gladstone was humiliated and the Liberal Party hopelessly divided. Russell was too weak and tired to repair the split: Gladstone was too obstinate and inflexible. The former wished to drop the Reform Bill: the latter firmly refused ... When Russell failed to obtain pledged support in the Party for a Reform Bill in the next session he wearily decided to resign, and did so on 26th June. The Queen invited Derby to form a government." (From *Democracy and Reform 1815-85* by DG Wright p. 71-72 Pub. Longman.)

When Lord Derby and the Conservative Party were invited to form a Government by the Queen, they did so only reluctantly. In the House of Commons they were in a minority position, and in the country they had to deal with a cholera epidemic and popular demands for reform, underlined by marches, demonstrations and even rioting in Hyde Park.

The leading figure in Derby's Cabinet and in the House of Commons at this time was Benjamin Disraeli. His attitude to reform was different from that of his party colleagues. Disraeli favoured extending the franchise so long as it did not mean handing over political power to the working classes. While many Conservatives may have wished to leave the potentially divisive reform issue alone, Lord Derby chose to act. He believed that the agitation in the country for reform was now so strong that his Government could not avoid the question. In addition, Derby took account of Queen Victoria's fear for the stability of the country in the absence of concrete reform proposals.

The Conservative Reform Bill was introduced to the Commons in March 1867 by Disraeli. Its proposals would have created an additional 400,000 voters by allowing household suffrage in the boroughs and by introducing so-called 'fancy franchises' for people with £50 in savings or who paid 20 shillings in tax. It was also proposed to reduce the county franchise from £50 to £15.

During the Commons debates on the Bill, Disraeli had to perform with great skill. He needed the support of the radicals within the Liberal Party as well as the anti-reformers within his own Party for the Bill to succeed. Disraeli convinced the Tory waverers that the Bill was essentially conservative, while the radicals were led to believe that the proposals could become even more sweeping.

The case for increased Scottish representation in the Commons was made by the Edinburgh MP McLaren. He

The Reform Debate

The Pro-Reform Lobby
Main supporters — Russell and Gladstone.

– Efficient government needs the support of a wider electorate.
– 'Respectable' working-class men deserved the vote.
– Rewarding the working-class elite with the vote would lead to its 'moral improvement'.
– The vote would turn working-class men away from Socialism.
– An extension of the franchise would break the power of the aristocracy.
– It would push the Liberal Party in a more radical direction.

The Anti-Reform Lobby
Main supporter — Robert Lowe.

– Working-class people were selfish and ignorant.
– They would use the vote in a self-seeking manner, destroying efficient government.
– Empowering the working-class would lead to attacks on property and the free market.
– Power must remain in the hands of the elite who know how to use it.
– Extension of the franchise would lead to a form of tyranny with attacks on traditional institutions.
– Only men of property have the intelligence to participate in politics.

argued that the Scottish quota of MPs should be increased from 53 to 68 since Scotland now contained one-ninth of Britain's population and contributed more than an eighth of taxation.

The Bill passed its third reading in the Commons without a vote and became law in August 1867, the House of Lords having made little alteration to its content.

The Second Reform Act 1867

This Act increased the electorate by 1,120,000 voters to approximately 2.5 million.

The Franchise
• In the boroughs, all householders with one year's residence and who paid rates got the vote.
• Lodgers living in accommodation valued at £10 annual rent got the vote.
• In the counties, the franchise was extended by reducing the £10 value for copyholders and leaseholders down to £5.
• Occupiers of premises which had a rateable value of £12 got the vote.

The Constituencies – The Act, plus measures taken in 1868, led to a number being disfranchised. The available 52 seats were distributed as follows – 25 went to the counties; 19 went to the boroughs; 1 went to London University; 2 went to Scottish Universities; and 5 were allocated to Scottish constituencies.

While it is clear that the Second Reform Act increased the numbers of men entitled to vote from one in seven in 1833 to one in three, it did not alter the balance of political power in Britain. The electorate still remained as before in both the boroughs and the counties, namely the middle classes: the shopkeepers and skilled workers, the landowners, tenant farmers, householders and local tradesmen. The most important change was the granting of the vote to occupiers in the boroughs. As a result, the electorate in some of the newer towns in England and Scotland increased dramatically.

The 1867 Reform Act gave the vote to many more men than had originally been intended by Disraeli, particularly in the towns. As a result, both political parties now understood that the traditional form of election campaigning would no longer be relevant. Thus in order to mobilise the support of the urban working class, both the Liberals and the Conservatives developed national organisations which in the future managed party activities on a nationwide basis. Increasingly therefore, fewer genuinely independent MPs were elected to the Commons. To be elected to Parliament, a man required the support and organisation of a national party.

While the Second Reform Act gradually moved the nation closer to democracy, the electoral system still had to free itself from the crooked practices of bribery, corruption and intimidation. Although the Chartists demanded a ballot to replace the traditional method of publicly declaring your vote from the hustings, a more democratic method of voting did not become an issue until the late 1860s. In the meantime, bribery during and between elections was rife, eg. in 1865 £14,000 was spent on bribing the 1,408 voters in the constituency of Lancaster.

The 1867 Reform Act

The Historical Debate

There are three different interpretations of the reasons for the passing of the 1867 Reform Act: the Whig school, the Socialist school and the Tory school.

The Whig School: Stresses the idea that political reform came about as a response to economic and social change in Britain. 'Whig' historians also emphasise the notion that popular pressure for reform led to the passing of the Act.

The Socialist School: Argues that popular agitation in 1866 and 1867 was responsible for the timing of reform. 'Socialist' historians say that the Reform League's campaign in 1866 and the Hyde Park Riot all combined to push both Gladstone and Disraeli in the direction of reform.

The Tory School: Emphasises party competition in the years following Palmerston's death as the reason for reform. They argue that neither Gladstone nor Disraeli was interested in creating a truly democratic system, rather they were more concerned with outplaying each other.

The idea of secret voting was criticised by individuals from both parties because, they argued, voting was a "privilege" and a "responsibility" which required to be carried out in public.

> "The motives under which men act in secret are as a general rule inferior to those under which men act in public."(From *The Constitutional History of Modern Britain* by Sir David Lindsay Keir p. 467 Pub. Adam and Charles Black.)

When a Parliamentary Enquiry into the 1865 General Election revealed the scale of electoral malpractice, Gladstone's Government brought in a Bill which, although rejected by the House of Lords in 1871, became law in 1872 as the *Ballot Act*.

Once voting was done in secret intimidation declined, although corruption was not completely wiped out. Between 1867 and 1885, 4 towns were disfranchised due to corrupt practices. It took a further measure from the Liberals in 1883 to deal adequately with the problem.

The 1883 *Corrupt and Illegal Practices Act* established:
- that a candidate's election expenses were determined by the size of the constituency.
- what campaign money could be spent on.
- that election agents had to account for their spending.
- a detailed definition of illegal and corrupt practices.
- that a breach of the law disqualified a candidate for seven years.
- that active involvement in corruption was punishable by a fine or imprisonment.

Having dealt with the problem of corruption, Gladstone's second administration now turned its attention to wider electoral reform, against a background of falling popularity and division within the Liberal Party. In 1883, Joseph Chamberlain, one of Gladstone's Cabinet Members, drew up a legislative programme for the next election which he promoted in a series of speeches across the country. Chamberlain advocated land reform, fiscal reform to cut the burden of taxes paid by the poor, and measures to democratise local government. However, the central feature of Chamberlain's programme was a Reform Bill which would grant equal voting rights for males in the counties with their borough counterparts.

While Gladstone was cautious about extending the franchise due to opposition within his own party, he was also well aware that an effective Reform Bill which removed electoral injustice could turn the tide of popular opinion in favour of his government. A Franchise Bill was therefore introduced to the Commons in 1884. Although the Bill passed all stages in the House of Commons, it was blocked by the House of Lords, who demanded that a scheme for the redistribution of seats be introduced at the same time. As protracted negotiations continued between government and opposition in both Houses of Parliament, there were some anti-peer disturbances in the autumn of 1884 in Birmingham, and protest marches in Scotland.

> "... These processions were pure street theatre, encapsulating more than anything else in the nineteenth century the character of proletarian Liberalism, and emphasising its civic and craft pride, its class

feelings against landlords ... The Glasgow demonstration of 1884, intended to put pressure on an obstructive Tory House of Lords involved 64,000 in the procession and another 200,000 gathering to greet them on Glasgow Green. They carried countless pictures of Gladstone and many of Bright ...The French polishers, for example, carried a miniature wardrobe, first borne in 1832, and a flag inscribed, 'The French polishers will polish off the Lords and make the Cabinet shine' ... The basic message was clear – the 'class' obstructed reform, the 'masses' were here to demand it." (From *A Century of the Scottish People 1830-1950* by TC Smout p. 245-246 Pub. Collins.)

Eventually it was agreed that there should be two Bills, one dealing with redistribution of seats and another which would tackle the extension of the franchise.

Representation of the People Act 1884
The effects of this Act can be summarised as follows:

- The electorate was increased from 2.5 to 5 million.
- In England and Wales two out of three men now had the vote.
- Male householders and lodgers in the counties with 12 months of occupation got the vote.
- Voting qualifications in the towns and counties were now identical, ie all householders and lodgers paying £10 per annum in rent could vote.

Redistribution of Seats Act 1885
This piece of legislation aimed to construct constituencies of approximately equal size.

- 79 towns which had a population of under 15,000 lost both their seats.
- 36 towns which had a population between 15,000 and 50,000 lost one seat.
- Towns with populations between 50,000 and 165,000 kept two seats.
- Universities kept two seats.
- The remainder of the country was divided into single member constituencies.
- The total number of MPs was increased from 652 to 670.
- Scotland's representation increased to 72 MPs.
- In Scotland 7 additional seats went to the counties.
- Lanark's representation was increased from 2 to 6 MPs.
- The counties of Fife, Perth and Renfrew each had their representation increased to 2 MPs.
- In the Scottish cities, Glasgow's representation increased from 3 MPs to 7, Edinburgh's from 2 to 4 MPs, and Aberdeen's increased from 1 to 2.

The Third Reform Act moved Britain closer to democracy, putting in place an electoral system which is very similar to that which presently exists. However, the country was far from being a democratic society. Women were still excluded from the system, as were male domestic servants, sons who lived at home, paupers on poor relief, soldiers living in barracks and those who had failed to pay their rates.

Between 1885 and 1918 there were few attempts to widen

the franchise, despite the suffragette agitation prior to World War I (see Chapter 3). The 1918 *Representation of the People Act* at last removed the discrepancies in the male franchise and gave the vote to women over the age of 30. Women eventually gained equal voting rights with men in 1928. Further twentieth century electoral reforms in 1948 and 1969 abolished University representation in Parliament and reduced the voting age from 21 to 18.

THE DECLINE OF THE LIBERALS AND THE RISE OF THE LABOUR PARTY

The decline of the Liberal Party and the rise of the Labour Party has been a lively source of controversy among historians for many years.

George Dangerfield, in his well-written, but essentially misleading work *The Strange Death of Liberal England*, published in 1936, was responsible for the view that the replacement of the Liberals by the Labour Party as the mouthpiece of the British working class was inevitable and the rift between Asquith and Lloyd George was merely an expression of and not the cause of this process. This view was to have considerable influence on later writers until the 1960s.

From a different standpoint, more recent historians such as Paul Thompson and Henry Pelling have come to the conclusion that the middle-class character of Edwardian Liberalism made it essentially incapable of accommodating its support at either national or local level. It was this factor which eventually ensured the triumph of the Labour Party. Thompson, in his book *Socialists, Liberals and Labour* (p.179), considered the radicalism of the Liberals in the 1900s to be an "increasingly outdated political concept". Pelling, an authority on the rise of the Labour Party, added that it, and not the Liberals, was better equipped "to take advantage of 20th century political conditions". (Quoted in *The Age of Lloyd George* by KO Morgan p.39 Pub. Allen & Unwin 1971)

On the other hand, some historians, notably Trevor Wilson, have rejected this view totally. In his work *The Downfall of the Liberal Party, 1914-1935*, he argued that the Liberal Party was still in a mainly healthy condition at the start of the war in 1914 when it was suddenly felled by the events of the war.

Kenneth O Morgan, in *The Age of Lloyd George*, concluded that during the difficult period of 1910 to 1914, "years of labour unrest, of the Ulster crisis and the Suffragettes' demonstrations", these challenges were directed more against the British constitutional system than the Liberal Party itself. Moreover, the Liberals, with Lloyd George in a key reforming position, were nowhere near exhausted. Morgan's conclusion was that "to view these years as a kind of Indian summer for a party on the verge of imminent collapse is a basic distortion of political history". (*The Age of Lloyd George*)

In 1974, Ross McKibbin, in his work *The Evolution of the Labour Party 1910-24* (Clarendon Press 1974), reinforced Pelling's view in addition to adding fresh research. McKibbin argued that,
- the growth and expansion of trade unions in the late 19th and early 20th century led to the rise of the Labour Party.
- as union membership increased after 1910, Labour's national structure and local campaigning changed, thus improving the party's electoral position.
- Labour was a real threat to the Liberals by 1914 and could have done even better had it not been hindered by legal impediments which affected the Party's ability to organise, and a restricted electoral system which continued to prevent large numbers of potential working-class Labour supporters from voting.

A recent work by Duncan Tanner, *Political Change and the Labour Party 1900-1918* (Cambridge 1990), reassessed all of the evidence and clarified the issues. He argued that,
- the success of the Liberal Party was due to its ability to attract working- and middle-class voters, rather than the ideology of the 'New Liberalism'.
- the Liberals were only under threat from Labour pre-1914 in specific areas of the country. The experience of war enhanced Labour's reputation in these areas.
- overall, the Liberals were defeated in 1918 due to their attitude to the war.
- although Labour became the major anti-Tory party after 1918, the Liberals still had a place in a new developing three party system.

FORCED FELLOWSHIP.

Suspicious-looking Party. "ANY OBJECTION TO MY COMPANY, GUV'NOR? I'M AGOIN' YOUR WAY"—(aside) "AND FURTHER."

Factors Promoting the Liberal Decline and the Labour Growth

1 The Liberals were split in 1886 over Gladstone, the Liberal Prime Minister, proposing Home Rule for Ireland. Ninety three Liberal MPs voted against the bill and many of them, calling themselves *Unionists*, gradually moved over to the Conservative side. The loss of Joseph Chamberlain, in particular, was a severe blow to the Liberals as he was their most radical spokesperson and was regarded as a natural successor to the ageing Gladstone. The Whig gentry, who had been a crucial element in Gladstonian Liberalism, were already shaken by the passing of the 1884 Reform Bill. They regarded the Irish Bill as the last straw and left the Party. Support was also lost in the centre of the Party among professional and academic opinion such as Arnold and Dicey. Gladstone, himself, seemed to be the only unifying factor in a party deeply split and disillusioned.

2 The attempt by the Liberal Party to remould itself in the late 19th century was another source of problems. With the adoption of the *Newcastle Programme* in 1891, which committed the Liberals to a vast range of reforms, there were now two contrasting views in the Party ie. 'Old Liberalism' and 'New Liberalism'. The former advocated the traditional individualism of Liberalism and the latter proposed the new collectivist or government interventionist thinking. (See chapters 6 and 7)

3 Imperial affairs also helped to weaken the Liberals in the 1890s. Divisions within the Party over Britain's policy towards the Empire came to a head in 1899 over the South African or Boer War. While the Conservatives were united in their approach to the war, the Liberals were split into three factions. Those who were opposed to the war, including Lloyd George, were called the National Liberal Federation; the faction who supported the war, including Rosebery and Asquith, were called the Liberal Imperialists; and the third faction, which observed an embarrassed neutrality, comprised the majority of the Party including Campbell-Bannerman. The ending of the war in 1902, however, concluded the most painful phase of Liberal disunity.

4 It can be argued that the Liberal landslide victory, the biggest since 1832, gave a misleading picture of its popularity and strength in 1906. Although the Party was now united under Campbell-Bannerman, historians and contemporaries have been puzzled to explain the reasons for this surprising election result. To a large extent the Liberals owed their triumph to the electorate's negative reaction to Conservative mistakes over the previous ten years. For example, the Conservative plan to end 'free trade', which had been the basis of Britain's industrial wealth until that point, and to introduce import duties on goods from non-imperial countries, split the Party and alienated many voters. Many voters thought that this would put up the cost of living as the cost of goods would have to be increased. Other important vote losers for the Conservatives were the importing of 'Chinese slaves' to South Africa, which upset humanitarians, and the 1902 Education Act which upset non-conformists.

Although the Liberals retained office in the two elections of 1910, their majority was greatly reduced. Indeed, they relied on the support of the Irish Nationalists and the new Labour Party to keep them in power.

5 In spite of the achievements of the greatest of all Liberal Governments, it can be said that they were a struggling party in 1914 as they were besieged on three fronts by an escalating militant suffragettes' campaign (see chapter 3), an increasing number of industrial disputes (see chapter 2), and by the twin possibilities of civil war in Ireland and the resultant mutiny of British army officers in Dublin.

Undoubtedly at this point the Government's reputation was badly shaken. Its record in by-elections was poor and the Conservatives anticipated victory at the next election. Nevertheless, the Party was very far from being dead as most contemporaries would have agreed. After all, the different challenges facing the Liberal Government were directed more at the constitutional system than at the Party itself. Moreover, Asquith's ministry was still overtly united and, with Lloyd George in the Cabinet and a new generation of younger men like Masterman and Simon, there were no signs of exhaustion.

6 With the arrival of the Labour Party in Parliament from 1906, the eventual demise of the Liberal Party was a strong probability. On the one hand, the middle-class character of Edwardian Liberalism and its basic incapacity to accommodate working-class support at local and national level would have made it difficult for the Liberals to hold on to

The Electoral Fortunes of the Liberal and Labour Parties 1906-1929		
	Liberals	**Labour**
1906	377*	29 + 24 Lib-Labs
1910 (January)	275*	40
1910 (December)	272*	42
1918	133 (Coalition or Lloyd George Liberals)	4 (Coalition Labour)
	28 (Asquith Liberals)	59 (Labour)
1922	57 (Lloyd George Libs.)	142
	60 (Asquith Liberals)	
1923	159	191*
1924	40	151
1929	59	288*

Table 5.1 (*Indicates the Party forming the Government)

the working-class vote. On the other hand, the potentially strong appeal of the new Labour Party to the working class on such important issues as social reform and trade union legislation made them, and not the Liberals, better equipped to profit from 20th century political conditions. (see chapter 2) However, this shift in the balance of working class support from the Liberals to Labour was likely to have been a gradual process.

7   Some historians have argued that World War One accelerated social and political changes rather than causing them. The Great War is often cited as having precipitated the decline of the Liberals and conversely the rise of Labour. Before 1914 the Liberals had won the three previous elections but after 1918 never held office again. Indeed by 1923 they had slumped to being the third party in the country. The demands of total war and Asquith's apparent inability to provide strong and effective leadership led to his resignation in December 1916. Lloyd George formed a fresh Coalition Government with the support of most of his Liberal and Conservative colleagues. However, lasting damage had been done to the Liberal Party as Asquith and his supporters felt betrayed from within by the new Prime Minister who, in their view, had conspired with the Conservatives. Unfortunately for the Party, the gulf between 'Asquithian' and 'Lloyd George' Liberals in the House of Commons extended to the constituencies. The growing rift continued in the 1918 Election when Lloyd George and his Liberal supporters stood for Parliament on a platform of continuing the Coalition Government with the Conservatives. Asquith and his supporters opposed him but were no match for the coalition parties. (see table 5.1) Indeed, in the course of this Ministry, Lloyd George was to become a prisoner of the Tories as they were largest single party with 389 MPs.

Although the war had caused problems within the Labour Party due to the different reactions of various groups, (see chapters 2 and 4) it gained Cabinet experience much earlier than could have been expected. Henderson became a member of the small, war Cabinet with eight other Labour members in the government.

DEMOCRATIC CHANGE IN THE TWENTIETH CENTURY - ONGOING ISSUES

Although the question of the franchise was largely settled by 1928, other areas of the constitution became the focus for reform and innovation. This is not surprising, since democracy implies that change is necessary and ongoing, and that it is carried out by consensus, through elected representatives, empowered by the voters and ultimately accountable to them.

Outside the area of the vote there are three sectors where change has been sought in order to enhance democracy. These are the House of Lords, the electoral system and the introduction of referendums.

Reform of the House of Lords

Parliament is made up of two chambers, the House of Commons and the House of Lords. The constitutional relationship between the two Houses has been the focus of attention at various times during the twentieth century. As constitutional precedent dictated, this relationship, until the late nineteenth century, was one in which an elected House of Commons initiated most legislation. The function of the largely hereditary House of Lords was to examine, criticise and revise untidy parts of legislation. The position of the Lords was recognised as being 'subordinate' to that of the Commons because the latter was elected by the people.

While the 1867 Reform Act had underlined this position of subordination, increasingly the Conservative dominated House of Lords became unwilling to pass Liberal legislation. As we have already seen, the Lords refused to pass the 1884 Franchise Bill without a redistribution scheme, and in 1893 it had rejected the Home Rule Bill. After 1906 the Lords rejected Liberal legislation on education, land valuation and Scottish smallholdings, and in 1909 rejected Lloyd George's famous 'People's Budget' in which the rich were to be taxed to pay for naval rearmament.

The Liberals perceived the behaviour of the Lords over the Budget as an attack on democracy and were determined to meet the challenge head on. In a famous election speech in 1910 Asquith described the Lords as a "doormat second chamber" which only woke up when "democracy votes Liberal". After two general elections in the space of two years, the Liberals, in 1911, introduced a Parliament Bill which only became law when the House of Lords was threatened with the creation of enough new peers to ensure a government majority. The resulting *Parliament Act* (1911) took away the Lords' power over Bills which concerned taxation and government spending – money Bills. They were left with the power to amend or reject other Bills, but only had the power of delay for two Parliamentary sessions. This delaying power was cut to one session by the *Parliament Act* of 1949.

Since then, the Lords have only rarely used their power, fearful that if they did so the Commons would cut their authority completely. In the 1970s the Upper House began to reassert itself by obstructing some Labour legislation.

There have been many schemes to reform the House of Lords. Proposals were mentioned in the King's speeches between 1920 and 1922, and reform has been the subject of several unsuccessful Private Member's Bills. The *Life Peerages Act* of 1958 created Life Peers and the *Peerages Act* of 1963 enabled Peers to give up their titles in order to stand for election to the House of Commons.

The last real attempt to democratise the Lords came in 1969 with Labour's Parliament (No. 2) Bill. It attempted to create a two-tier House in which Life Peers would be voting members and hereditary Peers would be non-voting members. The new House would also have had a six months power of delay on non-money Bills. The Bill, however, fell after its second reading in the House of Commons. Since then, ideas for reform have included outright abolition and election by proportional representation on a regional basis.

The Electoral System

Although the electoral system which evolved in the nineteenth century was simple and easy to administer, it was also unfair to minor parties. The system, as it has stood this century, has been overgenerous to the dominant parties, Labour and the Conservatives, leaving parties like the Liberals, despite a broad base of support across the country, with very few seats in Parliament.

While electoral reform is perceived as an issue of the 1970s and 80s, it has in fact been on the political agenda since World War I. In 1918 an all-party 'Speaker's Conference' proposed a form of proportional representation (PR) as a method of election which would more accurately reflect the wishes of the people. Although this proposal was dropped due to the 1918 election, proportional representation was again proposed in 1931 by the minority Labour Government as an inducement for Liberal support.

The Proportional Representation Debate

Listed below are the main elements of the debate which has developed over the years.

For PR	Against PR
• The present system is undemocratic because it is not representative.	• PR leads to a multiplicity of small parties.
• The unfairness of the present system discredits Parliament.	• Most governments would be coalitions.
• PR is fair.	• There would be political instability as a result.
• PR avoids extremism.	• PR leads to weak government.
• Other countries with PR are well governed.	• PR is too complicated

---

Since 1931 both the Labour and Conservative Parties have opposed electoral reform proposals which have favoured PR, convinced that any such scheme would be detrimental to their interests. In the 1990s interest in electoral reform revived in the Labour Party and also within some elements of the Conservatives. The Liberals have been enthusiastic supporters of PR as a means of reviving their political fortunes since 1922.

Referendums

A referendum is a ballot in which the voters are called to pass judgment on a particular question. Before the 1970s the use of a referendum as a form of democratic consultation had never been carried out in Britain. The idea, however, was not new. In the 1890s, the Liberal Unionists advocated the use of a referendum on the issue of 'Irish Home Rule'. Baldwin, in 1930, sought a referendum on the issue of 'protection', and in 1945 Churchill aired the possibility of a referendum over the question of continuing the wartime coalition until Japan was defeated.

The first referendum took place on 5th June 1975. It was initiated by the Labour Government which, in its election manifesto, had committed itself to renegotiating Britain's entry to the European Community and submitting the terms to the judgment of the people.

Labour claimed that the issue was unique in that one of the key elements to be considered was that of the sovereignty of Parliament: if Britain continued in the Community, Parliament's authority in some areas of legislation would be superseded by the Community. Thus, voters were asked to answer 'yes' or 'no' to the question "Do you think that the United Kingdom should stay in the European Community (the Common Market)?" The result was a two to one vote in favour of staying in the Community, a result which many opponents of the decision still argue has weakened the sovereignty of the British Parliament.

In 1977 the Labour Government agreed to referendums being held on devolution proposals for Scotland and Wales. (see p.127) In January 1978, a Commons amendment made the Scottish and Welsh referendums subject to the 'forty per cent rule', that is, if forty per cent of eligible voters did not vote 'yes', the legislation would fail. The Scottish and Welsh referendums took place on 1st March 1979, and in neither case was the forty per cent threshold achieved. At the time, Margaret Thatcher argued against the principle of referendums on the basis that they undermined the sovereignty of Parliament. George Cunningham, the architect of the forty per cent rule, had this to say:

"I do not say that referendums will become a regular part of our behaviour, but there is certainly a greater chance of that now than there was before and there are far more people who feel that a referendum is a useful tool in particular circumstances."
(From *The Constitution in Flux* by Philip Norton p. 214 Pub. Martin Robertson Oxford.)

Since 1979, there have been no further referendums.

The development of liberal democracy in Britain over the past 130 years was slow and piecemeal. The system which had evolved by 1979, while retaining many of the traditions of the past, had put in place most of the apparatus necessary to satisfy the democratic aspirations of the nation. Nevertheless, the essence of democracy is that of a system of government which promotes and encourages political change from below. Thus, issues such as electoral reform, devolution, the protection of human rights, the right to privacy and the promotion of equality, continue to be debated, explained and acted upon as part of our everyday, ongoing, democratic political culture.

6 Laissez Faire and its Critics in Late Victorian Britain

"Laissez faire is quite literally the only untried utopia"

(A W Macmahon quoted in J Bartlett Brebner - *Laissez Faire and State Intervention in Nineteenth Century Britain*, Journal of Economic History, supp. viii 1948)

In the next four chapters, we will be trying to explain the origins and growth of the welfare state from the late Victorian period until 1950 when the social welfare system was firmly in place. In this chapter, we will attempt to see if we can find the origins of the welfare state in late Victorian times from about 1870 until 1900. We will look at :

- the prevailing belief in laissez faire and the challenges to that belief by socialists, radicals, collectivists and social investigators;
- evidence of growing national and local government action to deal with the problems of poverty, education and public health.

For most of the 19th century, governments held firmly to the laissez faire principle ie. that the state should not interfere in the lives of the people or in the workings of the market economy. The individual should be free to run his or her own life unhindered by the tyranny of the state. If people were destitute, it was their own fault and due to their own moral failings. Poor relief in the workhouse was deliberately made so harsh that most of the poor shunned it.

This period, from about 1800 - 1870, was called the *'age of individualism'* by the historian AV Dicey. From 1870 until the end of the century though, the principle and practice of laissez faire or individualism came under increasing challenge. Britain was entering the *'age of collectivism'* when governments began to accept the need to regulate and care for their citizens in certain limited areas.

Dicey's attempt to parcel up the 19th century into neatly defined periods has been criticised by historians writing in the last 30 years. For example, it is quite easy to point out evidence of the persistence of laissez faire in the 'age of collectivism' and conversely the existence of state intervention in the 'age of individualism'. This is not surprising if we accept that the encroachment of the state into people's lives came about gradually and over a relatively long period of time. Below are some of the welfare reforms undertaken by governments round about the middle of the nineteenth century. Although this is usually considered to be firmly within the laissez-faire period, we can see that the state was gradually beginning to take some limited responsibility for the welfare of the people.

Early/Mid-Victorian Welfare Reforms

1840 Free vaccination against smallpox given on demand.
1842 *Mines Act* - prohibited the employment of girls, women and boys under 10 in the mines.
1844 *Factory Act* - prohibited children under 8 from working in factories. Children under 13 were only allowed to work up to 6 1/2 hours a day. Girls over 13 and women were restricted to working 12 hours a day. Machinery was to be fenced.
1847 *Ten Hours Act* - Women and young people up to the age of 18 were only to be allowed to work 10 hours a day. However, employers got round the law by working children in relays.
1848 *Public Health Act* - Local Health Boards were given powers to improve public health facilities eg. water supply, sewers. However, it was ineffective because powers were not compulsory.
1853 Vaccination of infants made compulsory.
1866 *Sanitation Act* - This strenghthened local authority powers concerning public sanitation. Authorities were now obliged to improve local conditions and remove nuisances.

Since there was no sudden abandonment of the non-intervention principle and because successive governments added to the list of welfare measures gradually, it is very difficult to pinpoint a precise transition period when laissez faire became less dominant and state intervention more accepted. However, if we look at Britain at the beginning of the 19th century and then at the end, it becomes clear that significant changes had occurred. As V Cromwell puts it:

"In 1800, England had virtually no government: the peace was kept and her shores defended. By 1900, no citizen could fail to be aware of the activities of government." (*Revolution or Evolution* by Cromwell p.3)

Nevertheless, laissez-faire ideas still dominated the thinking of most decision makers in the final decades of the 19th century, especially in the economic area. These ideas had been around for more than a century. In the next section,we will look at some of the leading political thinkers who provided the arguments and justifications for minimal state intervention - Adam Smith, Jeremy Bentham, James Mill and his son John Stuart Mill. At the level of popular culture too, laissez faire was deeply embedded in the Victorian values of self-help, thrift and hard work. Here, the writings of Samuel Smiles were particularly important and influential. However, we will also find out that the verdict on some of these writers is not clearcut. It is possible to cite passages from Bentham, J S Mill and Smiles which show that they were against the practice of laissez faire for its own sake - each in his own way came to believe that there were circumstances when government action was necessary. We will also argue against the view that self-help was exclusively a middle class value. There is ample evidence to show that skilled manual workers - the 'labour aristocracy' - were also in favour of mutual self-help eg. most belonged to trade unions and friendly societies. They were hostile to state welfare too as this meant suffering the stigma attached to the Poor Law and the workhouse. The better-off middle class preferred to relieve poverty themselves by voluntary acts of charity and philanthropy rather than looking to the state as the welfare provider. Only about 10% of the poor received public welfare assistance during the late Victorian period. The rest had to rely on the support of their family, what savings, if any, they had or on charity. This is what laissez faire meant to the less fortunate members of society at this time.

In the 1870s and 1880s, there were several periods of severe economic depression. During these times, it became clear that neither the state apparatus nor voluntary effort was able to cope with the mass ranks of unemployed poor. Social investigations also began to reveal the extent of poverty. These factual reports, as well as the more sensational journalistic exposés of slum life, stirred middle class consciences. Many began to realise that the combined efforts of public and private poor relief were woefully inadequate. Political thinkers, like T H Green, provided the intellectual ammunition for the new Liberals to challenge the classical individualist ideology. Socialist and collectivist ideas were being spread through groups such as the Social Democratic Federation and the Fabian Society. Another threat to the existing order came with the enfranchisement of the working class. The Liberals and Conservatives believed that the masses would have to be accommodated by some measures of social reform. Out of all these pressures for change emerged a trickle of new social legislation in the areas of public health, education and poverty relief.

The Ideology of Laissez Faire

Laissez faire originated as the basic belief of the classical economists of the late 18th century and was most powerfully expressed in Adam Smith's book *Wealth of Nations*, published in 1776. Smith believed that the interests of society as a whole could best be maintained if each individual pursued his or her own self-interest in accumulating wealth. Market forces ought to be allowed to work freely, with competition between each entrepreneur regulating prices. Only by each individual following his or her own self-interest, unhindered by state regulation, could society as a whole benefit. This was what Smith called the "invisible hand" ie. the sum total or the end product of all the selfish efforts of individuals competing to make a living. He believed that this and not state intervention promoted the general welfare. It alone guaranteed individual freedom. Smith's position on laissez faire is clear and simple. He had:

> "a strong presumption against government activity beyond its fundamental duties of protection against its foreign foes and maintenance of justice". (Smith *The Wealth of Nations* ed. E. Cannon 1904 p484)

In other words, the government should only be involved in providing for the defence of the country and law and order. All other activities were outwith its scope. Smith was primarily an economist and his ideas were influential into the 19th century. In the field of government and politics, Jeremy Bentham was the dominant figure. His followers developed a new school of thought called Utilitarianism. Bentham's political theory was based on his views of human nature. He believed that it was human nature to pursue pleasure and to avoid pain. If every individual was allowed to follow his or her natural in-

stincts, the result would be 'the greatest happiness of the greatest number'. (Can you see the similarities between Smith's 'invisible hand' and Bentham's 'greatest happiness' principle?) Benthamites called themselves 'utilitarians' because Bentham always applied the test of utility or usefulness to any institution or action. To the question, "What use is this activity?" the answer for him should always involve the greatest happiness of the greatest number. Bentham also believed in individual freedom and that it could best be preserved by the absence of government interference.

> "For taken by itself, government is in itself one vast evil." (From Bentham's *Constitutional Code*)

Bentham followed Smith in advocating laissez faire in the economic sphere ie. that governments should not be involved in the economic affairs of the country:

> "...nothing ought to be done or attempted by government for the purpose of causing an augmentation in the national mass of wealth...without some special reason. Be quiet ought on those occasions to be the motto or watchword of government."
> [Bentham *Institute of Political Economy (1810-4)* in W. Stark (ed) *Jeremy Bentham's Economic Writings* (1954) 111 p333]

Bentham and the Utilitarians were closely associated with the principle of laissez faire, at least in the first half of the 19th century. James Mill, a contemporary of Bentham, carried forward the laissez faire ideology in his *Principles of Political Economy*, which went through 9 editions between 1865 and 1873. Mill's son, John Stuart Mill, carried on the tradition in his book *On Liberty*. Here, he argues that people should be free to do what they like and that the only role for the state was in maintaining law and order:

> "The object of this Essay is to assert one very simple principle...The principle is, that the sole end for which mankind are warranted, individually or collectively in interfering with the liberty of action of any of their number is self-protection. That the only purpose for which power can be rightfully exercised over any member of a civilised community, against his will, is to prevent harm to others. His own good, either physical or moral, is not sufficient warrant...Over himself, over his own body and mind, the individual is sovereign." (J S Mill *On Liberty* (1859) p15-6)

Laissez Faire in Popular Culture

Although the ideas of Smith, Bentham and Mills were well known among the intellectual and political elite in Victorian times, the broad mass of people would have been quite ignorant about these great thinkers. However, laissez faire was alive and well-known to the general public in the familiar beliefs of thrift, hard work and self-help. The leading exponent of these mid-Victorian values was Samuel Smiles whose influential book *Self Help* was published in 1859, the same year as Mills *On Liberty*. Smiles was not an intellectual and his book was not written for an academic readership. He was a popular writer. *Self Help* was full of moralising articles and anecdotes about businessmen who had succeeded because of hard work and perseverance. It was written in a clear and simple style and was peppered with memorable quotes, gaining it a wide readership including many of the leading entrepreneurs of the day.

> " 'Heaven helps those who help themselves' is a well-tried maxim, embodying in a small compass the results of vast human experience. The spirit of self-help is the root of all genuine growth in the individual; and, exhibited in the lives of many, it constitutes the true course of national vigour and strength. Help from without is often enfeebling in its effects, but help from within invariably invigorates. Whatever is done for men or classes, to a certain extent takes away the stimulus and necessity of doing for themselves; and where men are subject to over-guidance and over-government, the inevitable tendency is to render them comparatively helpless." [S. Smiles *Self Help* (1903 ed.) pp1-3]

Laissez Faire Reconsidered

On first impressions, it would appear that Bentham, J S Mills and Smiles were all committed campaigners for the belief that the individual was of primary importance and that the government's proper role ought to be limited to the defence of the realm and the maintenance of law and order. On closer inspection though, the picture is not so clear. For example, although Bentham referred to government as 'one vast evil', he went on to qualify this by adding the following:

> "But wherever, by evil thus produced, greater evil is excluded, the balance takes the nature, shape and name of good; and government is justified in the production of it." (*Constitutional Code*)

In other words, Bentham appeared to be both condemning and condoning state intervention under certain circumstances in the same breath. Government action was bad but if it removed injustices or evil in society, then that action was good! This contradictory attitude towards the role of the state is reflected throughout Bentham's writings and makes it difficult for the historian to pinpoint exactly where he stood on the matter. As Dicey points out, if we accept that utilitarianism was the basic belief underpinning Bentham's thinking, then the greatest happiness principle could apply to a wide spectrum of policies from laissez faire through to state intervention. A J Taylor tries to resolve the problem by arguing that:

> "No Utilitarian believed in government for its own sake. What Bentham and his followers sought was not more but better government. In pursuing the greatest happiness of the greatest number, they were seeking in the last resort not the happiness of a collectivity but the happiness of individuals; and if this end could be achieved without the intervention of the state, so much the better. For the Benthamites, even the best government was a necessary evil."
> (A J Taylor *Laissez Faire and State Intervention in Nineteenth - Century Britain* p36)

Generally speaking, we can say that Bentham's followers during his lifetime were firmly in the laissez faire camp (eg. James Mill and Ricardo), whereas later disciples, like Chadwick in the 1840s who believed that the Board of Health had to intervene in public health matters to achieve the greatest happiness, were in favour of a degree of government intervention A V Dicey, in one of his later writings, argued that the underlying idea behind the Benthamites up to 1870 was individualism, *but during the next 30 years the balance moved decisively towards collectivism.* He gives 3 reasons for the drift towards "the authoritative side of Benthamite liberalism" ie. increasing state intervention:

> "Faith in laissez faire suffered an eclipse; hence the principle of utility became an argument in favour, not of individual freedom, but of the absolutism of the State. Parliament under the progress of democracy became the representative, not of the middle classes, but of the whole body of householders; Parliamentary sovereignty, therefore, came to mean, in the last resort, the unrestricted power of the wage-earners. English administrative mechanism was reformed and strengthened. The machinery was thus provided for the practical extension of the activity of the State ... Benthamites, it was then seen, had forged the arms most needed by socialists." (A V Dicey *The Debt of Collectivism to Benthamism* quoted in A J Taylor ibid p.18)

Like Bentham, the ideas of J.S. Mill do not all run in the same direction of minimal state intervention. Mill's later writings, and in particular his autobiography, published in the last year of his life, show a considerable shift of emphasis, even to the extent that some have seen him as an early socialist! In his *Principles of Political Economy*, he listed so many exceptions to the laissez faire principle that the reader is left wondering whether he still believed in non-interference at all.

> "Perhaps John Stuart Mill personifies the creeping mood of collectivism more vividly than most. Born in 1806, the son of James Mill, most fanatical of Benthamites, he inherited the moral leadership of the Utilitarians, but had, by his death in 1873, led them across the tutelary bridge to an acceptance of collectivism."
> (E C Midwinter *Victorian Social Reform* p50)

Samual Smiles also appeared to modify his populist doctrine of self-help when it came to matters of public health. He had met Chadwick as a young man and had become convinced that the state had to act on environmental issues which affected the whole population, both rich and poor. He was particularly concerned about the need for the authorities to crack down on the deliberate contamination of food and drink. In this sense, he mirrored the growing late Victorian concern over deprivation and abuses. But Smiles made a clear distinction between the virtues of economic laissez faire and the necessity of state intervention on social issues. On the latter, he wrote passionately:

> "When typhus or cholera breaks out, they tell us that Nobody is to blame. That terrible Nobody! How much he has to answer for. More mischief is done by Nobody than by all the world besides. Nobody adulterates our food. Nobody poisons us with bad drink...Nobody leaves towns undrained...Nobody has a theory too - a dreadful theory. It is embodied in two words: laissez faire - let alone. When people are poisoned with plaster of Paris mixed with flour, 'let alone' is the remedy...Let those who can, find out when they are cheated: caveat emptor (let the buyer

beware). When people live in foul dwellings, let them alone, let wretchedness do its work; do not interfere with death." (Smiles quoted in Asa Briggs *Samuel Smiles: The Gospel of Self-Help* in *History Today* May 1987 p42)

Laissez Faire Challenged

As Dicey has pointed out, belief in laissez faire was declining in the late 19th century. Democracy had been extended to working class men and the government machine was extending into more and more areas of life. All of these changes posed difficulties for the traditional party of laissez faire, the Liberals. There was clearly a need for a fairly major reinterpretation of the party's beliefs and values if it was going to survive the challenges of a modern industrial democracy. A key figure who helped to shape the New Liberalism was T H Green, an Oxford philosopher. Green developed a school of thought called Philosophical Idealism and, "between 1880 and 1914, few, if any, other philosophers exerted a greater influence upon British thought and public policy than did T.H. Green."
(M Richter *The Politics of Conscience - TH Green and his Age* p13)

He attempted to amalgamate the best ideas of both individualism and collectivism into a more moral creed. Green's purpose, according to one writer, was,

" to transform Liberalism from the social philosophy of a single set of interests seen from the point of view of a particular class into one which could claim to take account of all important interests seen from the point of view of the general good of the national community." (George H Sabine *A History of Political Theory* 3rd ed New York: Holt, Rinehart and Winston, 1961 p.737)

Unlike the old Liberals, he saw a positive, if limited role for the state:

"The purpose of state action is to free its citizens from hindrances or disabilities so that they may develop their moral potentialities."
(M Richter ibid p.284)

In his memoirs, Herbert Asquith, Liberal Prime Minister between 1908 and 1916, claimed that Green's Liberal version of Idealism had overtaken Utilitarianism as the accepted school of thought in the universities. One of Green's biographers, Melvin Richter further asserts that his ideas had come "close to a practical programme for the left wing of the Liberal Party." (Richter p13)

The Coexistence of Laissez Faire and State Intervention

Green became involved in the struggle to achieve compulsory state education through the National Education League. The League had been started up in Birmingham and by 1868 was being led by Joseph Chamberlain, a Birmingham screw manufacturer. Chamberlain, like Green, was attempting to move the Liberal Party forward to meet the challenges of the late 19th century. He quickly rose up through the ranks to become mayor of Birmingham in 1873. In his 3 years in office, Chamberlain carried out a

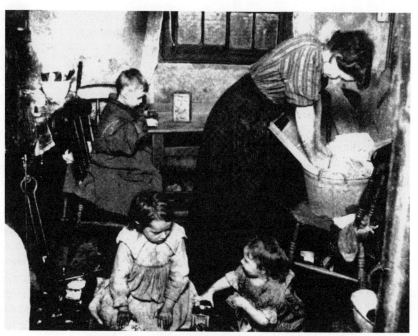

A common domestic scene in Victorian Britain

radical programme of social reform, turning Birmingham into the 'best governed city in the world'. He started by taking into public ownership the supplies of gas and water. The profits from gas were used to fund a huge slum clearance programme, as allowed under the *Artisans' Dwellings Act* of 1875, and sanitary measures were brought in to improve public health. (See p.70) The following figures show how effective Birmingham's improvement schemes were.

"The total area of land comprised in the Compulsory Powers was 93 acres. Eight acres of land acquired will be laid out in new streets and open spaces. The population of the unhealthy district was about 9,000 and the total number of artisans' dwellings purchased was 1,335. Of this number 298 have already been demolished...63 have been cleared away to make room for the new streets and 63 more are closed and marked out for speedy destruction. 434 dwellings, and shops used as dwellings, have undergone complete repair and sanitary inspection. The sanitary result of this improvement has been most striking."

Table 6.1 shows the death-rate in some of the streets in the area before the commencement of the operation and since the principle changes have been carried out.

	Average Death Rate	
	1873-5	**1879-81**
Bailey Street	97	25.6
Lower Priory	62.5	21.9
Rope Walk	42	24.9
Potter Street	44	28.8
Russell Street	55	19.1
Princess Street	46	13.2
Aston Road	40	15.0
Tasker Street	47	22.0

Table 6.1 (From *The Fortnightly Review* quoted in *The Bitter Cry of Outcast London* by Andrew Mearns p.147, pub. Leicester University Press)

At a more elevated level, Chamberlain built art galleries, libraries, museums and public parks.

Chamberlain was not the first municipal leader to introduce public facilities - other towns and cities throughout Britain were doing similar, if less spectacular, work. Almost in spite of central government, municipal authorities were tackling the social problems of the industrial revolution in a practical, non-ideological way. The very scale of the problems of installing basic amenities and providing a healthier environment demanded public rather than private action. What developed at the local level was 'collectivism by stealth'. By the end of the century, town councils were providing a wide range of social and technical services for their inhabitants.

If we are looking for the Victorian origins of the welfare state, many of the initiatives were coming from the local, not the national level. It is one of the great paradoxes of late 19th century Britain that the values of self-help and laissez faire coexisted with this creeping 'municipal socialism'. Advocates of the virtue of self-help could retain their faith undiminished by the evidence of local interventionism going on all around them at this time. In a brilliantly ironic passage, Sidney Webb, a leading member of the Fabian Society, introduces us to the individualist town councillor who is blind to the extent of social reform already in place. He will:

> "...walk along the municipal pavement, lit by municipal gas and cleansed by municipal brooms with municipal water, and seeing by the municipal clock in the municipal market that he is too early to meet his children coming from the municipal school, hard by the county lunatic asylum and municipal hospital, will use the national telegraph system to tell them not to walk through the municipal park, but to come by the municipal tramway to meet him in the municipal reading-room by the municipal art gallery, museum and library where he intends to consult some of the national publications in order to prepare his next speech in the municipal town hall in favour of nationalisation of canals and the increase of Government control over the railway system. 'Socialism, Sir,' he will say, 'don't waste the time of a practical man by your fantastic absurdities. Self-help, Sir, individual self-help, that's what made our city what it is."
> (Sidney Webb *Socialism in England* , 1889, p.116-7)

Having said that local authorities had been pioneering the introduction of social welfare services, we also need to recognise that at a national level too, both Conservative and Liberal governments had by 1870 already passed a formidable array of legislative measures designed to intervene in the social and economic life of the nation. The 'age of laissez faire' from 1830-1870 witnessed the unprecedented growth of government activity. Amongst other things:

> "the state maintained paupers, limited the employment of women and children, regulated emigration via the Passenger Acts, controlled pollution via the Alkali Acts, financed and supervised schools, reformatories, prisons and police forces, enforced nui-

sance-removal, vaccination and the civil registry of births, marriages and deaths."
(D Fraser *The Evolution of the British Welfare State* p.110-1)

The Victorian Welfare System - Philanthropy, Charity and the Poor Law

As we have seen, the late Victorian period saw a gradual shift away from the theory and practice of individualism towards collective action by national and local authorities. It was a period of transition and therefore, it is understandable that many people clung to established ideas of self-reliance in an age increasingly facing problems and demands no longer capable of being left in the private domain. More and more though, the beneficiaries of the industrial revolution, the urban middle class, were becoming aware of the inadequacy of the Poor Law to deal with the mass of people at the bottom of the social heap. However, the typical humanitarian response of the wealthy was to dispense private charity rather than to call for more public welfare. Philanthropy, not state-sponsored 'socialism' was the preferred middle-class remedy for the social ills of the day.

Although this acceptance of the need for private, voluntary giving was inspired by the individualist, rather than the collectivist impulse, it also marks a perceptible shift away from the first principle of laissez faire - self-help. It was an unspoken admission of the inadequacy of the Poor Law and of the inability of many, including the able-bodied, to provide for themselves. To fill the gap in the welfare system, a host of charitable bodies sprang up in the 19th century - such as the YMCA (1844), the Salvation Army (1866), Dr Barnardo's Homes (1869) and the RSPCC (1884). Many of these charities were motivated by a Christian or humanitarian desire to care for the suffering humanity only too evident in the industrial towns and cities. It is rather ironic that at a time when social Darwinism was becoming fashionable (i.e. the belief that only the fittest survive), evangelicals, Christian Socialists and humanitarians were also practising compassion for the weakest members of society. Moreover, few of these charities investigated very thoroughly the needs of applicants for relief. The Salvation Army for example, did not accept the Poor Law categories of 'deserving' and 'undeserving' poor.

By the 1870s , hundreds of organisations were striving to provide the sorts of social services that governments were unwilling to take responsibility for. The problem was that the 'private sector' welfare system lacked co-ordination and supervision. In 1867, the Charity Organisation Society was founded. Its aim was to attack the problem of poverty in a more coherent and rigorous way than hitherto. The leading figure in the COS was C S Loch. He had no truck with the 'indiscriminate alms-giving' practised by some charities.

> "Charity is a social regenerator...We have to use charity to create the power of self-help."
> (From *The Charity Organisation Register*, 27 Sept. 1884, quoted in K Woodroffe *From Charity to Social Work in England and the United States* p. 23)

According to Loch, aid should only be given to the deserving poor and then only after detailed investigation into the character and circumstances of the applicant. Financial assistance should help to restore the person's independence; indiscriminate aid, on the other hand, would only serve to demoralise the individual, robbing him of self-respect and initiative. By the 1890s though, even the COS had to moderate its hardline, laissez faire approach in the face of widespread economic distress. By advocating temporary job-creation schemes to tide people over during periods of economic depression, the COS was tacitly admitting that at least some poverty was unavoidable and could not be blamed on individual workers. Basil Kirkman Gray, who had been involved in charitable work in London wrote about the "exhaustion" of the COS approach in the face of extensive poverty. (*History of English Philanthropy*)

Just as the private distribution of aid was found wanting, so the public poor relief system was being exposed as inadequate to meet the needs of the day. *The Poor Law Amendment Act* (1834) was originally intended to achieve the following aims:

1 *To deter those not genuinely in need from getting poor relief.* This was to be achieved by stopping the able-bodied poor getting outdoor relief ie money given to the person in their own home. From now on, they would have to enter the workhouse. Conditions in the workhouse were also to be made deliberately harsh so that most people would regard it as a last resort. This was the principle of 'less eligibility'.

2 *To set up a more efficient, national system of relieving the poor.* Parishes were to be grouped into Poor Law Unions, each with their elected Board of Guardians, paid officials and Union workhouse.

3 *To save money on the poor rates.* By tightening up on the payment of poor relief, there was a significant reduction of about £1 million a year on the poor rates in the first decade of operation.

However, despite its financial 'success', the New Poor Law soon ran into difficulties, not least because its very aims seemed to be in conflict. How could a cost-cutting, harsh system also expect to fulfil its more humane function of relieving poverty? In the first decade of its operation, the Poor Law Commissioners tried to ensure that the system was implemented rigorously. This led to riots in the north of England during the trade depression of 1837-8. The factory workers in places like Bradford and Huddersfield were incensed because the new Poor Law rules allowed them no outdoor relief. They were not loafers or idlers but the victims of a downturn in the trade cycle - there was simply no work available. Newspapers like the *Times* began to criticise the Poor Law for failing to recognise the real causes of poverty and unemployment. As a result of the widespread protest, the Poor Law Commissioners were forced to relax the rules and a considerable amount of outdoor relief, even to the able-bodied, was administered. In Scotland, poor relief had traditionally been dispensed as outdoor relief but the *Scottish Poor Law (Amendment) Act* (1845) insisted that poorhouses should be erected in the more populous areas of the country.

Another problem arose over the conditions inside the workhouses. Families were segregated to different parts of the building; food was very poor, unappetising and often inadequate; no talking was allowed during meal times; no alcohol or tobacco were permitted; cards and other games were not allowed; strict hours for getting up, working and going to bed were enforced. Some workhouses were worse than prison and there was often a very high mortality rate. In 1862, 23% of the inmates resident in Scotland's poorhouses died during the course of the year. The *Scotsman* led the criticism, "... in our poorhouses we greatly fear that both quantity and variety (of food) fail ... In prisons the diet is much fuller than in these establishments ... We express a grave doubt whether aged, sick and brokendown paupers can be sufficiently fed on 3½d. a day." (*Scotsman* 7 May 1863)

The most shocking case of inhumane conditions concerned Andover workhouse in 1846. Here, the inmates were forced to work, crushing the bones of horses, dogs and other animals to make fertiliser for local farms. What follows is the evidence of one inmate, Charles Lewis to a public enquiry into conditions:

"9828 (Mr Wakeley) What work were you employed about when you were in the workhouse? - *I was employed breaking bones.*
9839 During the time you were so employed, did you ever see any of the men gnaw anything or eat anything from those bones? - *I have seen them eat marrow out of the bones.*
9842 Did they state why they did it? - *I really believe they were very hungry.*
9843 Did you yourself feel extremely hungry at that time? - *I did, but my stomach would not take it.*"
(*Parliamentary Papers* 1846 V quoted in *Victorian Social Reform* by EC Midwinter p76)

Conditions in the workhouses did improve from the 1850s onwards particularly for the old, the sick and the young.
• The old were often given outdoor relief. For those who remained in the workhouse, a more humane policy was adopted from the 1880s onwards when married couples over 60 were allowed to stay together, but in separate bedrooms.
• The sick poor began to receive specialised care in the 1860s. By the end of the century, separate infirmaries had been set up as general hospitals for the working classes.
• From the 1870s onwards, there was a growing belief that children should be removed from workhouses altogether and some kind of family life provided for them as far as possible. In Scotland, children were boarded out with working class families.

Despite these improvements, only a tiny percentage of those in need were willing to undergo the rigours of the workhouse and as a result, poverty remained largely untreated. In the 1880s, about 2.5% of the population were in receipt of relief at a time when something like 30% of people were in dire poverty. Furthermore, the workhouse was still a grim and forbidding place which was feared and hated by the poor. Charlie Chaplin, in his autobiography, described his experience in Lambeth workhouse in 1895 after his father, who was living apart, had stopped his weekly payments of 10 shillings:

"There was no alternative: she was burdened with two children and in poor health; and so she decided that the three of us should enter the Lambeth workhouse.

Although we were aware of the shame of going to the workhouse, when mother told us about it, both Sidney and I thought it adventurous and a change from living in one stuffy room. But on that doleful day I didn't realise what was happening until we actually entered the workhouse gate. Then the forlorn bewilderment of it struck me; for there we were made to separate, mother going in one direction to the women's ward and we in another to the children's.

How well I remember the poignant sadness of that first visiting day: the shock of seeing mother enter the visiting-room garbed in workhouse clothes. How forlorn and embarrassed she looked. In one week she had aged and grown thin, but her face lit up when she saw us. Sidney and I began to weep which made mother weep...Eventually she regained her composure...she smiled at our cropped heads...telling us that we would soon all be together again."

(Charles Chaplin *My Autobiography* p19, pub. The Bodley Head, London 1964)

As time went by, it became evident that the Poor Law was the wrong instrument for solving the social problems of an industrial nation. Above all, its approach to unemployment was fundamentally wrong, for it was no use trying to frighten an unemployed worker into finding work when no work was available. It was also failing to deal with the mass of untreated poverty revealed by the journalists and social investigators at the end of the 19th century.

The Investigation of Poverty

Middle-class consciences were aroused by the undeniable facts of poverty discovered through painstaking investigation by Charles Booth and Seebohm Rowntree. Booth was a wealthy Liverpool shipowner who took an interest in the poor. When he settled in London, he enjoyed walking through the East End, visiting pubs and music halls. He even lodged for a few days at a time with working-class families and developed considerable respect for them. He

Poor Law Statistics	
Year	Percentage of Paupers Relieved
1834	8.8
1850	5.7
1860	4.3
1870	4.6
1880	3.0
1900	2.5

Table 6.2

was spurred into action by the wish to disprove the Marxist HM Hyndman's 'incendiary' assertion that the wages of a quarter of working men were insufficient to keep them in health. The 1880s were undoubtedly years of economic depression and Booth was aware of it, but he was determined to collect precise statistical evidence about the extent of poverty in London. The first essential was a definition of poverty. Booth stated at the outset in very precise terms what he meant by 'the poor' and in doing so invented (almost by accident) the concept of a poverty line.

"By the word 'poor' I mean to describe those who have a sufficiently regular though bare income, such as 18s. to 21s. for a moderate family, and by the words 'very poor' those who from any cause fall much below this standard ... My 'poor' may be described as living under a struggle to obtain the necessaries of life and make both ends meet; while the 'very poor' live in a state of chronic want."

Booth's problem was to discover exactly how many people in London fell into each of these categories. He originally intended to use the census returns of 1881 but they proved useless for his purpose. In the end he turned to the School Board Visitors for information. Their reports, checked in various ways, formed the basis of his results.

Booth's Classification of People:

A	The lowest class - occasional labourers, loafers and semi-criminals
B	The very poor - casual labour, hand-to-mouth existence, chronic want.
C & D	The poor - including alike those whose earnings are small, because of irregularity of employment and those whose work, though regular, is ill-paid.
E & F	The regularly employed and fairly paid working class of all grades
G & H	Lower and upper middle class and all above this level

The proportion of the different classes shown for all London are as follows:

A (lowest class)	37,610	or	0.9%
B (very poor)	316,834	or	7.5%
C & D (poor)	938,293	or	22.3%

In Poverty 30.7%

E & F (working class comfortable)	2,166,503	or	51.5%
G & H (middle class and above)	749,930	or	17.8%

In Comfort 69.3%

	4,209,170	or	100.0%
Inmates of Institutions	99,830		
	4,309,000		

[Source: C Booth *Life and Labour of the People in London* (1892) Vol 11 pp20-1]

Over one million families were investigated by Booth's team and the monumental task took 17 years to complete (1886-1903). The results were contained in 17 volumes entitled *Life and Labour of the People in London*. Booth was shocked to find out that Hyndman's figures were an underestimate of the extent of poverty - about 30% of people in London were living below the 'poverty line'.

Booth had been able to show with devastating clarity that decades of private philanthropy and charitable effort had made little impact on the problem of poverty in London. His figures also challenged the Poor Law statistics, which seemed to imply that poverty had been steadily reduced to almost insignificant proportions. However, the reality was that about 3% of people in London at the turn of the century were being relieved through the Poor Law at a time when 30% of people were in poverty.

In other words, only about 10% of the poor were being helped by the Poor Law. The other 90% had to fend for themselves. Although Booth did attribute some of the blame for this poverty to moral failings (eg. the loafers of class A), it was clear that casual labour, poor pay and unemployment caused most of the distress – factors which were outwith the control of the individuals concerned.

"Charles Booth ... emerges as one of the most significant figures of the age. He pushed it very far towards a solution of the late Victorian dilemma: between the belief that the widespread relief of poverty undermined personal responsibility and fostered immorality, and the growing certainty that the very existence of that poverty threatened the political and economic foundations of the state." (R C Birch *The Shaping of the Welfare State* p.18)

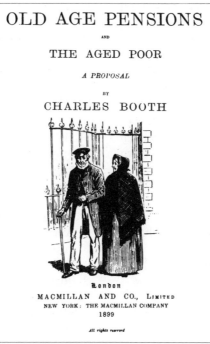

Booth's 1899 pamphlet advocating old age pensions

Seebohm Rowntree, the son of the cocoa and chocolate manufacturers who were known to have a charitable attitude towards the poor, carried on the investigation of poverty in his own town of York. He came up with a more satisfactory working definition of poverty:

"a) Families whose total earnings are insufficient to obtain the minimum necessaries for the maintenance of merely physical efficiency. Poverty falling under this head I have described as 'Primary Poverty'
b) Families whose total earnings would be sufficient for the maintenance of merely physical efficiency were it not that some portion of them is absorbed by other expenditure, either useful or wasteful. Poverty falling under this head is described as 'Secondary Poverty'."

Rowntree's study also added to the understanding of poverty by highlighting the fact that certain periods during a labourer's life were more likely to cause distress than others (see figure 6.1)

Rowntree determined the poverty line at 21s 8d (108p) ie. the minimum necessary for food, rent, clothing, light, fuel etc. - just enough "for the maintenance of merely physical efficiency". He was surprised to find that York had 27.8% of its population living in poverty in 1899.

"We have been accustomed to look upon the poverty in London as exceptional, but when the result of careful investigation shows that the proportion of poverty in London is practically equalled in what may be regarded as a typical provincial town, we are faced by the startling probability that from 25 to 30 per cent of the town population of the United Kingdom are living in poverty." (Rowntree - ibid p300-1)

While Booth and Rowntree were using careful investigation to define and quantify urban poverty, several other writers were publicising the squalor of much working class existence in more colourful and emotive language. Andrew Mearns in his *Bitter Cry of Outcast London* wrote about the capital's "pestilential human rookeries ... where tens of thousands are crowded together amidst horrors which call to mind what we have heard of the middle passage of the slave-ship." (Mearns (1883) quoted in Thane *The Foundations of the Welfare State* p17) Other accounts included *Horrible London* by G R Sim and *Darkest England* by William Booth of the Salvation Army.

The cumulative effect of all this literature was to create a greater awareness of poverty by the middle class. The climate of opinion was gradually drifting away from the individualist concern for renewed hard work and self-help by the lower class towards a collectivist belief in social reform. Some of this drift was motivated by fear of working-class agitation. The extension of the franchise to working-class men in 1867 and 1884 was also forcing the two established parties to take account of the new elector-

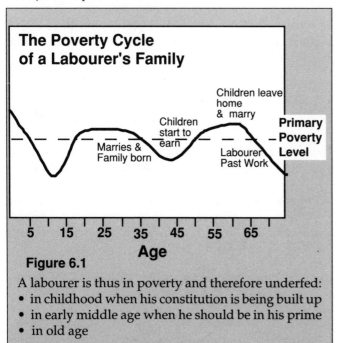

The Poverty Cycle of a Labourer's Family

Children leave home & marry

Children start to earn

Marries & Family born

Labourer Past Work

Primary Poverty Level

5 15 25 35 45 55 65
Age

Figure 6.1

A labourer is thus in poverty and therefore underfed:
• in childhood when his constitution is being built up
• in early middle age when he should be in his prime
• in old age

(Source: B S Rowntree *Poverty: A Study of Town Life*. 1901, p136 -7)

ate. As we will shortly see, both Conservative and Liberal governments carried out limited social reform measures in the last decades of the 19th century, moving very much with the prevailing tide of opinion.

The Socialist Challenge

From the 1880s onwards, the Liberals and Conservatives had to contend with and respond to the appeal of social-ism. For the previous 30 years, Marx and Engels had been asserting that the real cause of poverty lay with capitalism itself. Only when the capitalist system had been destroyed would the workers really enjoy the fruits of their labour. The Social Democratic Federation, founded by H M Hyndman, took a Marxist revolutionary line. Hyndman was suspicious of reforms which aimed to take the harsh edge off capitalism. Social welfare measures were only sops to the working class and helped employers to keep wages low.

The Fabian Society was a more moderate and gradualist organisation which included among its leading members the writers Sidney and Beatrice Webb and playwright George Bernard Shaw. They were in favour of more state intervention to relieve poverty. The Webbs helped to influence contemporary thinking on social problems through their books, pamphlets and frequent contacts with the political and academic establishment. In 1900, the Labour Party was in place. Like the Fabians, Labour did not seek the overthrow of capitalism. In the early years, the programme of the Labour Party was based on the protec-tion of trade union rights and interests. As Labour was the party of the working class, the Liberals and Conservatives would feel growing pressure to compete for their votes by proposing measures of social reform.

Historians disagree about the importance of the working class and socialist organisations in forcing the pace of social reform.

> D Fraser: "...socialism and the organisation of labour represented a threat to the other two parties in view of the more democratic franchise that existed. Though socialists were an infinitesimal minority of the elec-torate they had an influence far beyond their numeri-cal strength." (Fraser - op cit p.139)

> H Pelling: "...the pressure for social reform from the working class was politically negligible before the First World War." (Henry Pelling Popular Politics and Society in Late Victorian Britain p16)

Perhaps the reason why a 'politically negligible' working class had an inordinate influence is that the established parties believed (wrongly) that the workers would de-mand more state welfare and they acted on this belief by bringing in social reforms.

The Tories and Social Reform

In the twentieth century, the Liberals (1906-14) and Labour (1945-51) both contributed significantly to the develop-ment of the welfare state. But what about the Conserva-tives? They were in power for most of the last thirty years of the nineteenth century. Were they just the party of the aristocracy or did they really wish to provide better social conditions for the working classes? The evidence is mixed.

Certainly in terms of political reform it was a Conservative Government under Disreali which passed the 1867 Reform Act extending the franchise to include many working-class voters for the first time. Yet how would the Tories respond to and attract the working-class vote. Disraeli outlined the aims of the 'New Conservatism' in a speech at Crystal Palace in June 1872:

> "When I say 'Conservative', I use the word in its purest and loftiest sense. I mean that the people of England, and especially the working classes of Eng-land, are proud of belonging to a great country... Gentlemen, there is another and second great object of the Tory party - to uphold the Empire of England... Another great object of the Tory party is the elevation of the condition of the people...I venture to say that the health of the people was the most important question for a statesman...It involves the state of the dwellings of the poor. It involves their enjoyment of some of the chief elements of nature - air, light and water. It involves the regulation of their industry, the inspection of their toil. It involves the purity of their provisions..." (Quoted in Gladstone, Disraeli and Later Victorian Politics by Paul Adelman p. 89)

Disraeli hoped that the Tories could maintain their ascen-dancy over the Liberals by balancing the traditional inter-ests of the landed class with the pressing needs of the new industrial working clas. Tory reforms during Disraeli's second administration (1874-80) included:

Factory Acts 1874 and 1878: This Act further reduced the working week for women and young children from 60 to 56 hours per week. Thus the working week in the indus-tries concerned would be 10 hours on Mondays to Fridays and 6 hours on Saturdays.

Public Health Act 1875: This Act built on the earlier Liberal legislation of 1871. (See page 71) It put into a single code over one hundred previous regulations thus laying down "minimum standards of decency and cleanliness" for every local authority.

Artisans' Dwellings Act 1875: Local Authorities, if they wished, could demolish slums and then build council houses for rent.

Sale of Food and Drugs Act 1875: This Act, which prohibited harmful substances in food, was the first effective measure to deal with the serious problem of food adulteration.

Conspiracy and Protection of Property Act 1875: 'Peaceful' picketing during an industrial dispute was legalised.

Employers and Workmen Act 1875: After this Act a breach of contract by a workman was no longer a criminal offence punishable by fine or imprisonment. Such an offence became a matter for the civil court.

Education Act 1876: School Boards were to appoint Atten-dance Officers and to insist on children's attendance until the age of ten.

Enclosure Act 1876: Building on common land had to controlled in an effort to preserve, for recreational purposes, open spaces near large towns.

After a brief Liberal interlude, the Conservatives under Lord Salisbury held power for nearly 14 years between 1885 and 1902. Salisbury was of the old school of Tories, suspicious of democracy and social reform and always more interested in foreign affairs. The main hope for change lay with Lord Randolf Churchill, briefly Chancellor of the Exchequer in the first Salisbury Cabinet. In a speech at Dartford in October 1886, Churchill had advocated an impressive list of social reforms including "improvement of public health and housing, compulsory national insurance, smallholdings for agricultural labourers, reform of parliamentary procedure, and the provision of parks, libraries, art galleries, museums and public baths and washhouses." (*Mastering Modern British History* by N Lowe p. 297)

Clearly, these proposals were far too radical for Salisbury and when Churchill tendered his resignation over a disagreement concerning the budget in December 1886, Salisbury accepted it with relief. Another Conservative reformer who was highly critical of the Party's poor record on social reform was JA Gorst. He was also a strong advocate of 'Tory Democracy' by which he meant that:

"If the Tory party is to continue to exist as a power in the State, it must become a popular party ... The days are past when an exclusive class, however great its ability, wealth and energy, can command a majority in the electorate ... Unfortunately for Conservatism, its leaders belong solely to one class; they are a clique composed of members of the aristocracy, land owners, and adherents whose chief merit is subserviency ... They half fear and half despise the common people; they regard them more as dangerous allies to be coaxed and cajoled than as comrades fighting for a common cause." (From *Conservative Disorganisation, The Fortnightly Review*, vol 32, 1882 quoted in P Adelman p.94-5)

Not surprisingly, Gorst failed to make any headway to the top of the Conservative Party hierarchy. With Churchill and Gorst sidelined, Salisbury was able to lead the Conservative Party along traditional lines. Consequently, the 1880s and 90s saw few social reforms and little was done to improve the lives of the working class, although three important measures were introduced.

Housing Act 1890: This Act further extended the provisions of the 1875 Act for clearing slums and erecting new dwelling houses.

Education Act 1891: Free elementary education was introduced by increasing government grants to church and board schools.

Workmen's Compensation Acts 1897 and 1900: An employee could now obtain compensation for injury at work without having to prove negligence on the part of his employer. However, both acts only covered a number of occupations.

The Liberals and Social Reform

The overall record of the Liberal governments under Gladstone in introducing social reform in the closing three decades of the nineteenth century was a disappointing one. This was partly due to Gladstone's desire to keep down public expenditure, to his firm belief in individual self-help and to his preoccupation with the Irish Question which was to have unfortunate repercussions on his party. The Irish Question undoubtedly helped to split the Liberals and to place them in the political wilderness from 1886 to 1906 when they only held office between 1892 and 1894.

Nevertheless, the Liberals, like the Tories, did contribute to the growth of democracy in Britain when they introduced the *Ballot Act* (1872) which allowed secret voting; and in 1884 when they extended the franchise to male farm labourers and miners. (See p.57) In addition, a limited but useful number of social reforms were introduced.

1870 Education Act: This gave increased grants to the existing voluntary schools. New school boards were set up in areas where school provision was inadequate. School fees of a few pence were to be charged, but could be waived for poor children. The Scottish Education Act of 1872 went further. It made education compulsory for all children between the ages of 5 and 13.

1871 Vaccination Act: This followed and completed the legislation of 1841, 1861 and 1867 which made vaccination against smallpox compulsory.

1871 Local Government Board Act: Local government was now to supervise the work of the Poor Law and Public Health Authorities, eg. each local authority was to appoint a medical officer of health and a sanitary inspector.

1871 Trade Union Act: This act gave the unions certain legal rights such as allowing them to own property and having their funds protected from embezzlement by the courts.

1871 The Criminal Law Amendment Act: For trade unions this undermined the good work of the Trade Union Act as it made it difficult for them to picket during a strike. (See p.7)

1880 Education Act: This made attendance at school in England and Wales compulsory between the ages of five and ten.

1894 Out-Door Relief (Friendly Societies) Act: This allowed Poor Law administrators to give relief even to those who were receiving up to 5 shillings from friendly societies - indicating a less harsh attitude towards the treatment of the poor.

1894 Local Government Act: This introduced the idea of elections to parish councils which resulted in over 6,800 of them being established. On paper the councils had wide powers but these were greatly restricted by financial limitations. At least one great breakthrough for women was that those who were qualified to vote could be elected as well.

Thus, apart from a few exceptions the Old Liberalism of the Gladstone era, with its emphasis on the preservation of personal freedom by non-government intervention, was still very much in evidence.

"To many among the fathers of modern Liberalism, government action was anathema. They held, as we

71

hold, that the first and the final object of the state is to develop the capacities and raise the standard of living of its citizens; but they also held that the best means towards this object was the self-effacement of the state. Liberty is of supreme importance, and legal regulation is the opposite of liberty. Let governments abstain from war, let them practise economy, let them provide proper protection against violence and fraud, let them repeal restrictive laws ... such was their doctrine. The economics of Adam Smith and the philosophy of Bentham united to find a creed of noninterference which has inspired in large measure the politics of a century."
(From Herbert Samuel, *Liberalism.* 1902; Quoted in *The Age of Lloyd George* by KO Morgan p.130, Pub. Allen & Unwin)

We can perhaps see in the reforms of the late nineteenth century some very tentative steps being made to provide basic welfare facilities. The Education Acts stand out here as a noteworthy attempt to ensure primary education for all. The public health laws were also making inroads into the worst excesses of slum and insanitary areas of Britain's towns and cities. A great many problems still remained to be tackled though. For example, Joseph Chamberlain's grand scheme to clear Birmingham's slum areas was effective in cutting down disease but he left new house- building to the private sector and most of the tenants who had been cleared could not afford the new higher rents.

However, it was in the relief of poverty that we see the least movement from the Poor Law principle. Some of the harsher features of the system were modified but the system remained in place. For example, the provision of job creation schemes was a relaxation of the rules in exceptional times, not their abandonment. The notion that many of the poor were in that position due to unemployment which was no fault of their own, was still anathema to the Local Government Boards. Even the term 'unemployed' had as yet not entered common usage.

Nevertheless, the state was beginning to take more responsibility for the weakest members of society and those whom it thought to be deserving. On the other hand, we must be careful to avoid making too extravagent a claim for the Britain of 1900. This was still what we might call the *enabling state* rather than an early prototype for the *welfare state*. Voluntary action, private charity and self-help were still very much in vogue, but now local and national government were beginning to play a more positive part in enabling people to get back on their feet, while at the same time deterring 'scroungers' from abusing the system. The real turning-point was to come with the Liberal Government reforms between 1906 and 1914.

7 The Liberal Welfare Reforms 1906-14

The Liberals swept into power in January, 1906 with a massive majority of 356 (including Labour and the Irish Nationalists). They had defeated a Conservative Party which had been in government for most of the previous 20 years. (See p.60) It would be wrong though to imagine that the Liberals had won the election on a wave of 'New Liberalism'. (See p.59 & 65) Even in 1906, most Liberals were still committed to the causes of traditional Liberalism ie. to preserve personal freedom by non-governmental interference (laissez faire), keep the peace, collect taxes and secure the administration of justice. During the election campaign their main concern was free trade. Furthermore, Campbell-Bannerman, the new Liberal Prime Minister (1906-8) still very much believed in the virtues of Old Liberalism.

Key Liberal Ministers 1906-14			
Prime Minister	Chancellor of the Exchequer	President of the Board of Trade	Home Secretary
Sir H Campbell - Bannerman 1905-8 H Asquith 1908-15	H Asquith 1905-8 D Lloyd George 1908-15	D Lloyd George 1905-8 W S Churchill 1908-10 S Buxton 1910 -14	H Gladstone 1905-10 W S Churchill 1910-11 R McKenna 1911-15

However, from the turn of the century onwards, a small group of young Liberals began to campaign for more state action to help improve the conditions of the poor. Although the exponents of 'New Liberalism' were small in number, their influence was eventually to prove decisive in committing the Party to a programme of social reform. Extensive pressure was exerted from below by a group of highly influential individuals: Junior Ministers like Charles Masterman; journalists with the *Nation* newspaper, HW Massingham, HN Brailsford, LT Hobhouse and JA Hobson; social reformers like Sidney and Beatrice Webb and civil servants like R Morant and W Beveridge.

"What then is the matter with the Liberals? ... The political force of this Old Liberalism is spent. During the last 20 years, its aspirations and its watchwords, its ideas of daily life and its conceptions of the universe, have become increasingly distasteful to the ordinary citizen...Its worship of individual liberty evokes no enthusiasm. Its reliance on 'freedom of contract' and 'supply and demand'...now seems to work out disastrously for the masses, who are too poor to have what the economists call an 'effective demand' for even the minimum conditions of physical and mental well-being.

...Now the trouble with Gladstonian Liberalism is that, by instinct, by tradition..it 'thinks in individuals'...The principles were fresh once - in the last quarter of the 18th century. Their exponents' minds were fresh too - about the middle of the 19th century. But Adam Smith is dead, and Queen Anne and even Sir Robert Peel; while as to Gladstone, he is the deadest of them all." (Sidney Webb September, 1901 quoted in *The Age of Lloyd George* by K Morgan p.126-7)

Yet in spite of arguments from the New Liberals that the old Liberalism was out of date and could not cope with the present social problems, the achievements of the Campbell-Bannerman administration proved to be quite disappointing. Most of the period up to 1908 was concerned with traditional Liberal measures eg. the Education Bill. There were two main exceptions - the *School Meals Act* (1906) and provision for the medical inspection of children (1907). It was only with the advent of Asquith as Prime Minister in 1908 and the appointments of Lloyd George and Churchill to the Cabinet that the mood began to change.

During its lifetime, the Liberal Government brought in a series of new laws directed towards the young and the old. It insured many of those in work against unemployment and sickness and improved the conditions for millions of vulnerable workers. We will now look at the key social reforms undertaken during these years and attempt to gauge their significance as steps on the road to the welfare state.

The Young

The first social reforms to be undertaken by the Liberals were concerned with children and in particular dealt with the provision of school meals and medical inspection of pupils. Now that education was compulsory, it was all too obvious to teachers and the education authorities that large numbers of children were coming to school hungry, dirty or suffering from ill-health. Concern about the problem was widespread and efforts to provide school meals on a voluntary basis can be traced back to the 1860s. Arguments in favour of these reforms fell into two categories. Firstly, there were the *educational or humanitarian* arguments based on the adage 'Feed the stomach, then the mind'. One of the most fervent advocates of school meals was Margaret Macmillan in Bradford:

"The state compels the children to work (in school) - it makes the

General Election Results, 1906 - 1914						
	January 1906		January 1910		December 1910	
Parties	Seats	Votes	Seats	Votes	Seats	Votes
Conservatives	157	2,451,454	273	3,127,887	272	2,420,566
Liberals	377	2,757,883	275	2,880,581	272	2,295,888
Labour	29	329,748	40	505,657	42	371,772
Lib-Labs	24	-	-	-	-	-
Irish Nationalists	83	35,031	82	124,586	84	131,375

Table 7.1   (Source: D Butler and J Freeman *British Political Facts 1900-1968*)

Liberal Welfare Legislation 1906-14		
Group	Assistance Given	Legislation
Young	School meals.	Education (Provision ofMeals) Act 1906
	Medical inspection.	Education (Administrative Provisions) Act 1907
Old	Pensions.	Old Age Pensions Act 1908
Sick	Health Insurance.	National Insurance Act Part 1 1911
Employed	Compensation for injuries sustained at work.	Workmen's Compensation Act 1906
	Eight-hour day for miners.	Coal Mines Act 1908
	Minimum wages for 'sweated industry' workers.	Trade Boards Act 1909
	Half-day off for shop assistants.	Shops Act 1911
Unemployed	Help to find work	Labour Exchanges Act 1909
	Unemployment Insurance	National Insurance Act Part 11 1911

Table 7.2

demand for sustenance urgent, intolerable. But it does not compel parents to feed their children. Hence it is certain to some of these hungry little ones free education is less of a boon than an outrage.

Here, for example, is a group of very hopeful children. They have known what hunger is all their lives, but never have they been so hungry as now. When they were little they used to get scraps of food, and now and again a good meal, and this was enough to allow them to live a free, careless life in the fields or alleys. But at last the school board officer got on their track. They were led into a big school, and obliged to read, write, sing, calculate. Not one of these processes but involves a quickening of all the life processes, a new expenditure at a definite rate of nervous energy and living tissue. Lo! at noon all the children are ravenously hungry. The thought that dinner is a movable feast - that there is no dinner to be had - is now a dreadful one! Yesterday's hunger is a mild thing compared with today's." (*Margaret Macmillan, Prophet and Pioneer* by Albert Mansbridge 1932, p.41-2)

A study carried out in a poor district of Dundee in 1905 revealed that the children were significantly underweight and underheight compared to the national average:

"It may be fairly affirmed, after a dispassionate consideration of the facts disclosed by the Medical Reports, that there are in the Dundee schools a large number of children who should be under medical supervision, and whose future in life is imperilled for want of it; that many children, either from disease or lack of personal cleanliness, are a source of danger and serious discomfort to their companions; and that many derive little benefit from school attendance, because they cannot apply their minds to lessons while their stomachs are empty."
(T Ferguson *Scottish Social Welfare, 1864-1914* p. 565)

The second category of arguments for better treatment of school children had to do with the common belief at the turn of the century that *the people of Britain were suffering a physical decline.* Only a concerted campaign of 'national efficiency' could restore the vitality of the nation and this had to start in the schools. The poor physical condition of recruits during the Boer War (1899 - 1902) highlighted the problem. The minimum height requirement for entry into the army had to be dropped from 5 feet 6 inches in 1845 to 5 feet 2 inches before the Boer War. The leader of the Social Democratic Federation (SDF), Hyndman (see p.10), claimed at the time that 50% of urban working class recruits had been unfit for the war due to their poor physical condition. Table 7.3 shows the medical reasons why recruits were rejected for the army. Most of the defects listed below stemmed from the poverty and undernourishment of the mainly working class volunteers.

Two reports appeared in the wake of the Boer War - both stimulated by the alarm over the 'physical deficiency' of the British people. *The Royal Commission on Physical Training in Scotland* (1903) set out to investigate the physical condition of children in Scotland. It did this by comparing children's height and weight in Aberdeen, Edinburgh, Boston (USA) and Britain as a whole (see Table 7.4).

Although Aberdeen seems to have been about average compared to the rest of Britain, Edinburgh children were sigificantly underweight and height.* The Royal Commission recommended that "provision should be made for regular inspection of school children". It also came out in favour of education authorities providing school meals, working with the relevant voluntary bodies. In the following year, *the Report of the Interdepartmental Committee on Physical Deterioration* was published. It also recommended that "... a systemised medical inspection of children at school should be imposed as a public duty on every school authority...(and)...that definite provision should be made by the various Local Authorities for dealing with the question of underfed children..."

(* The findings of the Royal Commission stimulated another body, the Sanitary Institute, to produce its own *Inquiry into the Physique of Glasgow School Children* in 1904. Not surprisingly, it showed that Glasgow children were even more underweight than those in Edinburgh.)

The Education (Provision of Meals) Act 1906
Much of the credit for the school meals bill lies outside the Liberal Party - especially from the widespread public concern created by the two reports and from the new Parliamentary presence of the Labour Party. (See p.12) The Liberals had not campaigned on a platform of social welfare reform in the run-up to the General Election in December 1905 and there was little indication from their

Causes of Rejection of Army Recruits on Inspection (1891-1902)												Ratio per 1,000
	1891	1892	1893	1894	1895	1896	1897	1898	1899	1900	1901	1902
Under chest measure	93	96	108	110	126	140	89	74	66	60	49	57
Defective vision	40	42	41	42	39	40	41	42	41	36	35	39
Under weight	32	27	39	39	36	35	45	34	33	28	25	21
Under height	27	32	33	28	28	28	24	20	20	15	13	12
Imperfect constitution	18	10	9	5	3	4	4	5	6	5	3	4
Disease of veins	16	16	17	15	15	15	15	15	14	11	14	12
Disease of heart	16	18	17	19	20	18	17	17	15	13	16	17
Defects of lower extremities	15	17	14	17	18	18	18	17	13	10	16	12
Varicocele	13	12	13	14	12	13	13	12	11	11	14	12
Flat feet	11	9	12	14	13	17	16	12	12	9	11	12
Loss or decay of teeth	11	14	15	16	18	20	24	26	25	20	26	49

Table 7.3

manifesto that Britain was about to experience a period of radical social reform. Rather, the stimulus for action came from a Labour backbencher, William Wilson, the Chairman of the Amalgamated Society of Carpenters and Joiners. He introduced the school meals proposal as a Private Member's Bill and because it was so well received in the House of Commons, the Liberals decided to give it government time. The outcome was the Education (Provision of Meals) Bill which became law in December 1906. It was a cautious measure, allowing authorities to "take such steps as they think fit for the provision of meals" either in conjunction with voluntary bodies or on their own. Parents were to be charged if they could afford it or else the local authority could put a halfpenny on the rates.

The number of school meals provided rose from 3 million in 1906 to 9 million in 1910 and then to 14 million in 1914. By that time, the voluntary agencies had become overwhelmed by the scale of the scheme and most of the provision was in the hands of the local authorities, who in turn were in receipt of a 50% grant from the Treasury. So within a very short time, a publicly-funded welfare service administered by the Board of Education was beginning to replace a patchwork of local charitable efforts. There was still a long way to go, however, and by 1912 over half the local authorities had not set up a school meals service.

"This measure was important, first, because it was the first extension from the field of schooling into that of welfare of the principle that a publicly-financed benefit could be granted to those in need, free both of charge and of the disabilities associated with the Poor Law; second, it was a step towards recognition that parents were not necessarily culpable for the undernourishment of their children and that, with public support, needy children could be well cared for at home and did not require withdrawal into public or voluntary care."
(P Thane *The Foundations of the Welfare State* p. 75)

Education (Administrative Provisions) Act 1907
School medical inspection "owed as much to administrative pressure as to Liberal initiative" (H V Emy *Liberals, Radicals and Social Politics 1892-1914* p. 150) The Government was not at all enthusiastic about the proposal because it knew that inspection would inevitably reveal chronic health problems. This would lead to demands for publicly-funded medical treatment facilities which the Liberals felt they could not afford at that time. The administrative drive mentioned above, came from Robert L. Morant, the Permanent Secretary of the Education Board. During 1906, he

Pupils of the same London County School with 40 years between them, 1894 and 1934

Comparative Table on Height and Weight of British and American Schoolchildren Height (inches) Weight (pounds)				
	British	Boston	Aberdeen	Edinburgh
Height:				
Boys 6-9	45.67	46.15	46.0	44.52
Girls 6-9	44.64	45.89	45.4	44.51
Boys 9-12	51.68	52.10	51.2	50.20
Girls 9-12	50.96	51.72	50.09	49.93
Boys 12-15	57.07	58.34	57.3	55.26
Girls 12-15	57.74	58.74	57.4	55.65
Weight:				
Boys 6-9	49.6	49.6	51.1	46.1
Girls 6-9	47.1	48.2	47.9	45.6
Boys 9-12	66.6	66.32	64.0	59.5
Girls 9-12	61.8	63.9	60.9	57.76
Boys 12-15	83.7	89.1	84.5	74.0
Girls 12-15	86.7	90.9	83.3	78.4

Table 7.4

had been persuaded about the need for school medical inspection through contact with Margaret Macmillan.

"I have for some time past come to feel that for the good of the children and the public, what subjects are taught and how much they are taught *do not matter anything like so much nowadays* as attention a) to the *physical* condition of the scholars and the teacher and b) to the physiological aspect of the school...
Between us we shall do something, I am sure, if we can avoid a public hubbub against our efforts..."
(J R Hay *The Development of the British Welfare State, 1880-1975* p. 59)

Morant's influential position as Permanent Secretary enabled him to get his own way whilst avoiding the "public hubbub". It was his job to draw up the fine details of the Education (Administrative Provisions) Bill. He managed to smuggle the school medical inspection provisions into this rather innocuous Bill, which was passed into law in 1907. Under the Act, medical inspection of all elementary school pupils was to take place:

"...the statutory medical inspection...should take account of the following matters:
1 Previous disease including infectious diseases.
2 General condition and circumstances
   a. height and weight
   b. nutrition (good, medium, bad)
   c. cleanliness (including vermin of head and body)
   d. clothing (sufficiency, cleanliness and footgear)

3 Throat, nose and articulation (mouth-breathing, snoring, stammering, tonsillar and glandular conditions, adenoids).
4 External eye disease and vision testing.
5 Ear disease and deafness.
6 Teeth and oral sepsis.
7 Mental capacity (normal, backward, defective).
8 Present disease or defect."

As predicted, inspection revealed the disturbing fact that children were going untreated because their parents were too poor to afford the doctors' bills. The government was soon under pressure to treat the problems revealed by its own inspectors. In 1912, the Board of Education started to give grants to local authorities for treatment and school clinics were set up for the first time.

In Scotland, the medical inspection of children was authorised under the *Education (Scotland) Act* of 1908. The Act also gave School Boards the power to take action against parents who allowed their children to come to school in a filthy or verminous condition. Inspection was made compulsory and Medical Officers or nurses were hired for the purpose. Perhaps not unexpectedly, the first report of the school medical inspection service for Glasgow exposed both the level of ill-health amongst pupils and the lack of on-going treatment for their ailments.

"...it emerged that between 80% and 90% of the children examined had defective teeth; that about 9% suffered from rickets (due to inadequate diet); and that about 30% were verminous. It was found that 55% of children with defects had not had any form of treatment, while many of the others had not received the continuing treatment which they required."
(T Ferguson *Scottish Social Welfare 1864-1914* p. 571)

Children Act 1908

Like the *Education (Scotland) Act*, the *Children Act* made it a legal offence for parents to neglect their children. The Act also brought together and organised into a system a mass of previous rulings. It became known as the '*Children's Charter*'. Most of the provisions were for the protection of children eg.

- Children under 16 were forbidden to smoke or drink and stiff penalties were brought in for shops selling alcohol or tobacco to children.
- Children were forbidden to beg.
- Young offenders were no longer to be tried in the ordinary courts but in new juvenile courts.
- Remand homes were set up to keep child offenders out of prison while waiting for trial.
- If convicted, children were to be sent to borstal (a corrective school) rather than prison.
- Probation officers were appointed for the after-care of young offenders.

1908 - A Turning Point in the Pace of Reform

The first two years of the Liberal Government had seen only relatively minor reform measures, but between 1908 and 1911 several major social welfare reforms were passed. The turning point came in 1908 when Prime Minister Campbell-Bannerman was forced to resign due to ill-health. His replacement, Asquith, brought into the Cabinet two key figures who were to play a significant role in the next few years - Lloyd George (Chancellor of the Exchequer) and Churchill (President of the Board of Trade). Both were strongly committed to social reform and they were mainly responsible for the welfare legislation over the next 3 years.

As we saw in chapter 6, the Liberal Party itself was in the process of changing some of its fundamental values in line

Lloyd George c. 1910

Winston Churchill 1909

with *New Liberal* thinking (see chapter 6). Lloyd George outlined the broad principles now underlying the Government's policy in a speech at Swansea in October, 1908:

"It has not abandoned the traditional ambition of the Liberal Party to establish freedom and equality; but side by side with this effort it promotes measures for ameliorating the conditions of life of the multitude."
(Quoted in *The Development of the British Welfare State 1880-1975* , JR Hay, p73, Pub Edward Arnold)

Lloyd George himself was genuinely concerned for the welfare of the people because of his own background:

"I am a man of the people, bred amongst them and it has been the greatest joy of my life to have had some part in fighting the battles of the class from whom I am proud to have sprung."

Apart from this concern for social justice for the under-privileged, the Liberals had other motives for wanting to put social reform at the head of their policy agenda. In particular, they recognised the growing threat to Liberalism posed by the Labour Party. Lloyd George though was confident that Labour would only oust the Liberals if they failed,

"to cope seriously with the social condition of the people, to remove the national degradation of slums and widespread poverty in a land glittering with wealth." (Lloyd George speech at Cardiff 1906, quoted in *The Evolution of the Welfare State* p144 Pub. McMillan)

Churchill too was keenly aware of the challenge from Labour. He saw social reform as a means of halting socialism. In his by-election campaign at Dundee in 1908, he pointed out that:

"Socialism wants to pull down wealth, Liberalism seeks to raise up poverty...Socialism assails the

maximum pre-eminence of the individual - Liberalism seeks to build up the minimum standard of the masses. Socialism attacks Capital, Liberalism attacks Monopoly." (From *Winston Churchill Vol.II* by RS Churchill, quoted in *Evolution of the British Welfare State* p152, Pub. McMillan)

Finally, both Lloyd George and Churchill were influenced by the question of national efficiency. Lloyd George was particularly impressed by the advances made in Germany as a result of Bismarck's social legislation. He was also struck by the emerging military might of Germany and the way in which its national strength was directly related to an enlightened welfare programme. Churchill echoed this concern and in December, 1908 he informed Asquith that:

"There is a tremendous policy in social organisation. The need is urgent and the moment right. Germany with a harder climate and far less accumulated wealth has managed to establish tolerable basic conditions for her people." (From *Winston Churchill Vol. II* by RS Churchill, quoted in *Edwardian Britain* by K Benning, p20, Pub. Blackie)

All of these factors came together in and after 1908 and resulted in major steps forward such as old age pensions and insurance against sickness and unemployment.

The Old

The *Old Age Pensions Act* of 1908 was the culmination of more than 20 years of debate and enquiry into the subject of poverty amongst the elderly. Leading figures such as Charles Booth and Joseph Chamberlain had taken up the cause of pensions in the 1890s. Both were members of the Royal Commission on the Aged Poor (1893) set up to consider "whether any alterations in the system of Poor Law relief are desirable, and the care of persons whose destitution is occasioned by incapacity for work resulting from old age". The Commission was dominated by advocates of laissez faire and not surprisingly, the Majority Report (1895) came out against any major alteration of the current system. Chamberlain's contribution to the Minority Report contained cautious proposals - not for a universal system of old age pensions but :

"a tentative scheme which might develop into something much more complete, on a contributory basis, with sufficiently liberal help from the State to make the scheme attractive.

The scheme provides for a State Pension Fund, to which Parliament would make an annual grant, supplemented from the Poor Rate which old age pensions would ultimately relieve." (Chamberlain's evidence to the Royal Commission quoted in Sir A Wilson and G S Mackay *Old Age Pensions - An Historical and Critical Study*, 1941, p27)

During his evidence, Chamberlain cited two difficult hurdles which would have to be overcome before progress with old age pensions could be made. Firstly, he argued that the cost of a state scheme would create opposition:

"Mr Booth's scheme (ie. state pensions financed out of taxation) is logical and would do what it set out to do, but it would cost £20-£24 millions and the House of Commons would never provide the money." (Wilson and Mackay ibid p27-8)

Secondly, he feared opposition from the Friendly Societies who gained a great deal of business from providing pensions for the working class:

"I attach great importance to Friendly Societies. They are in touch with the thriftily minded section of the working class. Their criticism of any scheme would be very damaging: their opposition might be fatal. They have very great Parliamentary influence and I should myself think twice before attempting to proceed in face of hostility from so important and dangerous a quarter." (Wilson and Mackay ibid p27-8)

Chamberlain's words had a prophetic ring because these two issues were largely instrumental in delaying progress on pensions in Britain. In the meantime, Germany (1889), Denmark (1891) and New Zealand (1899) had all established their own systems of old age pensions before the coming of the twentieth century.

Cost to Government if pensionable age fixed at:			
	65	**70**	**75**
1901	£10.3 m	£5.9 m	£2.9 m
1911	£12.6 m	£7.4 m	£3.7 m
1921	£15.6 m	£9.5 m	£4.9 m

Table 7.5

Problems of Cost

In August, 1899 the Conservative Government set up a committee under Sir Edward Hamilton to look into the financial implications of an old age pension scheme. The findings of the committee are shown in table 7.5.

It is not clear how close the Government was to making a commitment to pensions but the financial implications of the Boer War put a stop to such costly 'adventures' . Bonar Law, writing in 1912 in defence of the Conservative Government, claimed that the Boer War made "all schemes of social reform impossible" and even up to 1905, "...the finances of the country had been so disorganised that even then such a scheme was impossible." (Wilson and Mackay ibid p. 38-9)

The Liberals also found that the cost of any proposed scheme was a significant factor. Asquith, the new Chancellor of the Exchequer would only commit the government to the introduction of a pensions bill once the budget was in surplus. Inside government, the Treasury had an important part to play in the final outcome. For example, when the Treasury balked at the cost of setting up and administering a contributory pension scheme, Asquith decided upon a non-contributory scheme financed out of taxation. When it was calculated that the cost to the state of pensions at 65 would be £17 million a year, the Treasury set an upper limit of £7 million. Again Asquith was forced to opt for the less generous starting age of 70, against his better judgement. Even then, the Treasury persuaded the Government to add in more exemptions to the final scheme in order to get the cost down further.

Friendly Society Opposition

The Friendly Societies were opposed to the state intervening to take over pensions because this would directly threaten their own vested interests. As we saw in chapter 6 though, the friendly societies were doing little more than reflecting the anti- state attitudes of their clientele ie. the 'better off' working class.

The Foresters was one of the largest friendly societies. The following quotation from their own journal is fairly representative of the views of most friendly societies towards state pensions. Notice also how the passage emphasises the ennobling virtue of working class mutual self-help:

"The aim of the working class ought to be to bring about economic conditions in which there should be no need for distribution of state alms. The establishment of a great scheme of state pensions would legalise and stamp as a permanent feature of our social life the chronic poverty of the age. The desire of the best reformers is to remove the conditions that make that poverty so that every citizen shall have a fair chance not only of earning a decent wage for today but such a wage as shall enable him to provide for the future...Employers have presented carefully organised barriers to the workmen getting more wages...We have always held that the only object of (reform) was to transfer the burdens from employer to labour...Man is a responsible being. To rob him of his responsibility is to degrade him. The working class should rise to the occasion and insist upon being capable of using their own wages to their own advantage." (*Foresters' Miscellany*, leader (June 1894) quoted in J R Hay *The Development of the British Welfare State, 1880-1975* p17)

However, public opinion began to shift unrelentingly in the direction of publicly- financed pensions and by 1903 the trade unions and co-operative movement had come to this conclusion. The friendly societies had also come to accept that old age pensions were going to be brought in soon and they reluctantly came down in favour of a non-contributory scheme.

The Old Age Pensions Act 1908

As with the children's legislation, the Liberals had not campaigned specifically for old age pensions during the election campaign in 1906. Nevertheless, there was growing public and pressure group demand for action. For example, the National Committee of Organised Labour for Old Age Pensions (NCOL) had been gaining support outside Parliament for pensions at 65 financed out of taxation. In the Commons, one of the Liberals' own backbenchers, the philanthropist soap manufacturer, W L Lever, attempted to force the pace by introducing a Private Member's Bill on pensions. Although the bill failed, there was widespread support for the principle in the House. The NCOL pensions campaign and Liberal inaction appeared to be benefiting Labour - at least the government seems to have interpreted its two by-election defeats to Labour in 1907 (at Jarrow and Colne Valley - previously safe 'Old Liberal' seats) in this way. It was a timely warning that action was necessary.

The Liberal *Old Age Pensions Bill* fell to Lloyd George, the new Chancellor of the Exchequer as of April, 1908. He had had an interest in this area for a long time, having been a member of the Chaplin Committee on pensions in 1899. That committee had looked in great detail at the New Zealand and Danish schemes, but Lloyd George was more interested in the German scheme and as soon as the pensions bill had been enacted, he paid a visit to Germany to see at first hand how the system worked in practice. The following passage shows how impressed he was - and not only with the pensions scheme but with the whole system of national insurance:

> "I never realised before on what a gigantic scale the German pension system is conducted. Nor had I any idea how successfully it works. I had read much about it, but no amount of study at home...can convey to the mind a clear idea of all that state insurance means to Germany...It touches the great mass of German people in well-nigh every walk of life. Old-age pensions form but a part of the system. Does the German worker fall ill? State insurance comes to his aid. Is he permanently invalided from work? Again he gets a regular grant whether he has reached the pension age or not." (E P Hennock *The Origins of British National Insurance and the German Precedent 1880-1914* in W J Mommsen *The Emergence of the Welfare State in Britain and Germany* p87)

Lloyd George successfully steered the Bill through the House of Commons and there was very little opposition except on detail. In the Lords, there was more evidence of hostility to the principle. This extract from the Earl of Wemyss' speech gives us a flavour of the laissez faire response to the origins of the welfare state:

> "The State invites us every day to lean upon it. The strongest man, if encouraged, may soon accustom himself to the methods of an invalid. He may train himself to totter, or to be fed with a spoon. Every day the area for initiative is being narrowed, every day the standing ground for self-reliance is being undermined: every day the public impinges - with the best intentions, no doubt - on the individual; the nation is being taken into custody by the State.

> ...It was self-reliance that built the Empire; it is by self-reliance....that it must be welded and continued."
> (Wilson and Mackay - op cit p43)

The Bill passed all its stages and became law in August 1908, with effect from January 1909. It entitled people over 70 with an annual income of between £21 and £31 to between 1 shilling (5p) and 5 shillings a week of a pension. The government were honest enough to admit that these payments were not meant to be a complete solution to the problem of poverty in old age. The maximum pension of 5 shillings a week was still 2 shillings short of what Rowntree considered to be the minimum necessary to remain above the poverty line and there were also exemptions. Any 70-year-old was entitled to the pension provided:

- they were British and had been resident in the UK for the last 20 years
- they had avoided imprisonment in the last 10 years
- they had not habitually avoided work
- they had avoided detention under the Inebriates Act in the last 10 years

The government miscalculated how many people would come forward for the pension. They estimated 500,000 - in fact 650,000 applied. By 1914, the number had increased to nearly a million. The government very quickly became aware of the level of poverty amongst the old - people who had worked all their lives and as Lloyd George said were "...too proud to wear the badge of pauperism." (M Bruce *The Coming of the Welfare State* p180)

Just how grateful many old people were for the meagre pension is vividly portrayed in Flora Thompson's book *Lark Rise*:

> "When the Old Age Pensions began, life was transformed for such aged cottagers. They were relieved of anxiety. They were suddenly rich. Independent for life! At first when they went to the Post Office to draw it, tears of gratitude would run down the cheeks of some, and they would say as they picked up the money, 'God bless that Lord George! (for they could not believe one so powerful and munificent could be a plain 'Mr') and God bless you, miss!', and there were flowers from their gardens and apples from their trees for the girl who merely handed them the money." (quoted in M Bruce ibid p100)

The Sick

> "The aged we have dealt with...we are still confronted with the more gigantic task of dealing with the rest - the sick, the infirm, the unemployed, the widows and orphans." (Lloyd George, speaking in Swansea on his return from Germany, 1908)

After his inspection of the German social insurance scheme, Lloyd George was in no doubt that Britain needed a more comprehensive system and he was determined this time not to be bullied by outside pressures. Instead, the government would construct its own policy on sickness and invalidity. He immediately instructed his civil servants to set out detailed proposals for a scheme similar to the German one. However, yet again, he was to come up against the resistance of powerful vested interests such as the friendly societies and the doctors and he had to modify his original scheme accordingly. As Chancellor of the Exchequer, Lloyd George was also acutely aware of the cost implications of national insurance and he had to provide for that in the 1909 Budget.

The People's Budget, 1909

"The wealth of this country is enormous. It is not merely great, but it is growing at a gigantic pace, and I do not think it is too much to expect the more favoured part of the community who have got riches so great that they have really to spend a good part of their time in thinking how to spend them, to make a substantial contribution to improve the lot of the poorer members of the same community to which they belong, because it is in their interest after all that they should not belong to a country where there is so much poverty and distress side by side with gigantic wealth." (*Hansard*, 25 May, 1908)

With these words in the House of Commons, Lloyd George signalled his intent to bring in a redistributive tax on the rich in order to finance the national insurance scheme which was in the pipeline. Income tax was made more progressive ie. the more you earned, the higher the tax rate. Income tax would start at 9d (4p) and go up to 1s 2d (6p) in the pound for average earners. The very rich earning over £5,000 would have to pay an extra supertax of 2d in the pound. Much more controversial was the proposed 20% capital gains tax on the sale of land and even land which was unused was to be taxed. Lloyd George justified these radical proposals in the budget speech:

"This is a War Budget. It is for raising money to wage implacable warfare against poverty and squalidness. I cannot help hoping and believing that before this generation has passed away we shall have advanced a great step towards that good time when poverty and wretchedness and human degradation which always follow in its camp will be as remote to the people of this country as the wolves which once infested its forests." (*Hansard*, 29 April, 1909)

The 1909 Budget was rejected by the House of Lords and a major constitutional crisis ensued, culminating in the Parliament Act (1911) which curbed the powers of the upper House. The budget was passed in 1910. The government now had the revenue to implement its social welfare programme. (See p.60)

The health insurance scheme was contained in Part 1 of the *National Insurance Act* (1911) and the main provisions are detailed in the box below.

Lloyd George admitted that the final scheme was a compromise and that more would have to be done for the disadvantaged in society. The following is a note to his private secretary, RG Hawtree, written on March 7, 1911:

"Insurance necessarily temporary expedient. At no distant date hope State will acknowledge a full responsibility in the matter of making provision for sickness, breakdown and unemployment. It really does so now, through the Poor Law; but conditions under which this system had hitherto worked have

been so harsh and humiliating that working -class pride revolts against accepting so degrading and doubtful a boon. Gradually the obligation of the State to find labour or sustenance will be realised and honourably interpreted." (Quoted in *The Evolution of the British Welfare State* by D Fraser, p156-7, Pub. McMillan)

In his famous speech in the House of Commons (10 June, 1911), Lloyd George used the mataphor of the ambulance wagon to make this same point:

"This year, this session..I am in the ambulance corps. I am engaged to drive a wagon through the twistings and turnings and ruts of the parliamentary road. There are men who tell me I have overloaded that wagon. I have taken three years to pack it carefully, I cannot spare a single parcel, for the suffering is great. There are those who say my wagon is half

---

'Insurance against Loss of Health and for the Prevention and Cure of Sickness'

Contributions

1 All workers up to the age of 70 who earned less than £160 a year had to insure themselves.
2 They could choose to be insured by any one of the "approved societies".
3 Male workers contributed 4d per week, to which the employer added 3d and the state 2d (Lloyd George called this ' ninepence for fourpence'). Female workers contributed 3d, making the total contribution for them 8d.
4 Those earning over £160 a year could also join the scheme but they would have to pay the employer's contribution themselves.
5 Each worker would receive a card which the employer would fill in with insurance stamps bought from the Post Office. Every three months, the worker had to take the card to the approved society, which would obtain the state's contribution.

Benefits

1 Insured male workers were entitled to sickness benefit of 10 shillings for the first thirteen weeks followed by 5 shillings for the next thirteen weeks. The corresponding rates for women were 7shillings and 6 pence (37 1/2p) and 3 shillings (15p). For men and women, benefits did not start until the fourth day of an illness (to stop people going off work for trivial illnesses). After 26 weeks of illness, workers would be entitled to a disablement benefit of 5 shillings (25p) a week. Maternity benefit of 30 shillings (£1.50) could be claimed. Dependants of insured male workers were not entitled to any benefits.
2 The insured were entitled to full treatment by a 'panel' doctor as well as treatment for tuberculosis at a TB sanatorium. TB was a serious problem at this time with 75,000 deaths a year. Local authorities were given £1.5 million to construct sanatoria. However, other general hospital treatment was not covered by national insurance, the reason being that the existing Poor Law and voluntary hospitals simply would not have been able to cope with the demand.

empty; I say it is as much as I can carry."
(Quoted in *Human Documents of the Lloyd George Era* by E Royston Pike, p110, Pub. Allen & Unwin)

Opposition of the Friendly Societies, Trade Unions & Industrial Insurance Companies

Lloyd George realised very quickly that his idea of a contributory scheme would be seen by the friendly societies as encroaching on their business and consequently, he decided to administer the system through the societies. Those trade unions which gave sick pay would also have to be included. However, the real problem came with the Industrial Insurance Companies (IICs). They were in business for profit and they objected to Lloyd George's proposal to include widows' and orphans' benefits. The IICs were a very important part of the existing insurance set-up, with large companies such as the Prudential involved. There were also about 80,000 door-to-door collectors throughout the country. In the weeks running up to the 1910 election campaign, the IICs waged a successful political campaign to secure pledges from candidates to back their claims and on 1 December Lloyd George was forced to back down and exclude the two 'funeral' benefits. The commercial interests had won this particular battle. They, along with the friendly societies, were designated 'approved societies' by the National Insurance Act, thereby enhancing their status with the public when conducting their other commercial business.

The Doctors

When Lloyd George brought out his proposals, the British Medical Association immediately put up objections. They were concerned that the government was simply going to reproduce, on a national scale, the existing unsatisfactory arrangement between the friendly societies and the doctors, whereby the doctors felt that they were being paid a pittance for treating the societies' working class clients. They also wished the medical side of the insurance scheme to be run by the profession and to be free from friendly society domination. Lloyd George met with the doctors and told them frankly that the societies were too powerful for him to resist, but that he was offering the doctors a higher contract fee of 4 shillings (20p) per patient and 2 shillings to cover drug costs. This was more than the friendly societies had been willing to concede. When the Act was passed, there was a rush by the poorer doctors to join the new 'panel' system. Many of them were able to double their income at a stroke. The House of Commons also came down on the doctors' side when it voted for an amendment putting the administration of medical benefit in the hands of Local Health Committees, later called Insurance Committees. All in all, the 1911 Act was so favourable to the doctors' case that it acquired the alternative title of ' the general practitioners' Act'.

The Unemployed

Up until the turn of the century, unemployment was still seen partly as a moral problem of individual idleness and partly as a cyclical or seasonal problem for certain industries such as construction and shipbuilding. As yet, few were willing to accept that unemployment might be due to structural factors outwith the control of individual workers. Thinking about the causes of unemployment was blinkered by the Victorian belief in self-help which went unchallenged for a long time because of a lack of accurate information about the scale of the problem. Nevertheless, attitudes were changing. The Chamberlain Circular (1886), encouraging local authorities to provide public works schemes, was a first step towards the state taking action on unemployment. T H Green argued powerfully that the state had a moral duty to intervene positively to help the weakest members of society. The unemployed, though were not as impotent as before. They now had the vote which compelled the established parties to take notice of their demands. Hunger marches and unemployment demonstrations took place during the trade depression between 1903 and 1905. The working class also had growing organisational strength with the coming of the Labour Party in 1900.

The Liberal Party came to power in 1906 with no policy on unemployment. The outgoing Conservative Government had passed the *Unemployed Workmen's Act* before they left office, but it was 1909 before a clear statement of intent emerged from the Liberals. They had preferred to set up the wide-ranging *Royal Commission upon the Poor Laws* (1905) and were content to wait for its conclusions. However, the members of the Commission could not agree and two documents were published, the Majority and the Minority Reports (see table 7.6). Lloyd George laid out the Government's plan for unemployment insurance during that important Budget speech of 1909. It steered a middle course between the voluntarism of the Majority Report and the socialism of the Minority Report. The Government had taken 5 years to finalise its unemployment policy enshrined in Part 11 of the National Insurance Act.

Royal Commission on the Poor Laws - Recommendations on Unemployment

Majority Report wanted:	Minority Report wanted:
National Labour Exchanges	National Labour Exchanges co-ordinated by new Ministry of Labour
Unemployment insurance	Non-contributory Benefits (not compulsory)
Training for the Unemployed	Training for the Unemployed
Better Technical Education	Better Technical Education
Temporary Public Works to be set up , designed to eliminate economic depressions	10-Year programme of Public Works only during times of very high unemployment
Juvenile labour to be reduced by introducing part-time education and raising the school leaving age	Juvenile labour to be reduced by introducing part-time education and raising the school leaving age
Labour colonies for the idle	Labour colonies for the idle

Table 7.6

The Unemployed Workmen's Act, 1905

The Liberals inherited the Unemployed Workmen's Act from the previous Conservative administration. It was designed to provide help for unemployed workmen by setting up Distress Committees in boroughs with a population over 50,000 (and equivalent burghs and counties in Scotland). The Committees had discretion to assist 'proper cases' ie unemployed workmen who had proved themselves previously to be thrifty, of good character and who had not received poor relief in the previous year. They could then set up public works schemes and give financial help for families to emigrate or find work elsewhere in the country. Some also bought up land to organise farm and labour colonies. For example, the Glasgow Distress Committee acquired 591 acres of land for this purpose in 1907 and for the next three years sent 200 men by train every day to the colony at Palacerigg. The Aberdeen Committee organised stone-breaking for 120 men at Dancing Cairns Quarry.

Nationally, the scheme was to be funded by voluntary donations and from the rates. A sum of £153,000 was raised through an appeal by Queen Alexandra, but the money soon ran out. A report by the London committees in 1907-8 concuded that "it is impossible to deal adequately with unemployment by local authorities and (we are) therefore of the opinion that in future legislation the question should be dealt with nationally." (quoted in H V Emy *Liberals, Radicals and Social Politics 1892-1914* p154) As the Queen's fund had been used up by the time the Liberals had come to power, it was decided to grant a further £200,000 from the Treasury coffers. Depending on how one interprets this decision, it was either a paltry gesture or a historic decision by the state to use national funds for the first time to deal with the problem of unemployment. In the short term, the temporary work schemes to 'tide people over' failed to get to the root of the problem. In the longer term, though, the government had set a precedent by taking some responsibility for the welfare of those out of work.

Labour Exchanges

In February 1909, two reports and a book were published, all advocating the establishment of labour exchanges throughout Britain. The two reports were the Majority and Minority Reports of the Royal Commission on the Poor Laws and the book was William Beveridge's *Unemployment - A Problem of Industry*. Beveridge argued that the current arrangement of men standing outside factories in the morning waiting to be chosen for casual work, was very inefficient. A Labour Exchange would enable employer and employee to register their requirements at one central location and their separate needs could then be met. The Exchange would also benefit from having detailed information about job vacancies.

Churchill had heard about Beveridge's ideas in advance of the publication of his book and managed to persuade him to join the Board of Trade team in July, 1908. Beveridge's remit was to lay out detailed plans for a *Labour Exchanges Bill*. These were ready in a few months and the bill passed all its stages in September 1909. By the following February, 83 Labour Exchanges had been set up; by 1913 there were 430 Exchanges throughout Britain. Despite wariness from both employers and employees, about 3,000 people were being fixed up with work every day by 1914.

Unemployment Insurance

Churchill envisaged Labour Exchanges as having two roles - firstly to register and find work for the unemployed and secondly to pay out unemployment benefit to those who were insured. It was to insurance that Churchill now

turned. The final scheme for unemployment insurance was worked out by Llewellyn Smith, Permanent Secretary at the Board of Trade, and Beveridge. Since there were no vested interests involved (like the doctors and friendly societies with health insurance), *Part II of the National Insurance Bill* had a relatively easy passage through Parliament. Churchill was not able to supervise the transition of the Bill into law as he was made Home Secretary in February, 1910. His successor at the Board of Trade, Sidney Buxton, remarked during the debate in the Commons: "...if the bill had been introduced ten years ago it would not have found ...a single supporter from either of the front benches." It was certainly true that the climate of opinion had changed. Charity and self-help were no longer seen to be adequate remedies for the evils of unemployment. Now the state was going to intervene to help the most vulnerable workers to insure themselves.

The Unemployment Insurance scheme got under way in July 1912 but benefits were not payable until January, 1913. Within two years, 2.3 million workers were insured. Although this was still a small proportion of the total working population, both Churchill and Lloyd George saw it as the beginning of a much more comprehensive system for dealing with the problem of unemployment.

Provisions of Part II of the National Insurance Act (1911)	
Contributions	worker 2¹/2d, the employer 2¹/2d and the state 3d per week
Trades involved	shipbuilding, mechanical engineering, building, construction, iron founding and sawmilling (the scheme was compulsory for these trades because of the cyclical/seasonal pattern of unemployment)
Entitlement	after a week of unemployment, the insured worker would get 7 shillings (35p) a week for up to 15 weeks in any one year
Payment	the insured worker had to register as unemployed at the Labour Exchange and he would get paid at the Exchange
Conditions	if a worker was dismissed for his conduct, then he would not be entitled to benefit

Table 7.7

The Employed

The Liberal Government also passed four laws which sought to improve workers' conditions, providing:

- compensation for injuries sustained at work;
- shorter hours to compensate for the dangerous and difficult job done underground by coalminers;
- minimum wages for exploited female labour in 'sweated industries';
- a half-day off for shop assistants who were mostly non-unionised.

Taken together, these measures constituted a significant improvement for millions of workers, many of whom had no one to speak up for them.

The Workmen's Compensation Act (1906) : This built on the previous Acts of 1897 and 1900 which had made employers in a few specified trades liable to pay compensation for injuries sustained as a result of conditions at the workplace. The 1906 Act extended this to cover nearly all employees. Employers were now also liable to pay compensation for the contracting of industrial diseases by their workforce.

The Coal Mines Act (1908): This gave miners an eight- hour day, for which they had been campaigning for 40 years.

The Trade Boards Act (1909): This set up Boards to negotiate minimum wage levels for the notoriously badly-paid and non-unionised 'sweated trades' usually employing women working long hours in four trades - tailoring, and box, lace and chain making. A total of 200,000 workers were involved in these trades. However, no attempt was made to define what a 'minimum' wage was.

The Shops Act (1911): This stated that shop assistants were entitled to a weekly half-day off and a reasonable break for meals.

As we have seen, the Liberals came into power with at first few definite plans for social reform. Perhaps because of this, the new Government seems to have been much more amenable to influence from outside bodies and individuals than previous administrations. Organisations like the BMA and the friendly societies and individuals like Beveridge, Morant and the Webbs were able to put pressure on Ministers and get their ideas enshrined in law. Especially in the complex areas of pensions and national insurance, the 'experts' and top civil service officials played a very important role in determining the final outcome of these bills. Since there were no guidelines for the shaping of the infant welfare state, the key reforming Ministers like Lloyd George and Churchill had to rely on a mixture of expert advice and acute political judgment. After all, there were political costs and benefits involved in every measure of social reform. These 'New Liberals' understood the dangers of excessive public expenditure and how that could alienate the old Gladstonian wing of the party. Even after such a modest step as old age pensions for the over 70s,

Lord Rosebery, the former Liberal Prime Minister condemned the scheme as 'so prodigal of expenditure as likely to undermine the whole fabric of the Empire'. On the other hand, social pressures were increasingly bearing down on all governments in the more democratic twentieth century. To do nothing was to invite the party of the working class into power. Liberal Ministers were keenly aware of the potential threat from the Labour Party and they considered their social reform programme to be a political antidote to socialism. Nevertheless, the working class were not wholeheartedly in favour of the efforts made on their behalf by the Liberals. Some saw the new insurance schemes and their attendant bureaucracy as little more than middle class interference.

Between 1906 and 1914, the Liberals introduced old age pension, unemployment and sickness insurance, labour exchanges, school meals and medical inspections, the eight-hour day for miners, minimum wages for 'sweated industries' and a half-day off for shop assistants. Taken together, this formidable list of social reform measures adds up to a significant shift away from minimum government. Some historians go further and argue that we can see the origins of the welfare state in the Liberal reforms. They justify this claim by saying that old age pensions and safeguards against unemployment and ill-health, which the Liberals brought in for the first time, are cornerstones of the modern welfare system. Other historians disagree with this interpretation. They argue that the Liberal reforms were very limited in scope and failed to deal adequately with such important welfare issues as education and housing and they did not attempt to set up a national health service or strive for full employment. Furthermore, the reforms passed were quite inadequate eg. pensions were too low, health insurance did not cover the employee's family and unemployment insurance applied only to seven trades.

Clearly the significance of the Liberal welfare reforms will continue to be debated. Certainly by the standards of the time, they were considered to be radical measures of social reform. On the other hand, looking back from the perspective of modern welfare Britain, the Liberal reforms appear to be very limited. However, it is important to realise that both Lloyd George and Churchill saw their reforms as only a first step.

8 The National Governments of the 1930s

The social and economic problems facing the National Governments of the 1930s had their origins in the twenties and before. Therefore, we will need to look at the preceding period before we can make any assessment of the governments of the thirties.

The origins of Britain's economic problems 1900-29
Between 1900 and the outbreak of the First World War, there were definite, if not indisputable, signs that Britain was no longer the pre-eminent industrial power it had been. As America and several European countries developed and industrialised, so they imported fewer British manufactured goods and themselves became competitors with Britain for foreign trade.

There were both encouraging and depressing lessons to be learned from Britain's trade performance with the rest of the world. For example, Britain's share of world export trade fell from 20% to 14% between 1880 and 1914. However, it was consoling to know that the country's total output for export was still rising at a decent 2% per annum. Coal still seemed to be doing well. Output was up from 223 million tons in 1900 to 287 million tons in 1913. However, the industry was hopelessly overmanned with over 1 million men working in the pits before the First World War. Cotton output was increasing and exports were improving, but how long could British markets in the Far East be secured when Japan, India and China were all building their own mills?

Altogether, then, Britain's place in the international league of industrial nations might have been slipping, but it was still a major force before the war. British industrialists, though, were not responding to the changing international circumstances and to stand still while other countries were emerging as serious competitors was shortsighted. What then, was wrong with British industry in the early years of the twentieth century?

Firstly, there were *too many small firms* - family businesses which had an in-built resistance to take-over. Being small and resistant to change, they were not investing enough money in the *modernisation and expansion* of their businesses - a better and safer return on profits could be had by investing overseas. With so many small businesses, it is difficult to see how British industry could quickly come to terms with foreign competition. For example, where were the 90 or so British motor manufacturers going to get the massive outlays of capital to invest in mass production line techniques like Ford in America?

The *entrenched attitudes of the Establishment and the upper classes* did not help either. They tended to look down on science, technology and business. The education system was similarly blinkered: the academically gifted children did classics and the rest did technical and craft. At university, the pattern continued. Whereas Germany produced 3,000 engineering graduates a year in 1913, Britain turned out less than 1,000 scientists in general.

Britain had been *the first industrial nation* and was considered to be the 'workshop of the world' by the end of the nineteenth century. Ironically, though, this fact was to be a hindrance to the country's progress in the next thirty years. Newly industrialising countries would use the very latest technologies, while British firms continued to use the original, but by now obsolescent, machinery and practices. It is understandable that the typical small to medium sized British firm would have been loathe to change. If they were making a profit, why use this money on so disruptive a process as re-equipping, which might come up against trade union resistance for fear of redundancy? It seemed better to carry on with existing machinery and techniques.

However, as the country emerged from the First World War, it was to find it increasingly *difficult to compete with overseas countries*. After a brief boom in 1920, the economy slipped backwards and was not to emerge into recovery again until the mid 1930s. The war itself dislocated British industry and manufacturing output only reached its pre-war levels in 1924. Interruption of overseas trade due to the war proved costly. Countries which had to do without British goods during the war either found other suppliers or set up factories to make the goods themselves.

Britain's staple or 'old' industries did not fare any better in the postwar world. Despite being overmanned, by 1924 the coal industry had actually added an extra 250,000 men to the million who were working at the pits before the war. However, throughout the 1920s, demand for coal steadily decreased as people and industry converted to other sources of power. Annual production fell from 287 millions tons in 1913 to 224 million tons in 1930. Similarly, exports dropped by a third from the prewar level to 61 million tons. Crisis was reached in 1925-6 when mines began to go bankrupt. When the mine owners put into operation the recommendations of the Samuel Commission report i.e. to reduce miners' wages and increase the hours, the miners called for other trade unions to come to their assistance. The result was the General Strike of May 1926. (See p.16-18) The strike collapsed after 9 days and the miners were eventually forced back to work, with lower wages, in December.

The other staple industries continued to have problems. Iron production fell from 10 million to 6 million tons between 1913 and 1930, due to overcapacity. Steel did better but was faced with strong competition from countries like Japan and India. These same problems dogged the shipbuilding industry. British yards were losing orders to their cheaper and more efficient Swedish and Japanese competitors. By the end of the 1920s, Britain's share of world shipping fell from 60% to 30%. Export of cotton cloth similarly fell from 6,500 million yards in 1912 to 2,000 million yards in 1937.

The government itself compounded exporters' difficulties by *the return to the Gold Standard* in 1925. The Gold Standard had been around since the 19th century. Those countries which subscribed to it were guaranteed a fixed rate of exchange with the pound, thus ensuring currency stability. In 1919, however, the Gold Standard was abandoned as it was feared that it might hinder Britain's postwar recovery. The result was that the pound, which had stood at 4.6 to the dollar before the war, began to fall. This made British goods cheaper to export and so it benefited British industry.

In 1925, Winston Churchill, the Conservative Chancellor of the Exchequer, announced that Britain would return to the Gold Standard at the prewar exchange rate between the pound and the dollar. For industrialists, this was a disaster. At a stroke, the cost of British exports went up by 10%. Given the difficulties outlined above regarding over-capacity and foreign competition, this decision could not have come at a worse time. The government and the Treasury seemed to be more concerned with protecting the financial interests of foreign investors in the City than in giving a helping hand to British industry.

Finally, *the attitude to the economy of successive governments in the 1920s* did not help matters. Conventional wisdom stated that the economy went in cycles. Just as winter melts into spring and summer, so a depression in the economy would almost naturally be followed (sooner or later) by recovery. Consequently, throughout the 1920s, governments rejected tariffs as a method of protecting British industry from overseas competition. The wartime controls on industry and agriculture were also quickly lifted. Even when unemployment went over the million mark, governments made no attempt to reduce it by spending money on public works or other job creation schemes. On the contrary, unemployment was to be tolerated as a necessary evil, helping to bring wages and thus costs down. Government, just like the family facing hard times, had to pull in its belt and practise economies.

Most historians would agree that these *deflationary and laissez-faire policies* carried out by governments in the 1920s may have hindered economic recovery. However, it is not clear that alternative remedies would have been more successful. The fundamental problem of the economy was that British industry was out-of-date, inefficient and thus unable to compete successfully for world markets. To protect British industry at this time would have served only to protect inefficiency. What was needed was fairly radical restructuring and modernisation especially of the 'staple' industries - and that was going to be painful. As for state intervention, very few economists or political thinkers considered that a viable option in the 1920s. *The debate between the orthodox economists (laissez faire) and those who wanted the government to stimulate the economy (Keynesians) only really got under way in the 1930s and even then, the former had the upper hand.*

Summarising the period up to 1930, therefore, we can say that Britain emerged into the twentieth century as the pre-eminent industrial and imperial power. Its very success however, only served to give industrialists and successive governments a blinkered attitude towards the fragility of the economy and the impending threat from foreign competitors. The failure to modernise and restructure industry and the dismissal of a measure of protection were symptoms of this blinkered attitude. On the other hand, can we really blame those decision makers for failing to see what we know now? At the time, economic difficulties were attributed to the whims of the trade cycle. Business would pick up in the near future. Of course, we know in hindsight that the agonies suffered by the 'old' industries were just the beginning of a longer term structural decline.

The 'new' industries (electricity, cars, chemicals) were as yet a small part of the economy and made little contribution to Britain's export effort. Governments throughout the period did little to help industry due to their continued faith in the unregulated free market. The return to the Gold Standard did nothing but harm.

The Second Labour Government 1929- 31

Ramsay MacDonald became Prime Minister for the second time in May 1929. As in 1924, the Labour Government did not have an overall majority of seats in Parliament, so it had to rely on the Liberals for survival. To make matters worse, MacDonald's term of office coincided with the onset of the world economic depression. The next two years were to see unemployment increase from 1.2 million to over 2.5 million and the Government itself was to come to grief over a financial crisis in August 1931. The performance of the second Labour Government has been criticised by historians ever since, but given the circumstances, would any of the parties have succeeded?

In this section, we will be looking exclusively at the domestic economic policies of the Labour Government and assessing why they failed. In particular, we will focus on the unemployment problem and the various remedies to solve it put forward by the parties, individuals and committees at the time. Secondly, we will investigate the causes and course of the financial crisis of 1931 and the government's handling of it. (See p.15-19)

Governments on coming to power rarely have a free hand to do as they wish. In MacDonald's case, the Labour Party had 'won' the General Election, but due to the quirks of the first-past-the-post electoral system, it secured 300,000 *less* votes than the Conservatives. The distribution of seats was - Labour 288, Conservatives 260 and Liberals 59. Given the fact that 14 million out of the 22.5 million electors had rejected the Labour manifesto at the polls, MacDonald felt, honourably, that he could not carry out the Labour pledges. In his opening speech as Prime Minister in the House of Commons he said, "I wonder how far it is possible, without in any way abandoning any of our party positions...to consider ourselves more as a Council of State and less as arrayed regiments facing each other in battle." (LCB Seaman *Post Victorian Britain* p.206) Some historians see this statement as evidence that MacDonald had been contemplating forming a National Government in 1929. More probably, it hints at his insecurity over the Government's weak position. One supporter unhelpfully advised him simply to "keep things going", but surely in the context of rapidly rising unemployment, this non-policy could only lead to disaster? Hoping for cooperation from the other parties was another blind alley. The Liberals and the Conservatives both had internal leadership quarrels based on policy differences. How did MacDonald expect to cooperate with parties so clearly in disarray?

The options available to MacDonald were few and far between. He felt he could not carry out Labour's preferred programme, the other parties were in no fit state to cooperate and to do nothing might be politically wise but would quickly lead the country to economic crisis. Unemployment was the key issue, but none of the parties had a solution for it - or at least, none of them had a solution that was politically acceptable at that time.

Plans for Unemployment

The Liberal leader, Lloyd George had set out his own plans to deal with the unemployment problem during the 1929 election campaign with his pamphlet, *We Can Conquer Unemployment.* He advocated massive government spending on roads, housing and other 'public works' schemes to stimulate the economy and thus put people back to work. It was an imaginative document and a real challenge to the policies of the other two parties. However, it had a fatal flaw - it came from the hand of Lloyd George, "...the most mistrusted man in politics." (R Blake *The Conservative Party from Peel to Thatcher* p. 229)

Oswald Mosley put forward his own proposals to fight unemployment in January 1930. Mosley was a relatively new recruit to the Labour Party, and came from a wealthy background. MacDonald brought him in as a junior MInister under JH Thomas, the Lord Privy Seal, who had responsibility for unemployment. When Thomas failed to produce a solution, Mosley presented his own memorandum to the Cabinet. Expanding on Lloyd George's ideas, Mosley proposed a £200 million public works programme, mainly on roads. Unemployment would be further reduced by raising the school leaving age to 15 and pensions and allowances would be made available to make it easier to retire early from industry. Further government intervention would come in the form of protective tariffs and from public control of the banking system.

Mosley's ideas were rejected by the Cabinet, mainly on the grounds that they would cost too much. In October, Mosley made a brilliant speech to the Labour Party conference in defence of his proposals, but here again he was defeated. Impatient for success, Mosley made a fatal move, consigning himself to the political wilderness by setting up his own 'New Party', later to become the British Union of Fascists. Many commentators reflect sadly on this episode and speculate that, if Mosley had not been in such a hurry, he might eventually have won the Labour Party round.

At the beginning of 1930, then, MacDonald was still no further forward in seeking a solution to the unemployment problem, so he set up the *Economic Advisory Council.* This was to be a committee of businessmen, trade unionists and economists who could provide him with advice independent of the Treasury. Unfortunately, this body found it impossible to agree among itself and so MacDonald was still unable to counter the "grim orthodoxies of Snowdon and the Treasury" (P Adelman *The Rise of the Labour Party 1880-1945* p.70) with practical advice on how to lower the unemployment rate.

Orthodoxy (Snowden and the Treasury) [see p.19]
versus State Intervention (Keynes)

Lloyd George and Mosley were both influenced by the ideas of the economist, JM Keynes. Keynes believed that the government should intervene during a period of depression to get the economy going again. As the depression was caused by the fall in demand, the quickest and most direct way to restore demand was for the government to finance public works schemes and increase pensions and other allowances. Government spending on public works would, of course lead to a deficit - unless it raised equal amounts of money by increasing taxation.

Keynes was against this even although there was a danger of inflation. He believed that it was more important to deal with the immediate problem of getting the unemployed off the dole.

Opposing these views were the Treasury and the Chancellor of the Exchequer, Philip Snowden. Snowden was very much on the right wing of the Labour Party. Although claiming to be a socialist, his idea of socialism as, "a principle, the principle of cooperation as opposed to competition" (P Snowden *Autobiography* p.760 quoted in A Wood *Great Britain 1900-1965* p. 267) was fairly woolly. He did not want to see capitalism destroyed - only to be made a little fairer. Furthermore, when it came to government intervention, he was strenuously opposed to the sort of levels of spending envisaged by Mosley. As Chancellor of the Exchequer, Snowden saw it as his responsibility to balance the budget and that meant cutting government expenditure. Unfortunately, the main target of the cuts would be the unemployed themselves. Ironically, the very people the Labour Party pledged to help at the election were to have their benefits cut.

Clearly, then, there was going to be no 'socialist' solution to the unemployment problem. Snowden's orthodox views were almost indistinguisable from mainstream Conservative thinking. The real issue dividing the Snowden and Keynes camps was not capitalism versus socialism, but *interventionist capitalism versus laissez faire capitalism.*

At the October 1930 Party conference, MacDonald put the blame for the prevailing economic crisis on the capitalist system: "We are not on trial, it is the system under which we live....It has broken down everywhere, as it was bound to break down." (AJP Taylor *English History 1914-1945* p.358-9). However, this did not signal his intention to tear down the great structures of capitalism. As Wood points out, "This...should have been the great opportunity for Socialism to prove its worth and for a Labour government to establish a comprehensive government control of the economy in sharp contrast to the anarchy of laissez faire amid the fluctuations of the trade cycle. The irony for Labour at this moment was that the senior members of the government could not cut loose from existing precepts and were thus condemned to policies which ran directly contrary to their ideological outlook." (Wood - op cit p.266)

Wall Street Crash 1929

MacDonald had referred to the breakdown in the capitalist system. This had originated in America with the Wall Street crash of October, 1929. The panic selling of shares on the New York Stock Exchange led to a catastrophic financial collapse throughout America. Banks folded, people's life savings were lost and businesses went bankrupt. Very quickly, the economic shock waves from America began to affect the employment situation in Britain. Demand for British goods in America dried up and workers had to be laid off. Unemployment increased dramatically from 1 million to 2.5 million in December 1930. How to tackle the problem was a grave test for the Labour Government, but since neither of the other parties was in very good shape, nor did they have viable alternative policies, the Government's position was not threatened. What did put the government at risk was the banking crisis precipitated by the Wall Street crash.

Banking Crisis 1930-31

The fate of most of the European economies was intricately tied up with the financial health or otherwise of the USA. Germany, for example, was dependent on loans from America under the Dawes Plan. Without these loans, German industry would not have been able to revive after the inflationary collapse of 1923. Germany's economic revival enabled it to pay reparations to France and Britain. The latter needed the reparations payments to pay American war debts. In this way, the economies of Europe and America were tied up in a circle of loans and repayments of debts. One break in the circle would affect everyone.

American loans had been keeping the German economy afloat since 1924 and when these eventually dried up in 1931, the German unemployment figure had reached 4 million. However, it was the collapse of the German banks that began to affect Britain. In March, 1931, the main Austrian bank, the Credit Anstalt collapsed, followed soon after by the German Danat and Dresdner Banks. The German government immediately froze all foreign assets in the country, including £90 million from London. The pressure then transferred to the Bank of England in mid-July. Foreign creditors began to withdraw their assets from London at the rate of £4 million in gold a day. As the Bank had relatively small reserves of gold, it was forced to seek loans of £50 million from France and America on 28 July. The pound was under heavy pressure and the bankers in the City began to look to the Government to help them restore international confidence in sterling.

The unemployed queuing at an Employment Exchange in the 1930s

The May Committee Report (see p.19)

By one of those pieces of bad historical timing, the banking crisis coincided with the publication of the gloomy findings of the May Committee. This Committee, under the chairmanship of Sir George May, was set up in February 1931 to explore ways of reducing government expenditure after it became known that the unemployment insurance fund had gone into debt of £90 million due to the rising levels of payouts of unemployment benefit. All three political parties were represented on the committee.

The May Committee reported on 31 July, just as MPs were going off for their summer break. It came out with the dire prediction that by April, 1932, the government would be in deficit to the sum of £120 million and recommended some stern orthodox measures in the form of cutbacks to remedy the situation. * They proposed to raise only £24 million by taxation and the rest, £97 million, was to be found, or more accurately lost, by reductions in government spending. Of that £97 million, £30 million was to come from cuts in the pay of the police, the armed forces and teachers (the latter to suffer a 20% decrease) and the remaining £67 million from a 20% reduction in unemployment benefit. (*The two Labour members of the Committee disagreed with the majority findings. They advocated increased taxation.)

The Report, and its timing, was a further blow to international confidence in the pound. What made matters worse was the fact that MacDonald made no statement on the May Report and promptly left London on holiday, allow-

ing the crisis to linger on. In the meantime, fears that Britain was heading for financial collapse led foreign investors to withdraw gold, which only added to the problem. MacDonald was forced to cut short his holiday in Lossiemouth and return to London on August 11. A meeting of the Cabinet Economic Committee was held the next day. They agreed to the £30 million cut in salaries but refused to take the distasteful step of cutting the standard rate of unemployment benefit.

Since the measures to be taken would need some degree of support from the other parties, MacDonald met with the Opposition leaders, Samuel and Baldwin, who rejected the Cabinet proposals as inadequate. On the 21 August, the Cabinet met again and a final figure of £56 million of cuts was reluctantly agreed. MacDonald knew that this was as far as his colleagues were prepared to go. Unfortunately, the financial crisis had taken a turn for the worse. Later that day, the Deputy Governor of the Bank of England, Sir Ernest Harvey, informed MacDonald that a further run on the pound meant that immediate loans would have to be sought from the U.S Federal Reserve Bank. These would only be granted if MacDonald could guarantee further tough cuts in government expenditure.

Increasingly hemmed in by circumstances outside his control, MacDonald recalled the Cabinet the next morning. It now seemed that the fate of the government lay in the hands of the American bank. The Cabinet, without committing themselves, asked MacDonald to find out if a further £20 million cut in government spending (involving a 10% cut in the standard rate of unemployment benefit) would be sufficient to release the necessary loan from the Federal Reserve. It was. The next day, Sunday 23 August, the Cabinet met. MacDonald now had the unenviable task of trying to persuade his colleagues to commit themselves to carry out these cuts which , he said, were, "...the negation of everything that the Labour Party stood for." (P Adelman op cit p.73) He went on to say that these vile measures were in the national interest and would help to rescue the country from the brink of collapse.

Twenty Cabinet ministers were present. Eleven voted for the cuts, nine against. There was no way that the government could now carry on and MacDonald left the meeting to hand in the resignation of the government to the King. Earlier that day, MacDonald had had a secret meeting with the King to discuss the possibilities in the event of a Cabinet split. The King had then seen the two Opposition leaders. They agreed that if the government were to collapse, a National Government should be formed with MacDonald as Prime Minister. The next day, Monday 24 August, MacDonald saw the King again and reluctantly agreed to head a National Government.

An Assessment of the Labour Government
We have been looking at two issues in this section - how the Government tackled the unemployment problem and secondly, its role in the financial crisis of 1931. On unemployment, we might have expected a Labour government to have made efforts to get the jobless off the dole and to improve and extend unemployment benefits. On neither count did the Government perform well. Certainly, the huge rise in unemployment during the period 1929-31 cannot be blamed on the Goverment. There were deeper causes relating to the poor state of British industry and the worldwide economic depression sparked off by the Wall Street Crash. *However, by sticking rigidly to the laissez faire policy, the Government offered no hope to the unemployed.* Taylor estimates that, at best, the Government found work for about 60,000 men - a paltry effort given the enormity of the problem. On the positive side, the Government passed the Unemployment Insurance Act in 1930. Those claiming benefit no longer had to prove that they were 'genuinely seeking work' and the number of people who could claim benefits was extended. Any good done here, though, was more than wiped out by the last act of the Government in voting for cuts in unemployment benefit.

Should we be so harsh on the government? After all, it was external circumstances - the world economic depression coupled with the banking crisis - that led the Cabinet to make such an unpalatable decision. It seemed that in August 1931, the government was in the hands of the Bank of England, the City and the foreign banks. On the other hand, if MacDonald had been more decisive in setting out an economic policy, those institutions might have had more confidence in the government. This point was made by representatives of the Bank of England who said that, "the cause of the trouble was not financial but political, and lay in the complete want of confidence in HMG among foreigners." (AJP Taylor op cit p.365)

Skidelsky is more critical of the government. He argues that the August 1931 crisis was largely self-inflicted. Labour had had two years to carry out practical policies to remedy some of the economic problems facing the country, but it had failed because its "commitment to a nebulous Socialism made it regard the work of the 'economic radicals' such as Keynes as mere 'tinkering', when in fact it was they who were providing the real choice". (R Skidelsky *Politicians and the Slump* p.12)

The National Governments of the 1930s
We have seen that the second Labour Government's policies between 1929 and 1931 could hardly be defined as 'socialist' - they were virtually indistinguishable from those of their Tory and Liberal predecessors. Economic orthodoxy, in the form of the balanced budget, and strict economies were the order of the day. MacDonald's government was just as laissez faire as previous governments, but more out of dithering inaction than conviction. No significant government action was taken to help or protect industry or the growing ranks of the unemployed.

Would the National governments of the 1930s tilt the balance in favour of government intervention, faced as they were with such massive problems? On the face of it, this seemed unlikely, especially after 1934, when the 'National' Governments were Conservative in everything but name. We might have expected to see more of the same ie. orthodox economic policies. In fact, we begin to see a significant trend away from laissez faire towards limited state intervention in certain areas. By the beginning of the Second World War, the British economy was more 'managed' than it had ever been in peacetime. In this section, we will find out why.

Prime Ministers and Chancellors of the Exchequer : National Governments 1931-9	
Prime Ministers	**Chancellors of the Exchequer**
Ramsay MacDonald (Lab) August 31 - June 35	Philip Snowden (Lab) August 31 - November 32
Stanley Baldwin (Con) June 35 - May 37	Neville Chamberlain (Con) November 31 - May 37
Neville Chamberlain (Con) May 37 - May 40	Sir John Simon (Con) May 37 - October 40

Table 8.1

The First National Government
The new National Government contained members of each of the three parties, although the majority of Labour ministers and MPs refused to support it. The Government's most pressing task was to restore international confidence by a policy of strict economy and a balanced budget. When the bankers were convinced that this would materialise, the promised loan of £80 million was raised in Paris and New York and the run on the pound stopped (for a few days).

Composition of Government August 1931	
MacDonald (Lab)	- Prime Minister
Baldwin (Con)	- Lord President
Snowden (Lab)	- Chancellor
Samuel (Lib)	- Home Secretary
Isaacs (Lib)	- Foreign Secretary
Chamberlain (Con)	- Health

On 10 September 1931, Snowden produced his balanced budget. Some of the main provisions were:
- income tax raised from 4s 6d to 5s (25p) in the £
- salaries of civil servants, armed forces cut by 10%
- teachers' salaries cut by 15%
- unemployment benefit cut by 10%
- a 'means test' introduced (see next section)

Just how insecure Britain's financial position was, can be seen in the events of the week following the budget. On the 15 September, sailors of the Atlantic Fleet based at Invergordon refused to fall in for duty in protest at the 10% cut in pay. News of a 'mutiny' in the Royal Navy spread panic amongst foreign investors. There was an immediate rush to withdraw gold from London. By 19 September, government stocks were down to only £130 million. In order to stem the flood, the Government was forced to come off the Gold Standard. Economic pundits predicted dire consequences, but they failed to materialise. The pound quickly stabilised at about two thirds of its previous value, dropping from £4.86 to £3.40 to the dollar. Incredibly, then, the government which had been put into power to maintain the Gold Standard only a few days previously was forced off it by 12,000 sailors in what seems to have been "the politest possible form of mutiny". (Seaman - op cit p. 222)

"A few days before, a managed currency had seemed as wicked as family planning. Now, like contraception, it became a commonplace. This was the end of an age." (Taylor- op cit p.373)

The Government had, "... thus unwittingly stumbled upon an important remedy: the consequent devaluation of the pound assisted exports, and the mild bout of inflation fostered economic expansion." (A Marwick *The Explosion of British Society 1914-70* p74)

The General Election, October 1931

The 'National' Government had failed to bring about national unity. The Labour Party was now irretrievably split. MacDonald and those who went with him were expelled from the party and branded as traitors. Similarly in the Liberal Party divisions had emerged - Lloyd George refused to have anything to do with the Government or the Liberals in it.

MacDonald appealed to the country for a 'doctor's mandate' ie. to heal the ailing economy. The election campaign turned out to be very bitter and also very confusing for the voters, as each of the parties fighting under the 'National' banner brought out their own manifestos. Nevertheless, the public gave the National Government a huge vote of confidence. As the figures show, the real winners were the Tories and the clear losers were Labour, who in the space of a month had gone from governing party to a rump of 52 Opposition MPs.

General Election Result, 1931			
National Government		**Opposition**	
Conservative	471	Labour	52
National Liberals	68	Lloyd George Liberals	4
National Labour	13		

Table 8.2

"... MacDonald asked for ' a doctor's mandate' ... In those days, before the development of modern remedies, all a doctor could prescribe for most ailments was rest, while natural recovery took its course, and this was much what the National Government did in the end." (Taylor- op cit p. 403)

If the National Governments of the 1930s cannot lay claim to having led Britain out of the Depression, there are other areas where they began to take a more 'hands on' approach to economic matters. The move from laissez faire to state intervention was to follow a more definite pattern over the next decade.

Ramsay MacDonald gave up his position as Prime Minister in 1935 due to ill-health and failing eyesight. He was replaced by the Conservative leader, Stanley Baldwin. This change at the top was unlikely to alter the balance of power because Baldwin had been very much in control in the latter stages of MacDonald's premiership. Another key Labour figure, Snowden had retired as Chancellor of the Exchequer in 1932 and he was replaced by another Conservative, Neville Chamberlain. The Cabinet was now dominated by Conservatives.

"...the Conservative-controlled National Government was... from the autumn of 1932 onwards, in uninterrupted command of the nation's affairs until the spring of 1940. The 1935 election, although it increased Labour's strength in the Commons to 154 seats, did not materially alter the situation." (Seaman - op cit p. 232)

General Election Result 1935		
	National	Opposition
Conservative	387	
Liberal	33	21
Labour	8	154

Table 8.3

Abandonment of Free Trade

As the economic depression began to bite, countries throughout the world put up tariff barriers to protect their own products. Britain joined in, with the passing of the *Abnormal Importations Act* of 1931. This put 50% import duties on woollen and cotton goods, to run for 6 months.

However, the real break with the policy of free trade came with the appointment of Neville Chamberlain as Chancellor in 1932. Chamberlain was a confirmed protectionist, following in the footsteps of his father Joseph, who had campaigned unsuccessfully with his Tariff Reform League in 1903. Britain's adherence to the doctrine of Free Trade, established in the 1840s and 50s by Peel and Gladstone, was ended at a stroke with the passage of Chamberlain's *Import Duties Act* in February 1932.

Duties of between 10 and 20% were imposed on about half the goods imported into Britain, with the exception of food and raw materials. Goods coming in from the Empire were exempted pending the outcome of the Ottawa Imperial Conference.

The Ottawa Conference took place in July and August, 1932 and attempted to revive the idea of imperial preference (again a favourite idea of Joseph Chamberlain at the turn of the century). Under this, it was hoped to organise a self-contained economic unit consisting of Britain along with its Dominions and Colonies. Britain would guarantee to buy primary products from the Empire and in return the colonies would provide an unrestricted market for British manufactured goods. Such a system failed to materialise at Ottawa. This kind of paternalistic trading relationship might have been possible a century before, but was inappropriate in the 1930s. Canada, for example, was developing its own industries and wanted to protect them against British imports. Furthermore, it was inevitably developing a strong trading relationship with its powerful neighbour, America. Limited agreements were signed, but fell far short of imperial preference. Nevertheless, trade with the Empire did grow over the next decade.

The abandonment of free trade by Britain was probably an inevitable reaction to the protectionist measures imposed by the other major trading nations. Not to protect British markets would only have serve to increase further the ranks of the unemployed.

"Although the abandonment of the gold standard and the establishment of protection had come as a shock to some, these moves were largely an immediate response to what appeared to be the dictate of economic expediency. They did not point to a new adventurous radicalism in facing the crisis of the depression." (Wood- op cit p. 282)

"...the whole affair was topsy-turvy. Protection was carried by the Conservatives who claimed to believe in free enterprise. It was opposed by Labour, whose programme demanded a planned economy". (Taylor - op cit p.411)

Government Intervention in Agriculture and Industry
Throughout the 1930s, the National Governments began to introduce a series of measures which, though limited in scope and only partially successful, added up to a marked shift in policy away from laissez faire to interventionism.

Agriculture
Free trade hit British farmers badly during the 1880s with the influx of cheap grain from America and refrigerated dairy produce from New Zealand. The Tory-dominated government was determined to help its traditional constituency, the farmers, by passing the *Wheat Act* (1932) which guaranteed the price of the home product. This was followed by a variety of measures, including direct subsidies and help to market farm produce:

- *Agricultural Marketing Act* (1933) set up marketing boards to buy up, market and sell milk, potatoes and bacon.
- *Cattle Industry Act* (1934) provided subsidies for cattle.
- *Sugar Industry Act* (1936) provided subsidies for sugar.

Although these protectionist measures helped farmers to increase output during the 1930s, they failed to stem the number of labourers leaving the industry - about 100,000 every year in the thirties. The government's policy also cost the country dearly. By 1939, it was spending £100 million to grow home-produced food which could have been imported more cheaply.

During the 1920s, coalmining had been in a very weak position, suffering the effects of foreign competition and overmanning. Subsidies were ruled out as being against good business practice, market forces had to be given free rein. However, when farming faced similar problems, the old arguments were quietly forgotten.

Industry
Government intervention in industry was more limited than in agriculture but again it signalled a changed attitude. The government concentrated on the 'old' industries. These were to be 'rationalised' i.e. the smaller, inefficient units were to be shut down or amalgamated to produce factories better able to deal with foreign competition.

- British Iron and Steel Federation, the National Shipbuilders Security and the Lancashire Cotton Corporation rationalised their respective industries

- A £9.5 million loan was given to help the building of ships for the North Atlantic Fleet

- *The Special Areas Act* (1934) provided £2 million and two commissioners to help attract new industries to the depressed industrial areas such as Clydeside, South Wales, West Cumberland and Tyneside. Rate, rent and income tax relief was given to employers starting up factories in these districts. However, even in spite of the Government increasing its support to £5 million, its policy generally did not succeed. This lack of success was more marked in Scotland where over 20% of insured workers in the Scottish Special Areas were unemployed, which was twice as high as the figure for England as a whole.

The Economic Recovery
There is a general consensus among historians that the economic recovery from 1934 onwards took place largely in spite of, rather than because of, government policies.

"The government naturally took the credit for this recovery. Probably the claim was unjustified. World trade generally recovered somewhat in 1933 for no apparent reason." (Taylor- op cit p.417/8)

Unemployment Figures			
Year	Unemployed (Millions)	Year	Unemployed (Millions)
1929	1.2	1935	2.0
1930	1.9	1936	1.7
1931	2.7	1937	1.4
1932	2.8	1938	1.9
1933	2.5	1939	1.3
1934	2.1		

Table 8.4 (Source:P. King *Twentieth Century History Made Simple* p128)

"In general economic activity, Britain's position in the thirties does contrast very favourably with that of such other countries as the United States and France. For this, the National Government can take at least some credit, though in the main its policies were fortuitous, or just irrelevant. Fundamental to British recovery (was)...the general picking up of world trade." (Marwick- op cit p73)

"How much (the government policies) contributed to the prosperity of the economy is anyone's guess. If they did, it was by accident rather than by design." (R Blake *The Decline of Power 1915-1964* p.169)

Circumstances outwith the Government's control helped Britain back on the road to recovery. World prices of primary products (especially foodstuff) began to fall and this lowered industry's costs and generally lowered the cost of living. Those in work saw their standard of living increase as a result (see p.93-94). Feeling better off, people bought more and this helped stimulate particularly the new industries. The government added to consumer spending in a limited way by restoring unemployment benefit cuts in 1934 and lowering income tax from 5s. to 4s.6d in the £.

On the whole, though, the Government continued orthodox policies of thrift and economy. For example, in 1932 it lowered interest rates from 6% to 2% with the intention of reducing its own debt charges. It saved £80 million on its War Loan. However, the effect of low interest rates was the reverse of what the government wanted. Industry was encouraged to start new projects with cheap loans and cheap mortgages stimulated a private housing boom.

For AJP Taylor, "the building boom was the outstanding cause for the recovery of the thirties." *(English History* p.426) Rather than encouraging building though, the government's orthodox remedy was to economise. In 1932, Wheatley's Housing Act, which had provided £9 million in state subsidies for the building of council houses, was revoked. However, cheap private houses, combined with easy mortgage rates and greater general affluence, more than cancelled out the government's policy. During the 1930s, individuals built 3 million private houses. This benefited construction and some of the new industries. Houses were now installed with electricity (there were 9 million users by 1938) and this in turn stimulated the electrical appliances sector (cookers, radios, vacuum cleaners etc).

In conclusion, we can say that, in marked contrast to the Five Year Plans of the Soviet Union and America's New Deal, the National Governments in Britain continued to believe that there was nothing much that they could do to promote recovery. Orthodox policies of economy and restraint were the conventional wisdom of the day, although we begin to see certain laissez faire beliefs abandoned, in particular the Gold Standard and Free Trade. Government subsidy and regulation of agriculture and industry, albeit in limited form, paved the way for the more radical departures of the Labour Government between 1945 and 1951.

The 1930s saw the National Governments straddling the

old orthodoxies of laissez faire and the interventionist consensus of the post-1945 welfare state era. The pressure on governments to intervene in the social and economic affairs of the country started with the Depression in the thirties and became irresistible during the 5 years of total war.

AN ASSESSMENT OF THE NATIONAL GOVERNMENTS OF THE 1930s

For historians who have grown up in Welfare State Britain where comprehensive care 'from the cradle to the grave' is taken for granted, the record of the National Governments must fall short of the standards of the post-war era.

By ideological inclination, the National Governments were loathe to spend money on social and economic problems. In fact, during the depths of the Depression, we have seen that unemployment benefit was cut. The prevailing belief, stemming from the laissez faire doctrine, was that people should fend for themselves and that the government's role was to curb its spending and tax people as little as possible. The welfare of the citizens would then be conditional on the success of the economy as a whole, where wealth would trickle from the rich downwards, and their own efforts.

The British capitalist system had always contained stark contrasts between the rich and the poor. During the first part of the 1930s, that system deposited vast quantities of human beings into the ranks of the poor. Their experience was harsh and perhaps made bearable only by the knowledge that they were not suffering alone. However, those unaffected by the scourge of unemployment had the completely different experience of a steadily rising standard of living.

In this section, we will look at the success or otherwise of the government in dealing with the following four social and economic problems:

- Unemployment   • Health   • Housing
- The general standard of living

Unemployment

As we saw in the first section, there were international as well as domestic causes of unemployment in the 1930s. On the international side, economic historians had observed that for many years Britain had experienced *cyclical unemployment* in line with the upswings and downturns of world trade. What compounded the problem in the thirties was the extra dimension of *structural unemployment* ie. persistently high levels of unemployment in the 'old' or 'staple' industries. We can see this quite clearly in table 8.5. In boom or slump, the old industries had markedly higher rates of unemployment compared to the average.

The decline in the number of workers involved in these industries was also part of a larger and longer-term process of *technological change*. As the British economy became more advanced and scientifically based, so it shed unskilled manual workers and took on more white-collar, non-manual workers. This disruptive period, when people's skills became redundant, was particularly marked in the 1920s and 1930s (as it was in the 1980s).

Percentage unemployment in staple industries compared to the national average				
	1929	**1932**	**1936**	**1938**
Coal	18.2	41.2	25.0	22.0
Cotton	14.5	31.1	15.1	27.7
Shipbuilding	23.2	59.5	30.6	21.4
Iron and steel	19.9	48.5	29.5	24.8
Average for all industries	9.9	22.9	12.5	13.3

Table 8.5 (Source: J Stevenson *British Society 1914 -45* p. 270)

Government measures

As we have seen, the government was not inclined to take radical action against the evils of mass unemployment. Like large sections of the population, including the victims themselves, they felt that the slump was a natural phenomenon and all they could do was to 'sit it out' and wait for the recovery.

Apart from the *Special Areas Act* and the restoration of the 1931 benefit cuts, little was done for the unemployed. On the negative side was the *Anomalies Act* of 1931, which tightened the regulations on who was allowed to claim benefit. Under it, over 130,000 married women lost their right to benefit. Most hated of all measures though, was the *'Means Test'*. Those on unemployment benefit could claim it for only 26 weeks. After that, they were transferred on to 'transitional payments'. To get this, the claimant had to undergo a 'household means test'. An official would visit the home to investigate the income and circumstances of the person as well as other money coming into the household, savings and other available assets - all this with a view to saving the government as much as possible in payouts. These officials did their job well, saving £24 million in 1931-2.

"The Means Test was specifically feared and hated by every unemployed worker. The regulations insisted that any member of a household who was working was responsible for the household - that it, he or she had to support the rest of the family. If any one in a house was working - including uncles, aunts, cousins and even lodgers sometimes - then unemployment benefit wasn't paid to the other people in that house.

It broke up families. Sons and daughters went to live away from home; fathers in work became bitter towards their children. Cases were reported in the newspapers where worry over the Means Test had actually led to suicide. It produced despair - and also the most massive demonstrations by the unemployed all over the country."

(Harry McShane *No Mean Fighter* p. 184 Pub. Pluto Press)

"One little collier boy fifteen years of age went home to his parents the other day and proudly announced that he had an increase of 3 shillings a week. The following week, the Board reduced the allowance of his unemployed father."

(Aneurin Bevin, Labour MP, writing in the *Daily Express* 23 April, 1937 quoted in J Patrick and M Packham *Years of Change* p. 253)

"The most cruel and evil effect of the Means Test is the way in which it breaks up families. Old people, sometimes bedridden, are driven out of their homes by it. An old age pensioner, for instance, if a widower, would normally live with one or other of his children; his weekly ten shillings goes towards the household expenses, and probably he is not badly cared for. Under the Means Test, however, he counts as a 'lodger' and if he stays at home his children's dole will be docked. So, perhaps at seventy or seventy-five years of age, he has to turn out into lodgings, handing his pension over to the lodging-house keeper and existing on the verge of starvation. I have seen several cases of this myself. It is happening all over England at this moment, thanks to the Means Test."

(George Orwell *The Road to Wigan Pier* p. 70-1 Pub. Penguin)

James Maxton, ILP leader and Labour MP for Glasgow Bridgeton, led a well orchestrated campaign against the Means Test as can be witnessed in his 1931 election campaign leaflet (see above). He clearly showed how various households in Glasgow would be seriously affected thus causing further financial hardship for the poor.

In December 1932 Maxton continued his attack on the Means Test in a debate on BBC Radio With the Conservative MP, Harold MacMillan. The latter defended means testing on the grounds that the payments were not tied to insurance contributions and in the present economic conditions there were limits to what the state could afford. Maxton could not accept the Tory argument. "He could understand a state which said, 'our total resources are very limited : it is impossible to allow anyone to have a very high income.' But he could not understand the state which said, 'our resources are limited : we must drive down the income of the whole working class to one dead level of poverty while other classes are left in affluence." (From *New Leader* 23 December 1932 quoted in *Maxton* by G Brown p. 251 Mainstream Publishing)

Regional Variations in Unemployment

At the height of the Industrial Revolution, the 'boom areas' of low unemployment were the north and west of England and southern Scotland, based on the location of the coalfields. During the 1930s, we began to see a reversal of the geography of affluence. The new industries, fuelled by electricity were located in the south and east where the markets were and the old industrial areas went into almost permanent decline.

In the worst affected regions, there were also marked

Percentage unemployed in regions of Britain			
	1929	1932	1937
London & SE England	5.6	13.7	6.4
SW England	8.1	17.1	7.8
Midland	9.3	20.1	7.2
Northern England	13.5	27.1	13.8
Wales	19.3	36.5	22.3
Scotland	12.1	27.7	15.9
Northern Ireland	15.1	27.2	23.6

Table 8.6 (Source: J Stevenson - ibid p.271)

localised variations in fortunes. Hardest hit was Jarrow with 67% of the workforce 'idle' following the closure of Palmer's shipyard. 'Jarrow' has since come to symbolise the darkest days of the Depression through the evocative images of the hunger march to London and the desperate plight of the people highlighted in Ellen Wilkinson's book *The Town that was Murdered*:

"Charles Mark Palmer started Jarrow as a shipbuilding centre without considering the needs of his workers. They crowded into a small colliery village which was hurriedly extended to receive them. They packed into insanitary houses. They lived without any social amenities. They paid with their lives for the absence of any preparation for the growth of such a town. And in 1933 another group of capitalists decided the fate of Jarrow without reference to the workers. A society in which the decisive decisions are invariably taken by one group, and in which those decisions are reached only by considerations of their own welfare, is not a just society."

(E Wilkinson *The Town that was Murdered* p. 171)

Towns dependent on single industries like Jarrow were worst hit eg. Merthyr relied on the coalfield and had 62% out of work in 1934. Manchester, on the other hand, had a variety of different industries and consequently fared much better. Halifax was doing very well with its machine-tool industries in contrast to the depressed woollen mill towns in the vicinity.

Life on the Dole

Writers like George Orwell, JB Priestley and Walter Greenwood described the degradation and misery of life on the dole:

"When I first saw unemployed men at close quarters, the thing that horrified and amazed me was to find that many of them were ashamed of being unemployed...The middle classes were still talking about 'lazy idle loafers on the dole' and saying that 'these men could all find work if they wanted to', and naturally these opinions percolated to the working class themselves. I remember the shock of astonishment it gave me, when I first mingled with tramps and beggars, to find that a fair proportion, perhaps a quarter, of these beings whom I had been taught to regard as cynical parasites, were decent young miners and cotton-workers gazing at their destiny with the same sort of dumb amazement as an animal in a trap. They simply could not understand what was happening to them. They had been brought up to

work, and behold! it seemed as if they were never going to have the chance of working again. In their circumstances it was inevitable, at first, that they should be haunted by a feeling of personal degradation. That was the attitude towards unemployment in those days: it was a disaster which happened to you as an individual and for which you were to blame."(George Orwell *The Road to Wigan Pier* p. 76-7 Pub. Penguin)

"There is no escape anywhere in Jarrow from its prevailing misery, for it is entirely a working-class town. One little street may be more wretched than another, but to the outsider they all look alike. One out of every two shops appeared to be permanently closed. Wherever we went there were men hanging about, not scores of them but hundreds and thousands of them. The whole town looked as if it had entered a perpetual penniless bleak Sabbath. The men wore the drawn masks of prisoners of war. A stranger from a distant civilisation, observing the condition of the place and its people, would have arrived at once at the conclusion that Jarrow had deeply offended some celestial emperor of the island and was now being punished. He would never believe us if we told him that in theory this town was as good as any other and that its inhabitants were not criminals but citizens with votes." (JB Priestley *English Journey* p 238)

"He was standing there as motionless as a statue, cap neb pulled over his eyes, gaze fixed on pavement, hands in pockets, shoulders hunched, the bitter wind blowing his thin trousers tightly against his legs. Waste paper and dust blew about him in spirals, the papers making harsh sounds as they slid on the pavements." (Walter Greenwood *Love on the Dole* p255 Pub. Penguin)

General Standards of Living

We can judge whether the standard of living was rising by looking at two areas of evidence.

- The 'real' incomes of people ie. what they could buy with their income compared to previous years.
- Evidence of increased spending on goods, services and increased saving and investment.

Table 8.7 provides fairly clear evidence that living standards for most people were rising during the 1930s.

Wages, prices and real earnings, 1930-38 (1930=100)			
	Weekly wage rates	Retail prices	Average annual real wage earnings
1930	100.0	100.0	100.0
1931	98.9	93.4	105.1
1932	97.9	91.1	105.7
1933	95.7	88.6	107.6
1934	95.7	89.2	108.1
1935	96.8	90.5	108.3
1936	98.9	93.0	107.7
1937	103.2	97.5	105.4
1938	106.4	98.7	107.7

Table 8.7 (Adapted from DH Aldcroft *The Inter-War Economy: Britain, 1919-1939* p 352 & 364)

93

Further evidence of rising living standards is given in the statistics below:

1 Working-class families on average spent 76% of their income on food, rent and rates in 1914; in 1938, they were only spending 44% of their income on these items.
2 One thousand million tickets to the cinema were sold in Britain in 1938.
3 Savings in building societies rose from £82 million in 1920 to £717 million in 1938.
4 Between 1935 and 1939, on average 350,000 houses were being built every year.
5 In 1931, 1.5 million cars were bought in Britain; in 1939, 2 million were bought.
6 Spending on food went up from £835 million in 1920 to £1177 million in 1939. Consumption of fruit went up by 88%, vegetables by 64%, butter and margarine by 50% and eggs by 40%.
7 The sale of vacuum cleaners doubled from 200,000 in 1930 to 400,000 in 1938.
8 Twenty million British people were taking a holiday by the sea by the late 1930s.

However, for many, poverty continued to be a problem throughout the thirties. Those unaffected by it were shocked because it existed alongside their growing affluence and also because, social investigators were revealing to the general public the true extent and depth of the problem. A study on London in 1934 found that 10% of the population were in poverty. Even in booming Bristol, Herbert Tout concluded that 19% had "insufficient income" and 10% were in poverty.

In 1936, Rowntree decided to survey the extent of poverty in York for a second time. His team of investigators used the same definition of the 'poverty line' as was used in his 1899 survey of the town. The results showed that there had been a considerable improvement in the people's standard of living during these 37 years. (See Table 8.8)

	1899	1936
Numbers in Poverty	7,230	3,767
Total population in poverty(%)	9.9	3.9

Table 8.8 (Source: RJ Cootes *The Making of the Welfare State* p. 68)

However, there were still some black spots. For example, Rowntree found that half of the working-class children were living in poverty. There were also some tragic cases of individual hardship:

"One family of five, all out of work, was found to be living on bread and margarine alone for more than half of each week. This was in spite of unemployment assistance and a widow's pension....An old lady of seventy-two, living alone, had no bed and had to sleep on an old sofa. After paying her rent and buying a bag of coal, she had 3s 3d a week for all her other needs." (RJ Cootes - ibid p.68)

Clearly, a safety net of welfare provisions to prevent the poor from falling below minimum standards of living still

had to be created. For too many of the unemployed, the elderly and the young, the thirties were the hungry decade.

Health

Evidence of improving health is given in the statistics below:

1 Life expectancy for those born between 1901 and 1912 was 51.5 (men) and 55.4 (women). Those born in 1930-2 could expect to live to 58.7 (men) and 62.9 (women).
2 In 1911, there were 6.2 doctors for every 10,000 of population; in 1941 there were 7.5.
3 Infant mortality rates went down from 67 per 1,000 live births in 1930 to 61 in 1940.
4 Tuberculosis (TB) killed 51,000 in 1910; 27,000 in 1940.
5 Two-thirds of prospective soldiers were declared unfit for service in the First World War; only one - third were rejected during the Second World War.
6 Deaths from measles went down from 389 per million of population in 1921-30 to 217 per million in 1931-9.

The government did play a limited role in helping the statistics along. A slum clearance programme was carried out in the interwar years which undoubtedly took people out of an insanitary and overcrowded environment. One and a half million families were cleared from the slums between 1919 and 1939. The *Public Health Act* (1936) continued and extended the previous work done by local authorities in improving the water supply and sewage systems. By 1935, 80% of the population of England and Wales was supplied with water by their local councils. The *National Health Insurance Scheme* (1911) had by 1936 been extended to 19 million wage earners who had free access to doctors and medical treatment. School milk, either free or subsidised, was being given to 3 million children by 1937. Four percent of children were now getting free school meals.

Much needed to be done though. The persistence of unemployment and poverty hindered overall progress in the health field. The following incident was witnessed by Frank Cousins. He encountered a young couple with child who were walking from South Shields to London to find work:

"They came into the cafe and sat down, and they fetched a baby's feeding bottle out, and it had water in it. They fed the baby with water, and then lifted the kiddy's dress up - it was a small baby - and it had a newspaper nappy on. They took this off, and wiped the baby's bottom with it and then they picked up another newspaper and put that on for a fresh nappy."
(From *The Listener*, 26 October, 1961 quoted in John Stevenson and Chris Cook *The Slump -Society and Politics during the Depression* p.6)

The middle class lived significantly longer than the working class. Poor areas had higher death rates than average. Merthyr, for example, had a 52% higher death rate than the average for the region; Jarrow was 30% higher. The infant death rate for England and Wales was 58 per 1,000 live births; poorer Scotland had a rate of 80 per 1,000; Glasgow had 104 infant deaths per 1,000.

Poverty then was a key factor affecting the health of the nation. If you were unfortunate enough to be working class or unemployed and living in the poorer north of the country, you were likely to have a below average health record and inadequate access to health care. Britain still lacked both a national health service and comprehensive free medical treatment.

Housing

Private housing : As we have seen, the 1930s saw an unprecedented house-building boom which contributed significantly to Britain's economic recovery. The bulk of building was in the private sector. Three million houses were built in the thirties, of which more than two-thirds were private. Owner occupation grew from 10% to 31% of the population between the wars. Despite the fact that the private semi-detached houses and bungalows on sale were relatively cheap with low mortgage rates on offer, it was only the middle class and the very top end of the working class who could afford to buy them.

Council Housing : After 1935, local authorities began to pick up on council house building, following the lifting of government cut-backs imposed during the worst years of the depression. Between 1931 and 1939, 700,000 council houses were built. By 1939, 14% of the population rented council houses compared to 1% in 1919. Building standards in the new council housing estates weregood and vastly better than the inner city dwellings many people had been used to. Houses were built with electricity installed, a piped-in water supply, giving hot and cold running water, inside toilets and gardens. Unfortunately, only the better-off skilled and semi-skilled manual workers and their families could afford to pay the rents charged by the local authorities. Many councils were unable to subsidise rents sufficiently to meet the needs of the poorest and ill-housed members of their community.

Housing the poor : The poor lived in private rented accommodation which was frequently damp, ill-ventilated, lacking in basic amenities and overcrowded. Here, George Orwell describes some of the housing conditions he found in Barnsley:

"1. House in Wortley Street. Two up, one down. Living-room 12ft by 10ft. Sink and copper in living-room, coal-hole under stairs. Sink worn almost flat and constantly overflowing. Walls not too sound. Penny in slot gas-light. House very dark and gas-light estimated 4d. a day. Upstairs rooms are really one large room partitioned into two. Walls very bad - walls of back room cracked right through. Window -frames coming to pieces and have to be stuffed with wood. Rain comes through in several places. Sewer runs under house and stinks in summer but Corporation 'says they can't do nowt'. Six people in house, two adults and four children, the eldest aged fifteen. Youngest but one attending hospital - tuberculosis suspected. House infested by bugs. Rent 5s. 3d., including rates.

2. House in Peel Street. Back to back, two up, two down and large cellar. Living-room 10 ft square with copper and sink. The other downstairs room the same size, probably intended as parlour but used as bedroom. Upstairs rooms the same size as those below. Living-room very dark. Gaslight estimated at 41/2d. a day. Distance to lavatory 70 yards. Four beds in house for eight people - two old parents, two adult girls ...one young man, and three children. Parents have one bed, eldest son another, and remaining five people share the other two. Bugs very bad - 'You can't keep 'em down when it's 'ot.' Indescribable squalor in downstairs room and smell upstairs almost unbearable. Rent 5s. 7¹/₂d., including rates." (George Orwell *The Road to Wigan Pier* p48 Pub. Penguin)

The government did take steps to deal with these problems. By 1939, 350,000 slum houses had been cleared, but the local authorities estimated that 600,000 slums were still standing. The problem was concentrated in the old industrial areas, with Scotland again breaking all records with ease. A survey of Scottish housing in 1936 found that 22% of the stock was overcrowded (defined as more than two people per room). Glasgow had 200,000 families living more than three people to a room.

Clearly, problems such as these would not be solved by market forces. The government believed that houses vacated by the lower middle class who were buying new houses, would be taken up by people further down the economic ladder. It did not happen because the poor could not afford the increased rent. Despite the record number of houses being built, demand still outstripped supply by 800,000 houses. The need was for cheap, affordable rented accommodation and it was not being supplied in sufficient quantities by the government and local authorities.

"Whatever the shortcomings of the new developments, there had been greater progress by the end of the thirties in providing an adequate solution to the housing conditions of the working class than in any previous decade." (J Stevenson - ibid p.223)

There is no doubt that the working class were better housed relative to previous decades. There is also no doubt that the government could have done a lot more to help those in the areas of multiple deprivation. Whether they should have done so is a matter of debate.

9 The Arrival of the Welfare State 1940-51

In the last three chapters, we have seen that the state began to take on more responsibility for the welfare of the people from the 1870s onwards. Now we will argue that the welfare state which was fully in place by 1951 was not the exclusive creation of the 1945 Labour Government. Its arrival has to be seen in the broader context of the total experience of the Second World War. Part of that experience involved Labour politicians pushing forward progressive ideas and plans. However, there was also a broad consensus among all three parties about what post war Britain should be like.

The war itself created a powerful unity of purpose in the country. Wartime leaders began to realise that, in a lengthy war, the British people needed an ideal to fight for as well as an ideology to fight against. If warfare was the weapon to conquer the evil of Hitler, welfare could provide the healing medicine to treat the backlog of ills persisting from the 1930s. The wartime Coalition Government mobilised the nation's resources and intervened in so many facets of people's lives that it would have been difficult for any post war government to have disengaged rapidly from such commitments. The Labour Government of 1945-50 completed the modern welfare state structure with a flurry of legislation carried out with great enthusiasm, but there is little doubt that had the Conservatives won the election, a very similar social services system would have been put in place.

The Impact of War

Evacuation

There had been a growing awareness of poverty as far back as the social investigations of Booth and Rowntree in the last decade of the 19th century. These were followed up, in the interwar period, with studies by Tout and the Bristol Trust. However, there is a difference between knowing the facts and seeing pathetic examples of urban poverty with your own eyes. It was the latter experience which stirred the conscience of many middle class families. When war broke out in September 1939, the government put its evacuation plan into operation. About 1.5 million people, mostly children, were moved from the major cities into the countryside. These were mainly from poor inner-city families who could not afford to move privately. The depth and extent of poverty which lingered on in Britain was revealed. About 20% of the children evacuated from Liverpool had lice. Many were clothed in little more than rags, were filthy and had very primitive sanitary habits.

> "Evacuation was part of the process by which British society came to know itself, as the unkempt, ill-clothed, undernourished and often incontinent children of bombed cities acted as messengers carrying the evidence of the deprivation of urban working-class life into rural homes." (D Fraser *Evolution of the British Welfare State* 4th ed. p.210 Macmillan)

> "...country people, and to a certain extent even the wealthy, learnt for the first time how the city poor lived. English people became more mixed up than before ... The Luftwaffe was a powerful missionary for the welfare state."
> (AJP Taylor *English History 1914-45* p556)

Neville Chamberlain, the Prime Minister at the start of the war and who had been Minister of Health between 1924-29, was shocked by what he experienced and admitted in a private letter that:

> "I never knew that such conditions existed, and I feel ashamed of having been so ignorant of my neighbours. For the rest of my life, I mean to try to make amends by helping such people to live cleaner and healthier lives." (quoted in Paul Addison *The Road to 1945* p72 Pub. Johnathan Cape)

Equality of Sacrifice

The long term effects of laissez-faire ideology and capitalism were to produce great inequalities in society and a reluctance by the ruling class to interfere with the mechanics of the market system. However, the war required great sacrifices from rich and poor alike and these common experiences brought about a change in the social attitudes of the country's elite. It produced a more egalitarian consensus which enabled people on both the left and the right of the political spectrum to come to similar conclusions about the need for a more caring and involved state apparatus.

Both the rich and the poor suffered during the blitz. Hitler's bombers were no respecters of class distinction. Four million houses were damaged or destroyed and over 61,000 civilians lost their lives. Even some of the better-off, who had hitherto extolled the virtues of hard work and self-help, were forced to rely on the benevolence of the state after their properties had been reduced to rubble. Rationing too had a levelling effect on society and there was popular support for it because it ensured fair shares for all. Everyone was reduced to the same basic level. Even the royal family entered into the spirit of sacrifice by eating spam.

War Socialism

The free flow of supply and demand was no longer adequate in wartime conditions. The government had to abandon laissez faire and intervene to control the distribution and price of food and clothing. More generally, the economy had to be managed and planned from the centre. A form of war socialism developed out of necessity. Production was coordinated; women were directed once more into the factories and farms; full employment was maintained. A whole new government bureaucracy had to be established to bring these changes about. Ministries of Supply, Home Security, Economic Welfare, Information, Food, Shipping and Aircraft Production were added to the existing administrative machinery. This indeed was a total war effort and out of it grew a popular belief that if the burdens were to fall equally on all, then peacetime Britain in turn ought to distribute resources more equally to all.

Changing Attitudes to Social Security

In one sense, there is an in-built conflict between capitalism and the welfare state since the former tends to distribute resources in the form of *rewards* whereas the latter distributes resources according to *need*. However, as we have seen, the workings of pure capitalism had to be modified during the war. At the same time, the needs of the whole nation had to be taken into account if the war was going to be fought efficiently. A healthy, well-fed workforce had to be supported. This meant that access to the nation's resources had to be open to all, not just to those who could afford to pay for them. During the war, the beginnings of a modern social welfare system were set up by popular demand.

> "In hotels, camps, factory canteens, hostels, railway trains, bars, restaurants, I listened and talked and argued. Topic Number One was probably the state of the war at the particular time; but Topic Number Two, running Number One very close, was always the New World after the war. What could we do to bring our economic and social system nearer to justice and security and decency? That was the great question..."
> (JB Priestly quoted in Addison *The Road to 1945* p 162)

> " The overall impact of the war was to increase the dependence of many even among the better-off on state services, and once this occurred, the remnants of the poor law and workhouse traditions that still underlay some of these services could not long survive." (CJ Bartlett *A History of Postwar Britain 1945-74* p6)

> "From assistance only to those most in need through poverty, the responsibility of the community had been extended, without discrimination, to all who needed its help; from marginal provision to the destitute and helpless, it had developed into a pooling of national resources to see all its members through any of the ills that social care could relieve."
> (M Bruce *The Coming of the Welfare State* p293 Pub. Batsford Books)

GOVERNMENT ACTION 1940 - 1942
Churchill's Coalition Government took over in May 1940 during Britain's 'darkest hour'. The country was now fighting alone against Hitler. Several historians see this period as a turning point in the advance towards a welfare state.

> "The resolution and uplifting of hearts that came with Dunkirk and all that it stood for brought also a mood of unity in sacrifice that was to colour the whole nation's attitude to social problems and ensure that things would never again be as they had been."
> (Bruce ibid p295)

> "Dunkirk, and all that the name evokes, was an important event in the wartime history of the social services. It summoned forth a note of self-criticism, of national self-criticism, of national introspection, and it set in motion ideas and talk of principles and plans". (Titmuss *Essays on the Welfare State* ch.2 quoted in D Marsh *The Welfare State* 2nd ed. p22)

Adding substance to this 'Dunkirk spirit' was the presence of the key Labour leaders in the Government - Attlee, Bevin, Cripps, Morrison, Greenwood, Dalton and Alexander. They were very prominent in the development of

social and economic policy on the Home Front. Several initiatives soon arose.

National Milk Scheme: This was set up the week after the evacuation at Dunkirk. The scheme granted nursing and expectant mothers half-price milk for all under-fives. By 1944, 95% of those eligible were participating in the scheme. 30% of mothers got free milk as their income was below £2 per week. The scheme was extended in 1941 to include the provision of vitamins, cod-liver oil and orange-juice.

Provision of school milk and meals: Before the war, school meals were provided for the poor, but the system was tainted with the stigma of the old Poor Law and charity. Now, the Cabinet was determined to supply a service for all:

> "There is a danger of deficiencies occurring in the quality and quantity of children's diets...there is no question of capacity to pay: we may find the children of well-to-do parents and the children of the poor suffering alike from an inability to get the food they need" (quoted in D Fraser ibid p211)

Thanks to government subsidies, the number of children taking school meals rose from 130,000 daily in 1940 to 1,650,000 in 1945 and school milk uptake increased from 19% to 46% during the war.

Immunisation: This was provided free from 1941 onwards and an intensive publicity campaign was launched by the government. Child deaths from diphtheria dropped from 3,000 before the war to 818 in 1945.

State Nurseries: These were set up during the war to enable mothers to return to war work.

Old Age and Widows' Pension Act, 1940 : This provided supplementary pensions for three-quarter million old people in need.

Determination of Needs Act, 1941: Under the old and hated household means test, husbands, parents, grandparents and children were legally bound to support those in need. Now, the dislocation of the war rendered this measure unworkable. The new Act provided a narrower, more humane form of means test.

The cumulative effect of these measures was to move the emphasis of the social security system away from *selective* benefits based on the old poor law towards *universal* benefits based on need. The foundations of the modern welfare state were being laid.

The Beveridge Report, 1942
More than any other person, William Beveridge's name is associated with the establishment of the blueprint for the postwar welfare state. Beveridge's *Report on Social Insurance and Allied Services* was published in December 1942. It created a great deal of public interest at the time and conditioned many to expect that the recommendations would be carried out if not immediately, then directly after the war. Incredibly, this rather dry report broke all records for sales of government publications, selling 635,000 copies.

The main principles behind the Beveridge Report were that the social security system would be:

- *comprehensive*   It would meet all the social problems faced by people from the cradle to the grave.

- *universal*   It would be open to everyone by right regardless of means.

- *insurance-based*   People would contribute weekly payments to finance future benefits

- *compulsory*   All people in work would have to be in the scheme.

- *integrated*   It would bring together all the individual schemes, to be covered by one payment.

- *involve flat-rate contributions*   Everyone would pay the same, regardless of income.

- *provide subsistence benefits*   Would provide the minimum benefit necessary for food, clothing and shelter.

- *would end means testing*   Benefits stopped or reduced depending on a person's financial means.

In essence, Beveridge advocated that all people in work would pay a single weekly flat-rate contribution into the state insurance fund. This would cover all possible contingencies that might befall people throughout their lives. In return for their contributions, a new Ministry of Social Security would provide people with subsistence in the form of sickness, medical, maternity, old age, unemployment, widows, orphans, industrial injury and funeral benefits.

Beveridge talked about the need to tackle 5 giant problems - *Want, Disease, Idleness, Ignorance and Squalor*. His Report only dealt with Want. The other problems still had to be conquered:
- *Disease* by the establishment of a new health service;
- *Idleness* by the state aiming for full employment;
- *Ignorance* by reform of the educational system;
- *Squalor* by a new house-building and slum-clearance programme.

Beveridge also took for granted that the government would introduce family allowances.

In a sense, it is understandable that Churchill should have been cool towards the Beveridge Report and the interest it had generated in the country. He was preoccupied with winning the war, whose outcome was by no means certain in late 1942. However, there is little doubt that Churchill misunderstood the public feeling and his handling of the issue was inept. In December 1942, a pamphlet explaining the Beveridge Report was issued to army units for discussion in 'current affairs hour', but soon after, orders were put out to return the pamphlets. The strong impression given was that the government was embarrassed by the Beveridge Plan and wished to shelve it. At home, six by-elections took place in February 1943 - a 'mini general election'. Despite a wartime truce between the major parties, the Conservative vote against Independent candidates went down in 4 of the seats, sending a clear signal to the government. Churchill then attempted to allay public fears by speaking to the nation on the radio in March. Again he blundered. On the one hand, he did commit a post-war Conservative Government to "national compulsory insurance for all classes for all purposes from the cradle to the grave" (P Addison *Road to 1945* p227), but nowhere did he mention Beveridge, nor did he convey great enthusiasm for the measures. The moment was lost. Churchill had passed up the opportunity to champion a universally popular idea. The public quickly perceived that Labour was more likely to put Beveridge's vision into practice. After Labour's House of Commons amendment for the immediate implementation of the Beveridge Report had been defeated in February, James Griffiths accurately predicted that "this makes the return of the Labour Party to power at the next election an absolute certainty". (Pauline Gregg *The Welfare State* p25)

Government Responses 1944-45

Beveridge, like the general public, believed that the government would quietly drop his proposals. However,

---

Views on the Beveridge Report

The author: "The scheme here is in some ways a revolution but in more ways it is a natural development from the past." (Beveridge)

The historians: "A country whose history had been so much concerned with freedom, the freedom to speak, to write, to vote, was now being given a new lesson in liberty, that true freedom lay in freedom from want, from disease, from ignorance, from squalor and from idleness. Here, in the totality of the vision, was the revolutionary element of the Beveridge Report."
(D.Fraser ibid p216)

"All this amounted to no revolutionary proposal. The Beveridge Plan...rounded off and carried to their logical conclusion all the established services, but made no extravagant demands on the State. In fact, it deplored the already accepted government responsibility for the long-term unemployed.." (Bruce *The Coming of the Welfare State* p.307)

The politicians: "A dangerous optimism is growing up about the conditions it will be possible to establish here after the war...The question steals across the mind whether we are not committing our forty-five million people to tasks beyond their compass...Ministers should, in my view, be careful not to raise false hopes, as was done last time by speeches about 'homes fit for heroes' etc."
(Winston Churchill - Conservative Prime Minister - Cabinet notes from 12 Jan 1934 from Churchill *The Second World War* p 861-2)

" Believe me, it is by acceptance or rejection of the plan that we shall be judged by this nation...It is because we are convinced that the nation wants this plan and that the nation ought to get it, and that we can afford it, that we have put down this Amendment." (James Griffiths [Labour] - speech in the House of Commons on 18 February 1943 proposing the immediate implementation of the Beveridge Report - amendment defeated - quoted in RC Birch *The Shaping of the Welfare State* p113)

Churchill came to the conclusion in late 1943 that detailed plans would have to be drawn up for peacetime Britain. Under the direction of Lord Woolton, the Minister for Reconstruction, three White Papers on Health, Employment and Social Insurance were drafted and an Education Act was passed in 1944 - all clearly influenced by the Beveridge Report.

The White Paper Chase 1943/4

Educational Reconstruction (July 1943) provided the basis for the Education Act in 1944.

A National Health Service (February 1944) proposed a comprehensive system of health provision which would be 'free' ie. financed out of taxation and available to all who wanted to use it. Discussions on the White Paper had to be suspended because of the war and were taken up by the new Labour Government.

Employment Policy (May 1944) committed the government to the maintenance of a "high and stable level of employment" after the war. For the first time, the state was admitting that it had a responsibility to intervene in order to avoid the sort of mass unemployment experienced after the First World War. If depression appeared to be approaching, the government would use public expenditure to stimulate the economy - in other words, use classic Keynesian methods.

Social Insurance (September 1944) was based largely on the Beveridge Report and proposed a comprehensive insurance scheme. Unlike Beveridge, however, benefits would not be based on the subsistence principle. The White Paper, with a few modifications, became the National Insurance Act of 1946.

During the war then, the Beveridge Report and the various White Papers laid down the principles and much of the legislative detail out of which emerged the post-war welfare state. Before the end of the war, two pieces of social legislation were enacted - *the Education Act and the Family Allowances Act.*

Education Act 1944

This was the major legislative achievement of the wartime Coalition Government in the area of social welfare. The Bill was skilfully steered through Parliament by the progressive Conservative RA Butler, then President of the Board of Education. The Butler Act, as it became known, set out the following provisions for England and Wales:

1 School leaving age to be raised to 15 by 1947 and 16 as soon as was practicable.

2 The school system to have 3 stages - nursery schools (attendance voluntary), primary schools (5-11 year olds) and secondary schools (11 years and over).

3 Attendance at primary and secondary school to be compulsory (until the Butler Act, parents had only been required to ensure their children's attendance for "efficient elementary instruction in reading, writing and arithmetic") .

4 Although not in the Act, it was recommended that secondary schools be divided into grammar, secondary modern and secondary technical schools, based on pupils' abilities and aptitudes. These would be tested at the end of primary school by an 'eleven-plus' exam.

5 Provision of school meals and milk to be compulsory.

6 A school medical service to be developed.

A parallel Education (Scotland) Act was passed in 1946. After the 'eleven-plus', pupils would go either to a senior secondary for an academic education or a junior secondary for a practical/technical education. Although the Act stated that there was supposed to be 'parity of esteem' between the different types of school, it was clear that a first-rate and a second-rate structure were being put in place, very much reflecting the persistence of social class divisions in society as a whole.

Family Allowances Act (1945)

During the time between the break-up of the Coalition Government and the election of the Labour Government, Churchill presided over a 'caretaker' government which brought in family allowances. It provided five shillings (25p) a week for each child after the first. Although Beveridge had included family allowances in his Report as one of the 3 'assumptions', the origins of the idea lay in a memorandum by an all-party group of MPs to the Chancellor of the Exchequer in 1941. It called for family allowances "to prevent the spread of discontent between the richer and poorer classes" (Pat Thane *The Foundations of the Welfare State* p241) Employers in particular wanted to keep wage claims down after the war and saw family allowances as a way of doing this. The memorandum. also advocated family allowances "to prevent a fall in the birth rate" (Thane ibid) A decline in the birth rate had been predicted by demographers in the 1930s. However, the amount of the allowance was very small, even by 1945 standards, and as such was likely only to have a marginal impact on family finances.

The motives of the MPs could hardly be described as high-minded and certainly had very little to do with the welfare of the poorest families. There was one enlightened aspect of the scheme though. Allowances were to be the legal entitlement of the wife, not the husband. This provision was added as a result of a campaign by the feminist MP Eleanor Rathbone who argued that if the male breadwinner squandered the weekly wage on beer, cigarettes and gambling, the wife would at least have control over the family allowance.

THE 1945 GENERAL ELECTION

Five years of coexistence and cooperation in the wartime government produced a remarkable degree of convergence between the two major parties on social welfare issues, as can be seen by comparing their respective manifestos.

Although there was nothing to choose between the parties on social policy, we have already noted that the public saw Labour as being more committed to the creation of a welfare state immediately after the war. This impression was confirmed by Labour's election campaign which concentrated on postwar domestic issues. Its manifesto,

Conservative Manifesto 1945

National Insurance
One of our most important tasks will be to pass into law and bring into action as soon as we can a nationwide and compulsory scheme of National Insurance based on the plan announced by the Government of all Parties in 1944.

Health
The health service of the country will be made available to all citizens...We propose to create a comprehensive health service covering the whole range of medical treatment from the general practitioner to the specialist...

Education
The Education Act set forth in the 'Four Years' Plan' has already been piloted through Parliament by Mr Butler. Our task in the coming years will be to remodel our educational system to the new law...

Labour Manifesto 1945

Social Insurance Against the Rainy Day
The Labour Party has played a leading part in the long campaign for proper social security for all...A Labour Government will press on rapidly with legislation extending social insurance over the necessary wide field to all.

Health of the Nation and its Children
Money must no longer be the passport to the best treatment.
In the new National Health Service there shall be health centres where the people may get the best that modern science can offer, more and better hospitals...

Education and Recreation
An important step forward has been taken by the passing of the recent Education Act. Labour will put that Act not merely into legal force but into practical effect...

appropriately called *Let Us Face the Future*, contrasted with the Conservative document *Mr Churchill's Declaration of Policy to the Electors*, which relied too heavily on their leader's wartime reputation. But there was a negative side to Churchill's war image, particularly his mishandling of the Beveridge Report. He was to do the Conservative Party further damage in the election campaign, when he launched a bitter attack on the Labour Party:

"There can be no doubt that socialism is inseparably interwoven with totalitarianism and the abject worship of the State...Socialism is in its essence an attack not only upon British enterprise, but upon the right of an ordinary man or woman to breathe freely without having a harsh, clumsy tyrannical hand clasped across their mouth and nostrils...(The Socialists)..would have to fall back on some form of Gestapo, no doubt very humanely directed in the first instance."
(Churchill radio broadcast 4 June 1945 quoted in *Life in Britain 1945-60* by L Coate and A Pike p5)

This sort of vindictive rhetoric was out of tune with the spirit of unity and consensus at the end of the war and it

backfired on the Conservatives. However, it is unlikely that either the broadcast or the Conservative handling of the campaign had a decisive impact on the final outcome of the election. Opinion polls conducted by Mass Observation showed a consistent Labour lead from 1942 onwards.

THE LABOUR GOVERNMENT 1945-50

With an overall majority in Parliament, the new Labour Government was able to carry out its social and economic policies to the full. The spirit of excitement at the beginning of the Labour era was captured in a House of Commons debate when the Attorney-General, Sir Hartley Shawcross stated:

"We are the masters at the moment, and not only at the moment, but for a very long time." (quoted in R Eatwell *The 1945-51 Labour Governments* p54)

Key Labour Government Ministers 1945

Prime Minister	Clement Attlee
Chancellor of the Exchequer	Hugh Dalton
Minister of National Insurance	James Griffiths
Minister of Health	Aneurin Bevan
Lord President	Herbert Morrison
President of the Board of Trade	Stafford Cripps

Table 9.2

We will now attempt to describe and evaluate the measures which the new 'masters' of Westminster and Whitehall took in Beveridge's 5 problem areas - social security, health, education, housing and employment. (See p.20-22)

General Election Result 5 July 45

Parties	Total Votes	MPs	% of Votes
Conservatives	9,988,306	213	39.8
(including Liberal Nationals)			
Labour	11,995,152	393	47.8
Liberal	2,248,226	12	9.0
Others	854,294	22	2.8
Total	25,085,978	640	100.0

Table 9.1 (From *Modern British History 1714 - 1987* C Cook & J Stevenson p78)

Social Security

National Insurance (Industrial Injuries) Act, July 1946

Labour inherited this Bill from the Coalition Government, which in turn had based its proposals on the Beveridge Report. Accidents at work were no longer to be a private matter between employer and employee, but the responsibility of society as a whole. Universality and compulsion were built into the scheme - all workers and employers would have to contribute payments (4d from the state, employer and employee). In return, the state would provide insurance against industrial injury. Benefits were set at a higher rate (45 shillings per week) than that for ordinary sickness.

National Insurance Act, August 1946

Like Industrial Injuries, the National Insurance Act was based on the 1944 White Paper. It offered comprehensive cover 'from the cradle to the grave'. The insured population would be entitled to unemployment, sickness, maternity and widow's benefit, guardian's allowance, retirement pension and a death grant for funeral expenses. Benefits were set at the rate of 26 shillings for a single adult and 42 shillings for a couple. Sickness benefits could only be claimed after 156 contributions and unemployment benefit could only be given for a period between 180 and 492 days.

National Assistance Act, 1948

The aim of the Act was to "make further provision for the welfare of disabled, sick, aged and other persons, and for regulating homes for disabled and aged persons...out of moneys provided by Parliament". In other words, national assistance was supposed to be a 'safety net' to meet the needs of those whose circumstances were not adequately catered for by the National Insurance scheme. The Act set up a National Assistance Board (replacing the Unemployment Assistance Board of the 1930s) to carry out these duties.

Criticisms of the Social Security System

In theory, national insurance was supposed to be comprehensive and the payments sufficient to meet the people's needs. National assistance was therefore designed only to provide a residual, back-up role to National Insurance. In practice, it did not work out like that. The government calculated and decided on benefit levels in 1946. These were to be fixed for the next 5 years, after which they would be reassessed. However, by the time the scheme came into operation on the 'Appointed Day' (5 July, 1948), prices of goods had increased significantly, thus reducing the purchasing power of the benefits. One historian has calculated that welfare benefits in 1948 were only 19% of the average industrial wage and therefore well below subsistence level. Because of this, many more people than expected, particularly the elderly, were forced into applying for national assistance. In 1949, 48% of all national assistance went to supplement retirement pensions. That figure had risen to 68% by the late 1950s. The problem here was that national assistance was means tested and many old people were reluctant to apply for it, fearing the stigma attached to the hated means test of the 1930s.

"This dependency of many recipients of National Insurance benefits on means-tested assistance - even if these needs tests cannot be compared with the notorious household means test - constituted a major inroad into the principle of universality and of benefits paid as of right as a consequence of the insurance principle."
(*The Social Policy of the Attlee Government* by J Heb in WJ Mommsen's *The Emergence of the Welfare State in Britain and Germany* p306)

Compared to the social security provision of the past, the system put in place by 1948 was a marked improvement, but looking back from the present, it is equally clear that there was still a long way to go before the problems of poverty and deprivation were to be adequately addressed.

Health

The National Health Service Bill was piloted through Parliament by the Health Minister, Aneurin Bevan and it became law in November 1946. During the debate in the House of Commons, Bevan spoke about the deficiencies of the existing system and the benefits of the new health service:

"The first reason why a health scheme of this sort is necessary at all is because it has been the firm conclusion of all parties that money ought not to be permitted to stand in the way of obtaining an efficient health service. Although it is true that the health insurance system provides a general practitioner service and caters for something like 21 million of the population, the rest of the population have to pay whenever they desire the services of a doctor ... and therefore tend to postpone consultation as long as possible (while) there is the financial anxiety caused by having to pay doctors' bills..In the second place, the national health insurance scheme does not provide for the self-employed, nor, of course, for the families of dependents— Furthermore, it gives no backing to the doctor in the form of specialist services—Our hospital or-

DOTHEBOYS HALL
" It still tastes awful."

ganisation has grown up with no plan, with no system; it is unevenly distributed over the country and indeed it is one of the tragedies of the situation that very often the best hospital facilities are available where they are least needed...One of the first merits of this Bill is that it provides a universal health service without any insurance qualifications of any sort. It is available to the whole population and....it is intended that there shall be no limitation on the kind of assistance given in the general practitioner service, the specialist, the hospitals, eye treatment, spectacles, dental treatment, hearing facilities, all these are to be made available free".

(Bevan in the House of Commons debate 30.4.46. quoted in M Bruce (ed) - *The Rise of the Welfare State* p260-1)

The NHS Act, like the other social services, was scheduled to come into operation in July 1948. Almost right up to the 'Appointed Day' though, the doctors campaigned vigorously for changes to the proposed health service. In a survey of British Medical Association members early in 1948, 40,814 doctors voted against the NHS Act and only 4,734 voted for it. Clearly, without their cooperation the NHS would not work. In the end, Bevan bought the doctors off, starting at the top with the consultants. Much to the dismay of the Labour backbenchers in the Commons, Bevan announced in February 1948 that consultants would be allowed to continue their private practices on a part-time basis as well as having their own lucrative pay-beds for private patients in NHS hospitals.

The ordinary doctors had two chief complaints. Firstly, they objected to the fact that the sale of private practices was prohibited under the Act. Bevan sugared that particular pill by setting aside £66 million to compensate the doctors for the loss of their private practices. The other main complaint was against the NHS becoming a completely salaried medical service. Bevan eventually agreed that GPs would be paid on the basis of a capitation fee for each patient on the doctor's list. With a fee of 15 shillings (75p) per patient, this would guarantee doctors an income of between £1,000 and £2,500. Doctors in 'unfashionable' practices would get an extra payment of £300. With all these concessions and sweeteners, doctors' reservations dwindled and by the 'Appointed Day', 90% of doctors had agreed to enter the NHS.

If many of the doctors joined up with some reluctance, ordinary people celebrated the arrival of the NHS. The following colourful extracts come from Paul Addison's book *Now the War is Over*:

Mrs Bond of Leeds recalled how her family reacted.

"When the National Health Service started, oh it was fantastic. My mother and dad had been having problems with their teeth for ages, and I think they were the first at the dentist, as soon as he opened, they were there for an appointment. And instead of having just a few teeth out, they had the complete set out. And free dentures. You know? Thought it was wonderful..."

Mrs Law of Manchester described her mother's reaction to the inauguration of the NHS:

"I can remember this particular day, everything was in the radius of a few minutes' walk and she went to the optician's, obviously she'd got a prescription from the doctor, she went and she got tested for new glasses, then she want further down the road... for the chiropodist, she had her feet done, then she went back to the doctor's because she'd been having trouble with her ears and the doctor said...he would fix her up with a hearing aid..." (Addison p104-5)

Stories like this were by no means uncommon and they highlighted the backlog of untreated problems which the NHS faced. Doctors, dentists and opticians were inundated with patients queuing up for treatment. Prescriptions rose from 7 million per month before the NHS to 13.5 million per month in September 1948. In the first year of the health service, 5 million pairs of spectacles were dispensed and 8 million dental patients were treated.

The enormous expense of the NHS came as a shock. From the beginning, the government accepted that National Insurance funds would be inadequate to meet the needs of the nation's health and that most of the money would have to come out of general taxation. In fact, National Insurance only contributed 9% of NHS funding in 1949. By 1950, the NHS was costing £358 million a year and the Labour Government were forced to backtrack on the principle of a free service by introducing charges for spectacles and dental treatment. The government, of course, was constrained by the economy, still recovering from the war. Plans for new hospitals and health centres had to be shelved. Nevertheless, despite the criticisms, the compromises and the constraints, the NHS was arguably "the greatest single achievement in the story of the welfare state". (RC Birch *The Shaping of the Welfare State* p63)

Education

Labour inherited the Education Act from the Coalition Government and they were charged with carrying it out. The most immediate problem was the shortage and poor condition of school buildings. About 20% of existing school stock had been destroyed or damaged during the war. Due to the scale of the problem and the economic constraints of the postwar period, Attlee was forced to concentrate on the replacement of schools bombed during the war and the building of new primary schools to accommodate the children resulting from the 'baby boom' of 1942-7. By 1950, 1176 new schools had been built or were under construction, 928 of which were primaries. At the secondary level, very few technical schools were built. Consequently, the proposed tripartite structure of secondary education in reality boiled down to a dual system of grammar schools and secondary modern schools.

"There were grammar school places for about 20% of children and technical places for no more than 5%, so most children were classified as nonacademic and allocated to the residual category of modern school." (E Royle *Modern Britain* p367)

Children were to be allocated to the three types of school after an 'intelligence' test at '11-plus'. This was supposed to be an objective and fair means of selecting pupils irrespective of their social class background. What it turned out to be was a socially divisive and highly contentious selection procedure for the limited number of prestige places at the grammar schools.

> "From the outset...(secondary modern schools) suffered from the crippling disadvantage that the grammar schools alone were geared, by tradition, organisation and staff, to the task of preparing their pupils for public examinations; therefore, only by going to a grammar school could a child be sure of obtaining access either to a university or to one of the professions. This made secondary modern schools inferior to the grammar school in that they offered their children fewer opportunities." (LCB Seaman *Post Victorian Britain* p454)

So why did the Labour Government do so little to enhance the opportunities for working-class children, most of whom left school at 14 (15 after 1947) with no paper qualifications? Several historians put this down to the educational background of the Labour leaders. On the one hand, Attlee, Cripps and Dalton had all been educated at public schools and had little understanding of the state system. Others like Bevin, Morrison and Shinwell had had little formal education. Tomlinson, who became Education Minister in 1947, had left school at 12.

Compared to the equality of opportunity and provision being carried out in the areas of social security and health, the Labour Government did little for the educational welfare of the working class. It was 1964 before the idea of comprehensive schools for all abilities and social backgrounds became Labour Party policy.

Housing

The chronic housing shortage at the end of the war was the most pressing problem facing the government. There had already been a serious shortage before the war and this was compounded by the destruction of 700,000 houses by Hitler's bombers and rockets. At the end of the war, the government's housing policy was hindered by the lack of building workers and the shortage and high cost of building materials. Timber had to be imported from Sweden and America. In 1947, the housing programme had to be cut back on Treasury insistence because of the effect of raw material imports on Britain's balance of payments.

The responsibility for Britain's housing problems fell to Bevan at the Health Ministry (Labour failed to create a Housing Ministry as promised). His policy was to help those most in need ie. the working class. Most of the scarce building materials were allocated to the local authorities to build council houses for rent. Between 1945 and 1951, 4 council houses were built to every 1 private house. The government also continued into peacetime the production of prefabricated houses as a temporary stop-gap to meet the crisis. Between 1945 and 1948, 157,000 'prefabs' were assembled. Despite all these efforts, there were still chronic shortages. Many desperate families, out of sheer frustration, took to squatting on disused army camps in the summer of 1946. The government wisely decided not to prosecute them and in fact, realising that this would help to reduce waiting lists, instructed the local authorities to provide basic services and amenities for these people.

Houses Built in England & Wales 1935-54			
	Local Authority	**Private**	**Total**
1935-9	346,840	1,269,912	1,616,752
1940-4	-	-	151,000
1945-9	432,098	126,317	588,415
1950-4	912,805	228,616	1,141,421

Table 9.3 (Source: *Modern British History* Cook &Stevenson p129)

The Labour Government's record on house-building does not compare well with prewar levels or with the achievements of the Conservatives in the 1950s. Poor housing and homelessness were still serious problems at the end of the Labour period. The 1951 census revealed that there were 750,000 fewer houses than households in Britain. This was roughly the same level of homelessness as in 1931. However, given the scale of social and economic problems facing the government in 1945, historians have tended to judge Labour less harshly than did the voters in 1951.

Employment

The 1944 White Paper on *Employment Policy* had committed the government to 'the maintenance of a high and stable level of employment after the war'. Beveridge had reckoned that unemployment could not be brought down below 3%, but by 1946 the figure was running at only 2.5%. Dalton, the first postwar Labour Chancellor of the Exchequer, claimed that full employment was "the greatest revolution brought about by the Labour Government" (Eatwell *The 1945-51 Labour Governments* p67) What is less certain is whether the government's economic policies or a mixture of postwar boom and Marshall Aid from America brought this about. As table 9.4 shows, stable levels of employment continued into the 1950s and beyond.

PREVENTION IS BETTER . . .

(Estimated additional expenditure on National Health Services for 1950—£129 millions
Proposed reduction in expenditure on Housing for 1950—£24 millions)

Unemployment Levels (000s) 1931-51					
1931	2630	1938	1791	1945	137
1932	2745	1939	1514	1946	374
1933	2521	1940	963	1947	480
1934	2159	1941	350	1948	310
1935	2036	1942	123	1949	308
1936	1755	1943	82	1950	314
1937	1484	1944	75	1951	253

Table 9.4   (Source: Cook & Stevenson p217)

The post war economy was not without its difficulties. Between 1945 and 1951, Britain experienced bread and potato rationing, fuel shortages during the winter of 1947, a 30% devaluation of the pound, inflation and balance of payments problems. Perhaps it is to the credit of the Labour Government that they completed the welfare state structure and maintained full employment under the shadow of such serious economic problems.

Labour's Role in Creating the Welfare State

Just how important was the Labour contribution to the building of the Welfare State? Certainly Labour's social security legislation and the creation of the National Health Service went a long way towards completing the social welfare system. By 1948, the five 'giants' of *'want'*, *'disease'*, *'idleness'*, *'ignorance'* and *'squalor'* were under severe attack. The state was now providing a 'safety net' which protected people of all classes 'from the cradle to the grave' against the five 'giants'. Hard evidence was soon available on the improvements brought about by the welfare state. When Rowntree investigated conditions in York in 1950, he found that primary poverty had gone down to 2% compared to 36% in 1936. On the other hand there was still a lot to do. In the austere world of post war Britain, adequate houses, schools and hospitals were in short supply. Labour had not ushered in a socialist utopia as many had expected. Deprivation and poverty had been reduced but not eliminated. The capitalist system, with all its attendant inequalities, continued on much as before despite the nationalisation of the 'commanding heights' of the economy. The welfare state, it is argued, was applying a bandage instead of carrying out the radical surgery needed to treat the ailing British patient.

From another point of view, Labour's contribution can be challenged if we look at the development of the welfare state over the long term, from its origins in the 1970s until its completion in 1948. During much of the time, Conservative and Liberal governments were in power and although reforms were limited and cautious, there were two periods when advances were made (the Liberal Government 1906-14 and the Coalition Government 1940-45). It can be argued therefore that Labour simply completed the welfare state originated by others eg. Lloyd George (Liberal), Churchill (Liberal and latterly Conservative), Beveridge (Liberal) and Butler (Conservative).

As well as individuals and parties we must not forget the forces which shaped the growth of the welfare state, especially the social impact of mass unemployment followed by war in the 1930s and 1940s. The two principal historians of the welfare state agree that the war was extremely important.

> "The decisive event in the evolution of the welfare state was the Second World War." (*The Coming of the Welfare State* by M Bruce p. 326)

> "The war was to have decisive influence in producing a common experience and universal treatment for it." (*The Evolution of the British Welfare State* by D Fraser p.207)

What the war helped to create for the first time was a popular and political consensus about how Britain's social problems should be treated and the role of the state in this process. In 1945, Labour, the Liberals and the Conservatives all came out with remarkably similar welfare proposals. In fact, it could be argued that if Churchill had become the first post war Prime Minister instead of Attlee, the historic achievement of the completion of the welfare state might have been attributed to the Conservatives rather than Labour. Nevertheless, the monumental task faced a Labour Cabinet lacking experience of government and hemmed in by serious economic problems in the immediate post war years. Labour's achievement was to complete the structure of the modern welfare state in a flurry of legislation between 1945 and 1948. Although that structure has been overhauled since then, the welfare state remains an important and popular part of the British political system.

10 Scottish Nationalism 1850-1979

"Nationalism, whether regarded as a 'natural' force
or a conscious political and social philosophy is the
joker in the pack of modern history. It has cohab-
ited with every 'ism', with socialism, liberalism,
convervatism...yet it cuts across all of them."
(*War, Peace and Social Change: Europe 1900-1955 Book 2* by Henry
Cowper et al.)

As the quotation above implies, nationalism is a complex
phenomenon and it would be unwise to attempt to define
the concept, especially since there are as many definitions
as there are nations in the world. Instead, we will chart the
rise and fall of the many different nationalist organisations
and movements which have appeared in Scotland since
the 1850s. In general, we will see that the early 'nationalists' were concerned more with cultural/emotive concerns than with economic and political matters. From the
1880s until the 1920s, the nationalist agenda was set by
those wishing 'Home Rule'. In 1928, the first nationalist
party emerged - the National Party of Scotland. The
Scottish National Party, as it became after 1934, was for the
next 30 years a very insignificant force in Scottish politics.
There followed 15 years of spectacular growth when the
SNP became the second largest party in Scotland and was
able to set the political agenda through much of the 1980s.

As we are looking here at Scottish nationalism over a very
much longer time span than a political commentator
would, we have two objectives. Firstly, to describe the
growth and development of nationalism from its origins in
the 1850s and secondly, to try to explain the rapid growth
of the SNP in the 1960s and 1970s.

However, first of all the question why nationalism *failed* to
take root in Scotland in the 19th century when it did
throughout Europe, needs to be addressed.

Why was Scottish
Nationalism absent between 1850-1914?

This question was first raised by Tom Nairn in his book *The
Break-Up of Britain*, published in 1977 at the height of the
nationalist/devolution debate. The book aroused a great
deal of interest. It is a thought-provoking work because it
takes a Marxist point of view and also because it looks at
Scottish nationalism from a European perspective.

So, why did political nationalism arrive relatively late in
Scotland ie. in the 1920s compared with the 'age of
nationalism' in Europe from the 1820s onwards? After all,
Scotland was well-placed for the development of a political movement - it had been an independent sovereign state
until 1707, it had a stock of heroic figures from its past like
Wallace and Bruce and it had retained its own religious,
legal and cultural institutions.

The Marxist explanation, however, does not accept that
there are 'natural' conditions for a nationalist movement to
arise, only material conditions. Throughout Europe, the
crucial trigger for awakening a nationalist movement was
*the impact of capitalism, industrialisation and modernisation on
hitherto backward or under-developed societies*. In particular,
the smaller European countries were shocked into nation-

alist reaction by coming into contact with French revolutionary ideas and English commercial dominance. They
were compelled to modernise. However, they demanded
that modernisation should be on their terms. Nationalism
was the result.

Scotland, according to Nairn, was unique amongst European nations in having modernised itself very rapidly
from a feudal society into a 'modern' civil society and
before the nationalist upheavals began in Europe. Scotland "...had progressed from fortified castles and witch-
burning to Edinburgh New Town and Adam Smith in only
a generation or so". (*The Break-Up of Britain* by Tom Nairn
p.107) Whether Scotland's renaissance was the result of
the Scots' own efforts or because of the beneficial effects of
the Union with England is irrelevant. For the most part,
Scotland was on a par economically, socially and cultur-
ally with England and as such would not encounter the
'hammer-blow' of progress experienced by the under-
developed countries of Europe. Consequently, a nationalist response did not arise between 1850 and 1914 - there
was nothing to respond to! As we will see, it took the shock
of the economic depression of the 1930s to jolt Scottish
nationalism into life.

1850-1885

Scotland, then, did not have a nationalist movement in
1850. However, there were recognisable stirrings coming
from a few individuals. The most notable of these was the
Rev. James Begg, a leading member of the Free Church of
Scotland. Writing in June 1850, Begg despaired at the way
Scottish society was degenerating. "We are sinking in our
national position every year....the Parliament of England
despising us." (*Scottish Nationalism* by HJ Hanham p.75) He advocated at best the re-establishment of a Scottish government, but if that was not possible, he would accept increased Scottish representation at Westminster.

A supporter of Begg's was James Grant, a historical novelist from Edinburgh. In 1852, he began a campaign against
the English, complaining that they had broken the terms of
the Act of Union of 1707 and that financially England was
benefitting more than Scotland from it. A more specific
grievance was England's improper use of flags. According
to the Act of Union, the Union Jack was to be used in all
circumstances, but England continued to display St.
George's flag in the Navy. What might nowadays seem to
be a minor point became a popular issue for many Scots. In
1853, the *National Association for the Vindication of Scottish
Rights* was set up to pursue the point more vigorously.
Although the politicians steered clear, support was forthcoming from the Convention of Royal Burghs and some
town councils. One meeting held in Glasgow attracted
5,000 people. Speakers called for the restoration of the
office of Secretary of State for Scotland and for a Scottish
Assembly to deal with exclusively Scottish affairs. However, the National Association failed to gain the sympathy
of the establishment who considered their nationalism to
be "an anachronism". It also failed to set up a grass-roots
organisation and with the onset of the Crimean War,
enthusiasm for *Scottish* issues faded.

The next campaign to surface in Scotland in the 1860s revolved around the desire of some patriots to have a monument to William Wallace erected at Abbey Craig near Stirling. Wallace had spearheaded Scotland's struggle for independence against English oppression before being defeated by Edward I in 1305. Now Wallace was being used as a nationalist symbol to revive Scottish pride in its glorious past. The campaign to build Wallace monuments spread throughout Scotland and into the ex-patriot communities in Australia and Canada. The real issue behind the monument campaign was a new English threat - the quiet but seemingly unstoppable assimilation of Scotland into the culture of England/Britain.

Along similar lines was the campaign initiated by a Glasgow solicitor, William Burns for the use of the term 'Scottish' rather than 'Scotch'. Again, this campaign was motivated by the fear that Scottish culture was being swamped and overtaken by the English. Even Scots at this time were in the habit of using the word 'England' when they meant 'Great Britain'.

To sum up so far, what we have seen in the decades after 1850 were a few individuals (Begg, Grant, Burns) and one short-lived organisation (the NAVSR) attempting to awaken the national consciousness of the Scottish people. As such, they were relatively successful in drawing attention to their causes. However, the issues they espoused were essentially symbolic and emotive rather than the economic and political causes adopted by modern nationalists. Very few of the early agitators could be termed political nationalists - Home Rule and independence had yet to enter the vocabulary of these men.

> "The inevitable consequence of the entente between emotive nationalisn and effective unionism was the impotence of political nationalism. Not only did it lack the economic grievances on which Irish and Welsh nationalism fed, but the religious and education institutions of the country...were committed to the Union and through it to the 'Greater Scotland' of the Empire." (*Scotland and Nationalism* by Christopher Harvie pp.40-1)

> "The economic advantages of the Union have...until recently always seemed so great that it was scarcely worthwhile to break the link with England. Indeed, during the Victorian age, Scotland enjoyed a prosperity so great by comparison with that of the past that unionist sentiment seemed likely to destroy Scottish national self-consciousness altogether." (*Scottish Nationalism* by HJ Hanham p. 10)

1885-1915

Agitation within the political establishment for better Scottish representation at Westminster continued throughout the 1870s, culminating in the creation of the post of Secretary for Scotland in 1885. (see chapter 11) Gladstone, though, was not sufficiently convinced about the new post to give it Cabinet status. However, 1885 - 1888 were watershed years. Before that time, Home Rule for Scotland had not been on the agenda. Now, Gladstone made up his mind that Home Rule was needed for Scotland and Ireland (although Ireland took priority). In 1886, the *Scottish Home Rule Association* was founded. Two years later, the Scottish Liberals became committed to the creation of a Scottish Parliament within the UK. From then until 1914, Scottish Home Rule was debated 15 times in Parliament and 4 Private Members Bills were introduced (none successfully).

The Scottish Home Rule Association (SHRA) attempted to mobilise public opinion by the production of pamphlet literature. However, the issue of Home Rule was very much a minority pursuit and failed to capture the popular imagination. On the other hand, the SHRA proved to be an important recruiting ground for future political leaders. Ramsay MacDonald had been Secretary of the London branch of the SHRA. Keir Hardie, who was instrumental in forming the Scottish Labour Party and committing it to a Home Rule policy, had been vice-president of the SHRA. RB Cunninghame-Graham, (see p.10) the novelist and adventurer, became the first president of the National Party of Scotland in 1928.

By the early years of the twentieth century, some form of legislative devolution had been adopted as policy by the radical Left in Scotland ie. Labour, the Liberals and the Crofter Party. Firmly in the unionist camp were the Conservatives, the Scottish nobility, most businessmen and the trade unions. It is difficult to see how the SHRA could progress from here now that the battlelines were drawn. The Liberal Party had been convinced of the case,

---

Scotland versus England

Hampden Park was the venue for the third round of the Football Association Cup on 30 October, 1886. The match was between Queen's Park and Preston North End (attendance 15,000). Jimmy Ross, a Scots player with Preston fouled the Queen's Park's centre forward, Harrower. The local crowd were incensed and invaded the pitch. Ross had to be smuggled out of the ground for his own safety.

The incident has some historical interest other than informing us that there is nothing new in the modern game of football. For some time, there had been simmering differences between the Football Association and the Scottish Football Association over the issue of professionalism in English football. The Hampden Park affair now brought the matter to a head and the SFA issued a declaration of independence, stating that 'clubs belonging to this Association shall not be members of any other National Association'. Scottish teams were to withdraw from the FA Cup competition.

The historical significance of this incident is explained by Christopher Harvie:

"The new, proletarian professional game was organised on national, not on British lines. 'Working class nationalism', James Kellas has written, 'is generally related to culture and football, not politics'. This consciousness stemmed from the 1880s. Had a British League come into operation in that decade, it might have been quite different."

(*Scotland and Nationalism* by Christopher Harvie p38)

but the urgency was not there - Ireland must come first. With the SHRA in a cul-de-sac, unable to force the pace of events at Westminster, a more vigorous group, the *Young Scots Society* emerged onto the scene in 1900.

The Young Scots Society was essentially a radical Liberal pressure group attempting to influence the parliamentary party to speed up the momentum for Home Rule. It published its own journal, *Young Scot* and a series of Home Rule pamphlets as well as holding numerous public meetings. Many of the leading Young Scots entered Parliament as Liberal MPs in 1906 and 1910. There, they formed a *Scottish National Committee* to promote their cause. Two other organisations were set up: the *Scottish Home Rule Council* to act as a publicity machine and the *International Scottish Home Rule Association* to attract funds from ex-patriots in America.

All this pressure began to have some effect. Even some Conservatives began to believe that devolution was a necessary evil to prevent the break-up of the UK. In April, 1912, the Liberal Prime Minister, Asquith, introduced the Government of Ireland Bill in the House of Commons and concluded with the remark that it was "only the first step in a larger and more comprehensive policy". The Irish Bill never reached the Statute book as the war intervened and Home Rule for Ireland (and therefore Scotland) was suspended for the foreseeable future.

Two of the leading historians of Scottish nationalism (Webb and Harvie) believe that if the war had not taken place, Scotland would probably have had its parliament. As it was, the whole Home Rule momentum was destroyed. Postwar Scotland and Britain were more hostile environments for the supporters of devolution. The Liberal Party, on which the Home Rulers had pinned their hopes, went into steady decline and disunity. The ascending Labour Party, on the other hand, saw its priority as articulating the interests of the British working class. Nationalism had few friends, being blamed by many for the War.

1918 -34 The Origins of Modern Political Nationalism

As figure 10.1 shows, four organisations emerged in the ten years after the end of the war, each in its own way attempting to promote the cause of Scottish nationalism. However, frustration at the lack of progress on the Home Rule front at Westminster led in 1928 to the formation of the first political party to focus exclusively on the issue of Scotland's political status. This was the National Party of Scotland (NPS). The Scottish National Party (SNP) in its present form arose 6 years later as a result of the amalgamation of the NPS with the more moderate Scottish Party. We will now look briefly at the organisations and parties which preceded the formation of the SNP.

The Scottish Home Rule Association (Mark II)

A new SHRA was set up in September 1918. Although it shared the same name as its prewar predecessor, this was a new organisation. Whereas the old SHRA had its ties with the Liberal Party, the postwar equivalent was mainly Labour, reflecting the changing balance of political forces in Scotland and Britain. The SHRA's founder and financial backer was R.E. Muirhead, the owner of a tannery in Bridge-of-Weir and himself a member of the Independent Labour Party (ILP). He became the Secretary of the organisation. RB Cunninghame-Graham was President of the SHRA for most of its life (remember that he had been a founder member of the Scottish Labour Party). Further evidence of the importance of the Labour/socialist connection can be seen from the fact that the majority of the organisational members of the SHRA comprised ILP and trade union branches and co-operative societies.

The SHRA's policy as stated at the inaugural meeting in 1918 was the "...demand for self-government in respect of Scottish affairs" (J Brand *The National Movement in Scotland* p.175) They also wanted the proposed Scottish Parliament to have its own revenue-raising powers. Like the prewar organisation, the SHRA intended to function as a pressure group via public meetings, the production of pamphlets and the lobbying of interested Parliamentary candidates and MPs. The Labour Party was the main target for persuasion and between 1918 and 1920, the party was sympathetic. Thereafter, support declined steadily and by 1924, neither Labour nor the Liberals considered Home Rule to be sufficiently important to include it in their election manifestos. Labour strategists began to see potential dangers in pursuing Scottish devolution too vigorously. In the 1924 election, Labour polled 41% of the Scottish electorate compared to only 33% of English voters. If a Scottish Parliament was set up, it might seriously weaken Labour strength at Westminster. Labour's ambivalence over the issue can be seen in the fact that while officially in favour of Home Rule, the party at the same time disapproved of its members joining the SHRA.

Lobbying of M.P.s was increasingly recognised as a doomed enterprise, so the SHRA decided to step up the pressure by calling a *National Convention* in November, 1924 with the

---

KEY ORGANISATIONS IN THE CREATION OF THE SNP

Pressure Group Phase 1918 - 1928

Scottish Home Rule Association Mark 2, 1918

Scots National League, 1920

Scottish National Movement, 1926

Glasgow University Student National Association, 1927

Political Parties 1928 onwards

National Party of Scotland, 1928

Scottish Party, 1932

Scottish National Party, 1934

The Duke of Montrose, Compton MacKenzie, RB Cunninghame-Graham, Hugh MacDiarmid, James Valentine and John MacCormick at the first public meeting of the National Party of Scotland, Glasgow 1928.

view of formulating a Home Rule Bill. The Labour MP George Buchanan's name had come out of the ballot for Private Member's Bills. He decided to sponsor a Home Rule Bill and agreed to accept SHRA help in drafting it. However, the Buchanan Bill was talked out on Second Reading. For the SHRA, this was a great disappointment especially as they believed the Labour Party could have done a lot more to assist the passage of the Bill. Its defeat proved to be a turning point in the strategy of the SHRA. Leading members began to talk openly about the need for a separate political party to pursue the Home Rule issue. Defeat in 1927 of Labour MP the Reverend James Barr's Private Member's Bill on Home Rule only served to confirm that neither Labour nor any other UK political party could not be relied upon to deliver legislative devolution for Scotland. A few months later, most of the SHRA's 3,000 members joined the new National Party of Scotland. The SHRA dissolved itself in September 1929.

The Scots National League

The SNL was more radical than the SHRA. Its stated aim was not Home Rule but "...the resumption of Scottish National Independence" (*The National Movement in Scotland* by J Brand p.185) The SNL seems to have come into existence in 1920, although records are very sketchy. Throughout its life in the 1920s, it had no more than 7 branches and at most 1,000 members. Such matters as organisational growth were not regarded as important by the intellectuals and propagandists who were dominant in the early days.

Two of the most prominent figures were the Honourable Ruaraidh Erskine of Marr and William Gillies. Erskine's numerous articles written in the 1920s show that he was very much in favour of the restoration of Celtic culture and the Gaelic language as well as the spread of the Roman Catholic faith throughout Scotland - all of which were hardly likely to endear him to most Scots. William Gillies had a similarly unorthodox background, being involved with the Highland Land League, the Gaelic Society and Irish Home Rule. Gillies became the first editor of the SNL's journal, the *Scots Independent*. (When the SNL

merged with the other organisations to become the National Party of Scotland and later the SNP, the *Scots Independent* moved with it to become the voice of Scottish nationalism.)

The SNL in the early 1920s was mostly concerned with cultural matters, much in the same mould as the first 'nationalists' of the 1850s. Erskine wrote several articles in *Liberty* magazine in 1920 attacking the use of the term 'British'. Gaelic and other linguistic matters were also to the fore. However, the organisation seems to have changed tack round about 1925. At the annual conference that year, the SNL voted in favour of running its own candidates at the next general election (despite the opposition of Erskine and the radical ex-patriots in the London branch).

Tom Gibson was the key figure in changing the character of the SNL. Gradually, under his influence, the organisation began to lay more emphasis on economic matters. Gibson's pragmatic approach became more prominent in his articles in the *Scots Independent*. In the September and November 1927 editions of the magazine, Iain Gillies and Tom Gibson respectively contributed pieces advocating the need for a National Party:

"The Scots National League has laid the foundations of a National Party - democratic, progressive and radical-minded - with a demand that will gain the support of all Scots save the reactionary....If and when the Home Rule Association boldly proclaims adherence to this policy, what is to prevent its co-operation in the League's work of putting forward and securing the return of National candidates? Such co-operation...would bring nearer that day when the Scottish people shall give to its National Party, to the majority of its representatives, a definite mandate to withdraw from Westminster and to establish on Scottish soil the National Government of our country."
('Scotland's Need: A National Party' by Iain Gillies in the *Scots Independent* p.5 Sept. 1927)

Gibson represented the SNL at the meeting which inaugurated the National Party of Scotland.

The Scottish National Movement

Of much less significance, but worth a brief mention in the history of the SNP is the Scottish National Movement (SNM). This small organisation with the grandiose title was founded by the poet Lewis Spense in 1926. Spense and Hugh MacDiarmid were two of the key figures of the Scottish literary renaissance in the 1920s. Both men effectively combined a strong sense of nationalism with a desire to express their poetry and literature in the Scots language. MacDiarmid was an active member of the SHRA and later the National Party of Scotland, while Spense had been a member of the Edinburgh branch of the SNL before breaking away to form his own SNM.

The main political aim of the SNM was, like the SNL, the re-establishment of an independent national parliament in Scotland. Its other aims were largely cultural, such as the revival of the study of Scottish history, the restoration of the Scots language and the advancement of Scottish art, literature and music. The SNM failed to make significant progress beyond the Lothian area, but because of Spense's journalistic connections, he was able to create a dispropor-tionate amount of publicity and propaganda. Like the SHRA and the SNL, the SNM quickly realised that the Labour Party was not going to deliver Home Rule and that the formation of a national party was the best way for-ward. However, it took another organisation, the *Glasgow University Student Nationalist Association* to provide the real catalyst which brought together all the groups to form the NPS.

The Glasgow University
Student Nationalist Association (GUSNA)
More by good timing than anything else, the fledgling GUSNA was pushed centre stage in the Scottish national-ist drama for a few weeks in 1928. The GUSNA was little more than a university debating club and had only been in existence since September 1927. Its founder, John Mac-Cormick, was to play a key role in bringing together the separate nationalist organisations and, as we shall see, he went on to become a central figure in the nationalist movement in the following 25 years.

In late 1927, MacCormick met with RE Muirhead of the SHRA to discuss ways and means of merging the various nationalist organisations without it appearing that any one of them was taking over the rest. It became clear that the student body could provide a non-threatening forum for the senior nationalist organisations to do business.

So it was that the GUSNA called a meeting of delegates from the SNL, the SHRA and the SNM on February 11, 1928 - MacCormick chairing the meeting. Towards the end of the proceedings, Gibson of the SNL put forward the proposal, "That this meeting of Scots men and women, having regard to the present deplorable conditions of national life and affairs in Scotland ... declares that the survival of Scottish life can only be effected by an inde-pendent parliament in Scotland and hereby constitutes itself as a National Party of Scotland". (J Brand *The National Movement in Scotland* p. 194) Although several stalwarts of the SHRA and the SNL refused to join the new party, the tide of events was running against them. The NPS was a reality and fighting elections against the English-dominated parties was the new priority.

The National Party of Scotland 1928 - 34
RE Muirhead became the first Chairperson of the party. His generous financial support was now transferred from the SHRA to the NPS. John MacCormick was rewarded for his role in the merger with the post of Secretary of the new party. It seems that the amalgamation of all the organisa-tions brought together only about 1,000 members in 12 branches, most of which were concentrated in the Glas-gow area. Over the next 4 years, there was fairly strong growth - by the end of 1928, 41 branches were in existence; by 1931, the party was claiming 70 branches throughout Scotland; by 1932, membership had increased to 8,000.

Along with Muirhead and MacCormick, Gibson was an influential figure in the NPS, particularly in the area of party policy. Coming from the SNL tradition, he success-fully pushed for the policy of complete independence for

NPS Electoral Performance 1929-33		
Date	**Constituency**	**%**
1929	Glasgow (Camlachie)	4.9
1929	Midlothian	4.5
1930	Glasgow (Shettleston)	10.1
1931	Edinburgh East	9.4
1931	East Renfrewshire	13.1
1931	West Renfrewshire	11.0
1931	Inverness	14.0
1931	Glasgow (St. Rollox)	15.8
1932	Dumbarton	13.5
1932	Montrose	11.7
1933	East Fife	3.6
1933	Kilmarnock	16.9

Table 10.1 (Source: J. Brand *The National Movement in Scotland* p.202)

Scotland, albeit still remaining under the Crown. The Party's official policy position was, "self-government for Scotland with Independent National Status within the British Group of Nations". (*Scottish Nationalism* by HJ Hanham p. 163) Gibson also took a hard line on the status of the NPS - it was a political party and as such was geared towards competing in elections against the UK parties. It was therefore inconceivable that a member of the NPS could retain membership of another political party. Dual mem-bership was accordingly outlawed.

The party's electoral performance in the General Elections of 1929 and 1931 and in various by-elections is shown in Tables 10.1 and 10.2. From a rather shaky start in 1929, the NPS candidates acquitted themselves reasonably well, getting into double figures and saving their deposits. Nev-ertheless, its entry onto the electoral scene did nothing to alter the policies of the major parties. On the other hand, it created new problems for the NPS. Now that the party was competing for power, the electorate might reasonably expect to know where it stood on economic issues as well as the issue of independence. If the party went left on economic issues (most of the leaders had an ILP back-ground), then it might divide its own membership and lose what little support it had with the Scottish electorate, which had swung decisively in favour of the Conserva-tives in 1931. (Table 10.2)

General Election Results (Scotland)		
1929		
Party	**Vote(%)**	**MPs**
Conservative	35.9	20
Liberals	18.1	13
Labour	42.4	36
NPS	0.1	0
Others	3.5	2
1931		
Coalition	63.9	64
Labour	32.6	7
Independent Liberal	-	-
NPS	1.0	0
Others	1.0	0

Table 10.2 Source: J. Kellas *The Scottish Political System* p.104

"...the very act of the nationalists entering the electoral arena had changed the logic of the situation. Prior to this, the home rule issue could be viewed by the major parties as a possible means of getting votes. The nationalists could pose a threat to the parties that could not be properly evaluated. In such a situation the party managers saw that it was an interest that at least ought to be deferred to if not actually accommodated. Having campaigned and failed badly, though, the nationalists exposed the inability of the home rule cause to mobilise the electorate, and thus allowed the major parties to take even less notice of it." (*The Growth of Nationalism in Scotland* by K Webb p. 52)

"Yet the options before the National Party were limited. The Scottish electorate was conservative, and a move to the left would alienate many potential supporters, particularly former adherents of the Liberal Party. It would also involve a competition - which the Nationalists could never hope to win - with the trade union-based Labour and Independent Labour Parties. They, and the Liberals, could still play the home rule card if challenged. The National Party would end up simply as the weakest section of the Scottish left." (*Scotland and Nationalism* by Christopher Harvie p. 49)

The Scottish Party 1932-34

The precise details of the origins of the Scottish Party are not known, but it seems to have come about after the Cathcart Unionist Association broke away from the Conservative Party in June 1932. The leader of the revolt was J Kevan McDowall. He believed in Imperial Federation and that within Britain, there should be devolution of powers to regional parliaments in England, Scotland and Wales. The Cathcart group was joined by some notable public figures, most of whom had their origins in the Conservative and Liberal Parties. During its 2 years of existence, the Scottish Party made no effort to develop itself as a party. In fact, it is debatable whether it was in any real sense a political party. No constitution was drawn up; branches were not formed; no elections were fought under the Scottish Party name and it is unlikely that there were ever more than 100 members. However, what the party lacked in electoral credibility, it made up for in terms of the important and 'respectable' figures who were willing to associate with it.

A further factor in the favour of the new Scottish Party in 1932 was that its moderate, Home Rule image coincided with the line taken by the *Daily Record* and the *Scottish Daily Express* which were conducting a circulation war at the time. Each paper tried to outdo the other in proclaiming its Scottishness, but they stressed that it was Home Rule, not the independence of the more extreme NPS, that they desired. All of this would not have escaped the attention of the NPS Secretary, John MacCormick, who was on the Home Rule wing of his own party. The advantages of a merger of the two parties were immediately clear to him.

"The Scottish Party was just the sort of party MacCormick approved of. It boasted a great name (the Duke of Montrose), a notable public figure (Sir Alexander MacEwen), a patriotic lawyer (Andrew Dewar Gibb) and a first rate lawyer (Kevan Mc Dowall). It had good press connections. And its policy was a gradualist one that pointed to Home Rule rather than independence." (*Scottish Nationalism* by HJ Hanham p. 159)

SCOTTISH NATIONALISM 1934-62

It is important at this stage to make a distinction between *Scottish nationalism* and *Scottish national consciousness*. The former deals with those organisations attempting to achieve more political devolution or independence; the latter is "as assertion of Scottishness on the part of an amorphous group of interests and individuals, whose identity is caught up with that of Scotland." (*The Scottish Political System* by J Kellas p. 128) Although it is more difficult to pinpoint or measure, many observers over the last 50 years have noted a steady growth of Scottish national consciousness throughout all sectors of Scottish society. This heightened sense of 'Scottishness' has not always spilled over into votes for the SNP. In fact, we will see that nationalism since the 1930s has not been a matter of steady growth, but rather a series of peaks and troughs affecting the various nationalist organisations.

In this section, we will look at the changing fortunes of the SNP and the rival organisation, the *Scottish Convention*. It is also worth noting that there were a great many fringe nationalist organisations around at this time. Although some of them had dubious credentials, there has been no tradition of violence associated with Scottish nationalism except for a few isolated cranks.

Timetable of events leading to the formation of the SNP

September 1932   Scottish Party held its first meeting. Policy of party much more moderate than the NPS. They stressed need for "a responsible Parliament in Scotland" but wished "to maintain, unimpaired, Scotland's loyalty to the Crown and Empire." (*The National Movement in Scotland* by J Brand p. 215)

October 1932   At Scottish Party Conference, a much stronger statement calling for a Scottish Parliament for all Scottish affairs was accepted. Scottish Party moving more towards NPS policy.

November 1932   NPS Special Conference gave MacCormick authority to start merger negotiations with the Scottish Party.

May 1933   At NPS Annual Conference, basic policy on independence was diluted from extreme position of a separate sovereign state to a Scottish Parliament for 'all Scottish affairs' (to all intents and purposes, the same as the Scottish Party policy)

July 1933   Key NPS hard-liners, outraged by the softening of party policy, were expelled at the instigation of MacCormick. About 20% of NPS members left in sympathy.

September 1933   NPS and Scottish Party put up a joint candidate, Sir Alexander MacEwen, at the Kilmarnock by-election. Best ever result of 16.8%.

January-March 1934   Various joint meetings about the details of the merger.

7 April 1934   New party, called the Scottish National Party formed.

110

The SNP 1934 - 42

The early years of the SNP's history were neither spectacular nor glorious. This was due mainly to the fact that the party was disunited. The merger of the NPS and the Scottish Party had simply brought all the moderates and hardliners under one roof. Not surprisingly, cracks began to appear on the facade quite early on and culminated in the exodus of a large number of members at the 1942 Party Conference. Three main issues divided the party over this period:

- whether SNP members could also be members of another party
- the personality and role of John MacCormick
- the attitude of the party towards conscientious objection and Scottish neutrality during the war.

The Membership Issue

When the NPS and the Scottish Party merged, it appeared that you could not be a member of the SNP and another political party at the same time, although a firm policy had not been worked out. However, it did not take long for the membership issue to come to the fore. On 4 May, 1935, the *Glasgow Herald* published a letter by the Duke of Montrose advocating a merger of the SNP and the Liberal Party. (see above) What was so shocking about this was that the Duke, who was President of the SNP, had not consulted his colleagues on the proposed amalgamation and more importantly, it was revealed that he took the Liberal Whip in the House of Lords. A special conference was hastily convened to clarify party policy. What the conference revealed was an unbridgeable gulf between the hardliners and the moderates, who were willing to allow dual membership. At the national conference in 1936, a vague 'compromise' position was adopted, stating that: "Only those persons who believe that self-government is the most urgently required political form for Scotland should become members of the party". (J Brand *The National Movement in Scotland* p. 236) Clearly, this statement could be construed to allow dual membership and Tom Gibson resigned from the party. Other hardliners remained to carry on the fight.

The background to the Duke of Montrose's merger proposals only came to light in 1977 in an article in the *Scotsman*. The Duke appears to have been a rather eccentric member of the landed aristocracy. He certainly did not feel the need to keep on good terms with the left-wing of the SNP when he used the columns of the *Scots Independent* to lambast the hikers who disturbed his grouse moors!

Just like the hikers, the right-wing Duke wanted to get rid of the 'extremists' from the SNP's territory. His attempt to secure an electoral pact with the Liberals in 1935 was motivated by a desire to isolate the leftwing of his own party. The irony of the situation was that, while seeking a deal with the Liberals, the President of the SNP was still taking the Conservative Whip in the Lords. It eventually dawned on the Duke that he could not continue to have a foot in three camps. In a letter to an SNP colleague, he wrote: "My position is illogical. It cannot be right for me on the one hand to be president of a party which stands for self-government for Scotland and then, on the other hand, actively to support a party which is pledged against the government of Scotland by the Scottish people". (*Weekend Scotsman* May 14, 1977 p.1)

The Duke's parting with the SNP was a bitter affair. He initiated a lawsuit in the Court of Session against the party over the recovery of a guarantee he gave in 1935 for a bank overdraft facility for the party. In an article in a nationalist pamphlet, an anonymous writer summed up the Duke's party career: "His connection with the Party has always been unfortunate. About 1928, he was in the National Party of Scotland but departed in a few months with a blast of publicity as damaging as could be made. He returned when the National and Scottish Parties united in 1934, lasted a little longer, but again quit. All through, his association with the Movement has been damaging in every part of the country where big land monopolists and hereditary nobles are not well regarded". (Source: *Quarter in Review* (no date), *Scottish Nationalist Papers* 7, Aberdeen University Library)

The Issue of John MacCormick

There is evidence going back as far as 1933 that MacCormick was resented in certain quarters in the party. At that time, some of the hardliners in the NPS felt that he was bending too much to the moderate Scottish Party line in the merger negotiations. There were also allegations that he had spent far too much of the party's meagre funds on the East Fife by-election in 1933. Stung by the personal criticism, MacCormick used his position in the party to engineer the expulsion of two of his most forthright critics, McColl and Clark in July of that year.

Throughout the 1930s, MacCormick consolidated his position in the party. In his favour was the undoubted fact that he was an accomplished and powerful speaker and he was able to use this talent both at public rallies and to influence colleagues on the National Council. His enemies began to accuse him of running a 'kitchen cabinet' without consulting the rest of the party. Certainly, like the Duke of Montrose, he had no authority to enter into negotiations with key Liberal figures in 1935. Several attempts by the anti-MacCormick faction to curb the powers of the National Council over the annual conference failed. MacCormick's departure from the party at the 1942 Conference was full of personal animosity and mutual recriminations, reflecting a history of simmering resentment over his 10-year dominance of the SNP.

The Neutrality Issue

At the 1937 annual conference, a resolution was passed to the effect that, "...all male members of the SNP of any military age hereby pledge themselves to refuse to serve with any section of the Crown forces until the programme of the SNP has been fulfilled". (K Webb *The Growth of Nationalism in Scotland* p. 57) For the next 5 years, there was a running battle between the pro- and antiwar factions within the party. On the antiwar wing were RE Muirhead, who was a pacifist and Arthur Donaldson who set up the *Scottish Neutrality League*. Both were imprisoned for their stance. On the pro-war side was the MacCormick group. After 1937, MacCormick attempted to modify party policy to accommodate both sides. However, the more he manipulated, the more the anti-war group was joined by the anti-MacCormick group. By the time MacCormick took the rostrum at the 1942 Conference, suggesting that the party should abandon the electoral strategy in favour of attempting to influence the Labour and Liberal Parties to adopt Home Rule, he had alienated too many party members. (See p.49-50)

The 1942 Split

Realising that his days were numbered, MacCormick stood down as Party Secretary. He then nominated his preferred candidate for the post of Chairperson, William Power. Another nominee was put up - Douglas Young, a lecturer in Greek at Aberdeen University. Young was a recent recruit to the party, but he had gained a reputation for taking a stand against conscription, for which he was subsequently jailed for 8 months. The vote was won by Young and his followers. MacCormick retaliated by calling on his supporters to resign from the party. About half of the delegates did so.

In a rearguard action, MacCormick claimed in a well-circulated 'private' letter that an organised faction had been plotting against him for the last year and more

---

Some of the Fringe Nationalist Organisations 1934-55

1   The Democratic Scottish Self-Government Organisation
2   The Scottish Self-Government Federation
3   The Anti-Conscription League
4   The Scottish Neutrality League
5   United Scotland
6   Scottish Watch
7   Scottish Patriots
8   The League of True Scots
9   The Scottish Secretariat
10 Scottish Congress

---

seriously that fictitious branch delegates were planted at the conference to vote against him. Both allegations were strenuously denied, notably by Arthur Donaldson:

> "...I am putting it on record here as untrue for the benefit of those who have seen your letter. I am told indeed by others you mentioned that the whole statement is false and that there are other misstatements and misrepresentations in the letter....It would seem, in fact that, far from there having been a successful conspiracy to unseat you, the result was as big a shock (but more pleasant) to your opponents as it was to you. It would appear to have been due, first to a genuine realisation within the SNP that a continuation of your dominance, however disguised, meant an early demise for the Party; and second, to the ineptitude, petulance and latterly vindictiveness shown by you at the Conference."
> (Open letter to JM MacCormick by A Donaldson [undated] *Scottish National Papers* op cit)

Bitterness over MacCormick's role in the splitting of the SNP was still evident two years later in a *Scots Independent* article entitled 'On a North British Devolutionist'. The following verse was mischievously inserted:

> *They libbit William Wallace*
> *He gar'd them bleed*
> *They dinna libb MacFoozle*
> *They dinna need*

gar'd = made *libb* =castrate
(Christopher Harvie *Scotland and Nationalism* p.235)

Due to the 1942 split, mainstream Scottish nationalism until the mid-1950s was represented by 2 organisations: the SNP, containing those who wished to reassert the fundamental policy of complete independence, to be achieved by fighting elections; and the Scottish Convention, containing those who wished a measure of Home Rule within the UK, to be achieved by pressure on the major political parties.

The Scottish Convention

The Scottish Convention from beginning to end was John MacCormick's project. It was to be an all-party organisation whose aim was to pressure the major parties to grant a Scottish Parliament. A Scottish National Assembly was held in 1947. About 600 delegates from different backgrounds attended. At this meeting, the idea of a plebiscite of the Scottish people on the issue of Home Rule was discussed. Two years later, at the Third National Assembly, a Scottish Covenant was drafted and duly signed by the delegates. The last paragraph read:

> " ... we solemnly enter into this Covenant whereby we pledge ourselves in all loyalty to the Crown and within the framework of the United Kingdom, to do everything in our power to secure for Scotland a Parliament with adequate legislative authority in Scottish affairs." (J Brand *The National Movement in Scotland* p. 246)

The Covenant was a huge success with the Scottish people in 1949. About 2 million signatures were recorded, of which at least 1.5 million were genuine. But from the

Labour Government's point of view, what did the Covenant prove? Signatures were not votes. As Webb points out:

> "Without votes in a Parliamentary election, Government was not going to recognise nationalism as a political force...Thus, while the Scottish Convention and the Covenant Association were splendid failures, they were always doomed to fail." (K Webb *The Growth of Nationalism in Scotland* p. 61)

The SNP Eclipsed 1942-62

For most of the 20 years after 1942, the torch of Scottish nationalism was carried by the Scottish Convention, leaving the SNP very much in the shade. There was one brief glimmer of light when Dr Robert MacIntyre became the first SNP MP at the Motherwell by-election in April 1945. However, this victory was achieved during the unnatural conditions of a wartime political truce by the major parties. MacIntyre was unceremoniously ejected from his seat 2 months later at the first post war general election.

With the MacCormick Home Rule faction out of the way, the SNP fell into the hands of the fundamentalists, led by Arthur Donaldson and MacIntyre. These two increasingly took control of the party. They were intent on establishing a clear line of policy and on purging the party of those elements who had reduced the effectiveness of the organisation in the past. The SNP was to be an election-fighting party and independence for Scotland was the aim. In essence, the SNP was reverting to the NPS position of 1928. From the hardliners' point of view, the merger with the Scottish Party in 1934 had caused nothing but trouble.

If the leaders of the SNP could take satisfaction in the new-found unity and purity of the party, they failed to realise that the vast majority of the Scottish people did not want complete independence. Consequently, the SNP almost disappeared from sight in the 1940s and 1950s. Membership of the party hovered between 1500 and 2000 and there were probably fewer than 20 branches throughout Scotland. Brand quotes a source as saying that there were only 2 fully operational branches in the whole of Scotland at the end of the 1950s. As table 10.4 shows, the SNP's electoral performance was disastrous. Less than 1% of the electorate supported the SNP during the 1950s. No matter how many signatures were appended to the Scottish Covenant, the only statistics which mattered for the government were votes for the SNP - and they clearly indicated a lack of commitment to Home Rule and independence.

SNP Electoral Performance 1945 -59		
General Elections	Number of Candidates	% of Votes
1945	8	1.2
1950	4	0.4
1951	2	0.3
1955	2	0.5
1959	5	0.8

Table 10.4

The turning point in the SNP's fortunes came in 1961-2 with the Bridgeton and West Lothian by-elections. Ian MacDonald gained 18.7% of the vote at Bridgeton in November 1961 - by far the best SNP result for a long time. Enthused by the result, MacDonald, a wealthy farmer, offered his services to the party for a token salary. Thus, he became the first full-time National Organiser in June 1962. Immediately, he gathered together a core of young activists to canvass the West Lothian constituency. To everyone's amazement, the SNP candidate, Billy Wolfe polled 9,450 votes and came second to the formidable Tam Dalyell (Labour). Both the Liberal and Conservative candidates lost their deposits. From now on, the major parties could not discount the SNP as an irrelevance and the voting public began to alter its perception of the SNP. A vote for the SNP might not be a wasted vote.

THE RISE AND FALL OF THE SNP 1962-79

After West Lothian, the SNP turned its attention to increasing party membership and putting the organisation on a sound, efficient footing. Two years previously, the National Council had initiated a membership drive by intro-

The eleven SNP MPs elected at the October 1974 General Election

113

Membership of the SNP 1962-83			
1962	2,000	1967	80,000
1963	4,000	1968	120,000
1964	8,000	1971	70,000
1965 (June)	16,000	1974	85,000
1965 (Nov)	20,000	1983	c.20,000
1966	42,000		

Table 10.5

ducing a business reply card system. However, the whole process was accelerated by the energetic new National Organiser. Largely due to MacDonald's efforts, the number of branches nearly doubled every year until the peak of 500 branches was reached in 1968. The membership of the party also showed nearly geometric progression up to 1968.

On the fund-raising side, the SNP had Angus MacGilliveray, a former West Lothian baker. He started up the Alba Pools which netted the party £200,000 in the first 5 years and publications run by him turned over more than £50,000.

Growth in Number of SNP Branches			
May 1962	18	December 1967	484
May 1963	41	April 1969	500
1965	140	March 1971	518
December 1966	205		

Table 10.6

EXPLAINING THE GROWTH OF NATIONALISM

In this last section, we will look at some of the contending theories put forward to explain the rise of the SNP and Scottish nationalism in general.

The Protest Vote Explanation

According to this theory, those who started voting for the SNP in the late 1960s and 1970s were not 'genuine' Scottish nationalists but were temporarily disillusioned with their own preferred party. Their vote was essentially negative and usually directed against the party in power. The protest voter rarely changes allegiance from one major party to the other, because the ideological distance between Labour and Conservative is too great. As a compromise, he or she protested by casting a vote for a third party. In Scotland, the SNP become a viable repository for the protest vote from the late 1960s.

Some facts seem to fit the theory. The theory states that protest voting usually takes place at by-elections when the outcome will not affect the governmental ambitions of the protest voter's preferred party. At the general election, the voter usually returns to his or her original party. This seemed to have occurred to the SNP when they did very well at the Pollock and Hamilton by-elections in 1967, yet only achieved 11% of the vote nationally at the 1970 General Election.

Criticisms of the Protest Vote Theory
If the SNP benefited from the protest vote in the 1960s and 1970s, why didn't the other third party, the Liberals benefit too? Of course, this can be answered by the observation that the Liberals benefited in the 1980s, at the expense of the SNP. (see Table 10.7)

The protest vote is, by definition, very volatile since it is made up of people with no firm allegiance to the party and who tend to switch back to their preferred party at general elections. We would therefore expect the SNP vote to fluctuate wildly. It has not. The SNP percentage of the vote declined by 16% between 1974 and 1987. This was the same as the Conservative decline between 1964 and 1974.

The protest vote theory relies too heavily on analysing election statistics and fails to account for underlying social, economic, political and historical causes.

The theory assumes that the SNP is the passive recipient of votes when, in fact, we know that the party, by its own energy and organisation, caused at least some of its own success.

Key Dates and Electoral Statistics 1964 - 79

1964	At the General Election, the SNP put up 15 candidates, 8 of whom saved their deposits.
1966	At the General Election, the SNP put up 23 candidates, 16 of whom saved their deposits.
1967	At the May municipal elections, the SNP won 16% of the vote and 23 seats. In November, Winnie Ewing (SNP) won the Hamilton by-election to become the first post-war SNP MP.
1968	At the municipal elections, the SNP made 103 gains, mostly at the expense of Labour. The SNP won 30% of the vote. In Glasgow, SNP councillors held the balance of power.
1969	SNP polled only 22% at the municipal elections. Glasgow councillors gained a poor reputation - several were frequently absent from meetings.
1970	SNP polled 20% at the South Ayrshire by-election and only 12.6% at the local elections. In June, at the General Election, the SNP share of the vote was 11.4%. Hamilton was lost, but Western Isles was gained (Donald Stewart).
1971	The SNP candidate came second to Labour with 34.6% in the Stirling, Falkirk and Grangemouth by-election.
1973	Victory for Margo MacDonald at the Govan by-election in November. This had been a safe Labour seat
1974	The SNP gained 21.9% of the vote and 7 MPs at the February General Election. At the subsequent General Election in October, the SNP reached its peak with 30.4% of the vote and 11 M.P.s The party was now the second largest in Scotland after Labour
1978	SNP failed to win both the Glasgow Garscadden and the Hamilton by-elections.
1979	The SNP lost all but 2 of its MPs at the General Election and its share of the vote dropped to 17.3%.

Colonial Explanations

If the protest vote theory can be criticised for being too narrow, only looking at voting statistics and also taking a short-term view of nationalism, the colonial explanations go deeper and take a longer perspective.

Decline of Empire Theory

Scotland benefited from the 1707 Act of Union. It enabled Scots to participate in and profit from the English colonial trade. However, as Britain shed its Empire in the post-1945 period and the country sank economically from great power status, it put great strains on the UK. Scots who no longer benefited from the Union felt less need to maintain a British identity. Perhaps the logical end-point of the decolonisation process should be the break-up of the UK into its constituent nations? After all, other small nations in Europe were flourishing. Maybe Scotland would be better off as an independent state and no longer dependent on the poor economic performance of 'Great' Britain? Such feelings were heightened in the 1970s during the successful 'It's Scotland's Oil' campaign when the nationalists claimed that Scots would be much better off if the oil wealth was shared among 5 million instead of 55 million people.

Flaws in the Theory

The theory implies that Britain's economic and political status declined as a result of the loss of the Empire. In fact, Britain's economic position was declining long before it shed the Empire - arguably at the turn of the century and certainly after the First World War. As we saw in Chapter 8, Britain's poor economic performance was due mostly to internal problems - lack of Government policies, outdated technology, overmanning, lack of investment etc. By the 1970s when the SNP made their greatest gains, Empire was a dead issue. The decolonisation process was complete and Britain had voted itself into the EEC.

The Internal Colonialism Theory

This was proposed by Michael Hechter in 1975. He claimed that the small peripheral Celtic regions of the UK are in a colonial relationship with the major core area of England. Scotland is portrayed as an exploited culture, economically dominated from south of the border. Hechter (like Nairn) sees *nationalism as a reaction to this exploitation and domination*.

One of the weaknesses of Hechter's thesis is that it claims a colonial relationship has existed for some 300 years, but it does not offer convincing evidence why Scottish nationalism lay dormant for so long. (Remember that Nairn explains Scotland's lack of a nationalist movement in the 19th century by the fact that Scotland did very well out of the relationship with England and the Empire at that time.) It is also difficult to accept that Scotland has been exploited in terms of its language and religion, as Hechter claims. Unlike Welsh nationalism, there has never been a strong demand for Gaelic to be protected in Scotland. As for religious domination, it simply has not been an issue. This is because the largest Protestant organisation, the Church of Scotland had its position as the established church guaranteed by the Act of Union.

There is better evidence for Hechter's proposition that the Scottish economy has become increasingly controlled from outside (although not necessarily from England). According to Webb, 59% of Scottish manufacturing industry in the 1970s was outwith Scottish control. This was particularly true in Clydeside where shipbuilding and heavy engineering dominated. As the 'old' industries were progressively replaced by the new industries in 'Silicon Glen', the pattern of overseas ownership was even more marked. Of course, it could be argued that foreign penetration and the rise of the multinational company were features of all the developed economies and not unique to Scotland. Hechter does not provide convincing linkages between economic domination and the rise of the SNP. In fact, he says that nationalism in the Celtic periphery is expressed more broadly as the anti-Conservative/Unionist vote. If we accept such a general definition, then we can see that Scotland has been displaying nationalistic tendencies throughout the 1970s and 1980s. During that period, the Conservative vote has never risen to more than about 30% and especially during the years of the Thatcher Government (1979 - 1990), it pushed the Conservatives into third place.

The Realignment of Scottish Politics Explanation

Both Webb and Brand, writing in the mid-1970s at the crest of the SNP wave, concluded that many Scottish voters no longer acted in similar ways to voters in the rest of the UK Three basic propositions can be detected in their books. Firstly, UK voters as a whole and Scottish voters in particular, have become more and more disillusioned with the two major parties. The evidence for this is clear. In figure 10.2, the aggregate percentage of votes for Labour and Conservative since 1945 are shown.

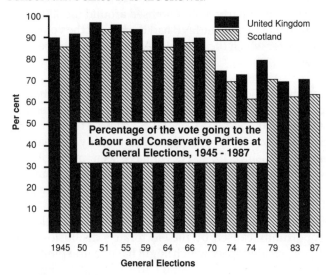

Figure 10.2

We can see that the two major parties' share of the vote in the UK generally has gone down from over 90% in the early 1950s to a consistent failure to reach 80% of the votes from 1974 onwards. The two-party system is not dead, but there has been more scope for a third party to do well (in votes if not in terms of MPs). In Scotland, this trend has been even more marked. Notice how up until 1964, Scots voted in even greater numbers than the UK as a whole for the two big parties. However, since then they have turned towards the third parties (ie. Liberals and the SNP). Table 10.7 below shows the Scottish electoral statistics for the period after 1964 when the key changes appear to have started.

115

Share of the Vote Received by Parties (%)						
Election	Cons	Lab	Lib	SNP	Cons & Lab	Lib & SNP
1964	41	49	8	2	90	10
1966	38	50	7	5	88	12
1970	38	45	6	11	83	17
1974	33	37	8	22	70	30
1974	25	36	8	30	61	39
1979	31	42	9	17	73	27
1983	29	34	25	12	63	37
1987	24	42	19	14	66	34

Table 10.7

We can see that although both major parties suffered loss of support, the Conservative vote simply collapsed. This is in marked contrast to the UK pattern. Whereas the UK electorate returned 3 successive Conservative Governments in 1979, 1983 and 1987, more than two-thirds of Scottish voters rejected the Tories. Irrespective of whether this anti-Conservative vote reflects higher levels of nationalism than the SNP vote alone, it is certainly true that it puts a strain on the Union and keeps alive the issue of devolution.

Since 1964, the Labour Party has been dominant in Scotland, but table 10.7 shows us that Labour has generally lost about 10% of its share of the vote since then. This leeching of votes from the 'big two' has benefited the Liberals and the SNP. If we combine the votes for the two minor parties, we can see a clear change in their fortunes after 1974. Before then, they hovered around in the 10-17% range, but after 1974, they have only once gained less than a 30% share. This compares favourably with Labour's and Conservative's individual scores. It would appear then, that the 'third party' vote stabilised around the 30% mark. Within that figure, the SNP had the bulk of the votes up to 1979, after which the Liberals/Alliance were the beneficiaries.

Another indication of the disillusionment with the two-party system is the turnout of voters at general elections. At the 1950 and 1951 General Elections, the turnout in Scotland was 81%. The figure has steadily decreased to about 75% since 1974. As we have seen, many of those voters who did continue to vote, turned away from Conservative and Labour and chose first the SNP and later the Liberals. As Webb says, "The success of nationalism in Scotlan ... was not due solely to the arrival of an electoral opportunity caused by the electorate's disillusion. This merely created space which might have been exploited just as successfully by the Liberal Party as it was by the SNP."
(K Webb *The Growth of Nationalism in Scotland* p. 98)

This brings us to the second proposition which is that *the SNP itself created opportunities to exploit growing disillusionment with the UK parties.* We have already noted much of the evidence for this. There was the concentration on the build-up of grass-roots organisation during the 1960s; branches, membership and party finance all shot up; the party structure was reorganised to take account of this transformation of the SNP into a mass political party; by-elections were fought vigorously with young activists bussed in to canvass constituencies thoroughly; the discovery of North Sea oil was ruthlessly and successfully exploited by the party in the early 1970s.

The third proposition is that *there has been a shift away from voting according to the social class a person identifies with, towards a 'national identification' which benefited the SNP.* Both Webb and Brand observed such a trend in the 1970s. However, it has to be said that with the decline of the SNP in the 1980s, this proposition does not appear so convincing.

For the last 50 years, political scientists have consistently observed a clear relationship between a person's social class and their voting behaviour. For example, if you happened to be an unskilled manual worker who was a trade union member living in a council house on a large council estate, the likelihood that you would vote Labour was very high indeed. Conversely, the more middle class a person was, the greater the chance that he or she would vote Conservative. However, we have seen that there has been a weakening of support for the two 'class parties' in the last 20 years. The SNP undoubtedly saw the opportunity to attract voters from all social classes by promoting a national, classless image. Certainly in the 1970s, there was good evidence to show that the party's 'catch-all' strategy was paying off, as table 10.8 shows.

Social Class and the Vote - June 1975				
	AB	C1	C2	DE
Conservative	56	40	23	22
Labour	14	23	39	48
Liberal	10	6	6	6
SNP	20	30	32	23
Other	-	1	-	1

Table 10.8
(Source: Based on an ORC survey for the *Scotsman* June 1975)

People are classified according to whether they have high-status professional occupations (AB) to unskilled manual occupations (DE). Conservative and Labour still appear to attract a class-based support, but the SNP vote is spread across the whole spectrum of society.

All of the above led both Webb and Brand (writing before the 1979 General Election) to believe that there had been a restructuring of Scottish and British politics.

"The desire for increased autonomy has probably since the Union always been widespread in Scotland, but it has not been felt intensely and neither has it been high on the list of priorities. But it has been there, and its emergence now must indicate that there is a permanent realignment of the British political structure."
(K Webb - *The Growth of Nationalism in Scotland* p. 104)

"The crucial connection seems to have been forged by a gradual restructuring of the political consciousness of the Scottish electorate in such a way that they began to perceive themselves as Scots in terms of their political interests rather than as, for example, members of the working class."
(J Brand *The National Movement in Scotland* p. 301)

"Evidence of Scottish nationalism was seen in a ... survey of national identity, reported in the *Glasgow*

Herald (18 Aug. 1980). In response to the question 'Which of the statements best describes how you regard yourself?', 69% gave predominantly or exclusively Scottish identity, with only 10% a predominantly or exclusively British identity."

(J Kellas *The Scottish Political System* p. 266)

After the 1979 General Election, the SNP's fortunes declined both in 1983 and 1987. The party in 1987 received less than half its October 1974 vote. So, does this invalidate the three propositions we have put forward? I think not. It is still in the interest of the SNP to portray itself as a classless, national party (proposition 3). The dilemma it faces is this: to take votes away from the largest party (Labour), the SNP must produce left-of-centre policies. The more it does this, the less it is able to claim to be a 'national' party.

As for proposition 1, Scottish voters have, up till 1991, continued to reject the two major parties in significant numbers. The most serious effect of this was the collapse of the Conservative Party vote in Scotland while the rest of the UK returned three consecutive Conservative Governments - the so-called *Doomsday Scenario*. Both Labour and the SNP claimed that the Conservative Government had no 'mandate' to rule in Scotland and there were renewed attempts to get devolution put back on the political agenda.

Perhaps the weakness of proposition 2 is that it assumes that only the third parties could exploit the disillusionment with the major parties. The fact is that all the parties are in competition with each other and it is unrealistic to assume that, for example, Labour would passively allow the SNP to grow at its expense. The SNP had everything going its way up until about 1975 with the campaign for 'Scotland's oil'. However, the Labour Government then took the initiative by putting forward the *Scotland and Wales Bill* in 1977-9. This effectively stole the SNP's thunder. There was little point in voting for the SNP if the Labour Party was going to deliver a Scottish Assembly. The SNP were also forced to take a stance on devolution, which served to split the party once again between the Home Rulers and those wishing complete independence. The rest of the story is well known (and is told in more detail in Chapter 11). The Scottish electorate failed to vote in sufficient numbers for a Scottish Assembly in the referendum of March, 1979. The SNP vote slumped dramatically in the subsequent General Election in October. This prompted the independence faction in the SNP to set up the '79 Group' with the aim of breaking the devolutionist stranglehold on the party. The '79 Group' were expelled at the 1981 Party Conference. In the meantime, the public image of the party had changed - the SNP was seen to be riven with conflict and therefore unworthy of support. Party membership and finance slumped. The 1983 and 1987 General Election results do not encourage the view that the party is reviving.

The major constraint on past and future progress for the party is the fact that there has never been more than 20% of the Scottish public in favour of complete independence. If the SNP goes down the independence road, it may well be that it is a dead end - it can never expect to gain a majority of seats in Scotland. On the other hand, the more moderate it becomes, the less distinctive it appears to voters. After all, both Labour and the Liberal Democrats have a firm commitment to devolution as evidenced by their participation in the Scottish Convention. The Convention finally reported in September 1990, advocating a Scottish Assembly with strong revenue-raising powers. Where this leaves the SNP is difficult to say. There is no doubt that it has overcome the credibility problem. The other parties take the SNP seriously and it has had a permanent presence in Parliament since 1967. This is a significant achievement. If we reflect back to the 1850s and indeed to many of the intervening years, we can say that Scottish nationalism in all its aspects has been on the rise and shows little sign of going away.

11 Scottish Devolution 1850-1979

In this chapter, we will be looking at the history of *administrative and legislative devolution* in Scotland since the mid-19th century. In order to do this with some understanding and clarity, it will first of all be necessary to find out the precise meanings of these terms. *Administrative devolution in Scotland is concerned with the granting of certain administrative powers by and from central government to the Scottish Office and the Secretary of State for Scotland.* In the first section then, we will be studying the background to the creation of the Scottish Office in 1885 and the subsequent growth of that Office up till 1979. We should also be clear that, although the Scottish Office has seen an increase in its staff and its role in Scottish affairs, it is still part of the central government apparatus and its powers are defined by and from the centre.

By legislative devolution in Scotland, we mean the granting of law-making powers by and from central government to a Scottish legislature. Unlike administrative devolution, which has been ongoing for the last 100 years, Scotland had not by 1991 achieved a devolved legislature. Consequently, the second section of the chapter will seek to trace the background to as well as the various attempts to gain a Scottish Assembly.

The term 'devolution' is relatively modern, only really gaining currency in the last 30 years. Before then, politicians used the term 'Home Rule' to indicate what we nowadays would call legislative devolution. Confusingly, another term was incorrectly used up until the 1930 ie. Federal Devolution. This term was used to mean the granting of Parliaments to all the nations within the United Kingdom with the Imperial Parliament continuing to manage the common business of the whole country. A more accurate description of this proposal was the term 'Home Rule All Round'.

ADMINISTRATIVE DEVOLUTION

1707 - 1850

Scotland's claim for 'special treatment' of its affairs goes back to the Act of Union of 1707. Scotland, it is important to note, was not completely submerged into the UK political system. It retained its own legal and educational systems and the established Church of Scotland. Having a separate and distinctive legal system in particular meant that the interests of Scots law would have to be represented in London; hence the Lord Advocate, Scotland's chief law officer, held the position of government minister after 1707. Scotland also kept its Secretary of State and Scottish Departments. Although Parliamentary Union was complete in the sense that there was now only one Parliament in London, as far as the administration of Scottish affairs was concerned, Scotland retained a good deal of autonomy. In other words, administrative devolution was built into, or arose out of, the Act of Union

So what happened between 1707 and 1850 to create new demands for the devolution of administrative powers to Scotland? Firstly, the post of Secretary of State for Scotland was abolished in 1746 in the aftermath of the Jacobite Rising. In 1707, there had been those, like Daniel Defoe, who feared that Scotland would not be wholly integrated into the Union as long as it had its own government ministers, and the '45 Rising proved to be the last straw. (The last incumbent, the Marquess of Tweeddale did not help his own case when, three weeks after Bonnie Prince Charlie had landed at Eriskay, he wrote to the Lord Advocate that it was "very doubtful if the Pretender's son be himself actually landed in Scotland". (Sir David Milne *The Scottish Office* p.11))

From 1746 until 1782, Scotland was run by the Northern Department and for the next century by the Home Office. While the Secretary of State for the Home Office was now officially responsible for the running of Scottish affairs, in practice real political power lay with the Lord Advocate and the 'Scottish Manager'. By the early 19th century, the Lord Advocate had acquired considerable political power, prompting one English newspaper to write:

> "Arrived in Edinburgh - the Lord High Chancellor of Scotland, the Lord Justice General, the Lord Privy Seal, the Privy Council and the Lord Advocate, all in one post chaise, containing only a single person."
> (Sir David Milne *The Scottish Office* p. 12)

In practice though, the Lord Advocate was usually bound up with his legal responsibilities, leaving little time for political business.

This is where the 'Scottish Manager' comes in. His was an unofficial post which fell to the Scotsman who happened to be in the Cabinet at the time. He was expected to oversee Scotland's political affairs. If the 'Manager' wished, he had a great deal of political power to wield, in particular the power to appoint many top posts. The most famous (or notorious) of the Scottish managers was Henry Dundas. At the height of his 'reign' in 1802, he controlled the nomination of 43 out of the 45 Scottish MPs returned at the general election. Opinions about Dundas and his effect on Scottish political life differ widely:

> "... a man of considerable administrative capacity as well as influence, who towered over Scotland."
> (Sir David Milne *The Scottish Office* p.11-12)

> "As totalitarian regimes went, the 'Dundas despotism' was more clumsy than savage and its increasing unpopularity stemmed more from its incompetence ... than from its viciousness."
> (Christopher Harvie *Scotland and Nationalism* p.82)

Whether one is inclined to the former or the latter view, it is surely true that Scotland was at this time being governed in an autocratic manner. Power was centred in the hands of one man who was accountable only to his Cabinet colleagues. Few, if any, in the Cabinet were particularly interested in the minutiae of Scottish affairs. After 1827 though, there was no one to take up the position of Manager and consequently responsibility for Scotland reverted to the Home Secretary. This led to complaints from Scotland that it was being neglected. According to one historian, Scots had become "among the least governed people in Europe". (HJ Hanham *The Creation of the Scottish Office* in *Judicial Review* p.205, 1965) They were also poorly represented. The Lord Advocate was no longer a member of the Cabinet so, apart from the Home Secretary, there was no one to take Parliamentary responsibility for the control of Scottish administration.

1850 - 1887

With the widening of the franchise in 1832 and 1868, and the introduction of the secret ballot in 1872, there was considerably less scope for corrupt practices or 'management' of the system. Increasingly, Scottish MPs set the agenda for Scottish politics. By the late 1860s, both Liberal and Tory MPs had agreed that something must be done about the neglect of Scottish affairs. As far back as 1853, the National Association for the Vindication of Scottish Rights had called for the restoration of the post of Secretary of State. In 1869, a majority of MPs wrote a letter to Gladstone (then Prime Minister) pointing out the need for a Scottish Minister. Gladstone duly set up a Royal Commission of Inquiry, under Lord Camperdown, to look into the matter. The Commissioners recommended what the MPs had been advocating. Neither Gladstone nor Disraeli when he became Prime Minister in 1874, acted on this recommendation.

As we have seen, Scotland had had a raw deal. Up until the 1820s, it had relied on a patronising 'manager'; for the next 50 years, it had no manager at all. The need for efficient administration was ever more pressing. With the onset of industrialisation, the existing social service agencies (the Church, charity, local government) were not able to deal with rapid social and economic change. Alongside this antiquated local provision were a number of administrative Boards based in Edinburgh. These Boards were only loosely controlled by central government and were in need of coordination and political control.

Boards in existence prior to the Scottish Office

1 Board of Manufactures 1726 - 1906
2 Fisheries Board 1808 - 1939
3 Board of Supervision for Poor Relief
   1845 - 1894
4 General Board of Commissioners in Lunacy
   1857-1913
5 Prison Commission 1877 - 1928

It was in the context of the persistent neglect of Scottish affairs and the inefficiency of the Scottish administrative system, that political pressure was reapplied in 1881. The key figure was now the Earl of Rosebery, a young Liberal politician who had the advantage of being a good friend of Gladstone. Rosebery and the Earl of Fife spoke in the House of Lords about the need for a minister of Scottish affairs, with Rosebery warning that, "The words Home Rule have begun to be distinctly and loudly mentioned in Scotland". (Sir Reginald Coupland *Welsh and Scottish Nationalism - A Study* p. 295) Gladstone reacted by appointing Rosebery as Parliamentary Undersecretary of State at the Home Office with the remit of reorganising Scottish administration. Here Rosebery met with considerable opposition from both the Home Office and the Treasury. They maintained

that since there was hardly any Scottish business transacted through their Departments, the effort and expense required to set up a separate Scottish Office would outweigh any advantages gained. The existing practice of the Home Office was simply to send "the whole of the Scotch Papers" to the Lord Advocate, whose secretary was left to sort them out. Rosebery tried to persuade the Home Office that this was an unsatisfactory way to treat Scottish matters, but to no avail. His appeal for the appointment of a clerk to supervise Scottish business was also turned down.

Since he was making little headway with the Home Office, Rosebery now resolved to accelerate the campaign for an independent Scottish Office and a Scottish Secretary with a seat in the Cabinet. Gladstone was opposed to this, but as a concession agreed to put the matter to a Select Committee of Enquiry in April 1883. Rosebery interpreted this as a delaying tactic and resigned a month later. He wrote:

"From the day of the first meeting of the new Parliament until the present day of its third session...not one minute of Government time has been allotted to Scotland or Scottish affairs. Can you be surprised that the people of Scotland complain?"
(Sir Reginald Coupland *Welsh and Scottish Nationalism* p. 295)

Rosebery's resignation seems to have been a futile gesture because first the committee of enquiry and then the Cabinet came down in favour of the creation of a Scottish Office. However, the necessary legislation to bring this about was blocked in the Lords in June 1883 and the following year in the Commons. The *Secretary for Scotland Act* was finally passed by the new Conservative Government headed by Lord Salisbury in August 1885. By this time, Rosebery had lost interest and the post of Scottish Secretary fell to the Duke of Richmond and Gordon. Ironically, the Duke had, up until this time, been firmly opposed to the idea of a Scottish Secretary. Replying to Salisbury's offer of the post, he wrote:

"You know my opinion on the office, and that it is quite unnecessary, but the Country and Parliament think otherwise - and the office has been created and someone must fill it. Under these circumstances, I am quite ready to take it and will do my best to make it a success (if that is possible!)" (HJ Hanham *The Creation of the Scottish Office* in *Judicial Review* p. 229, 1965)

The powers of the new Secretary for Scotland and his department, the Scottish Office, were decided over the two years after 1885. Here again, the Treasury and the Home Office fought a rearguard action to retain as much power as possible at the centre. Most contentious of all was the question of education. The position here was that the Scottish educational system had kept its distinctive qualities under the Act of Union. However, after the Education Act of 1872, Scottish education was administered by the Scotch Committee of Council for Education and the Scotch Education Department, both of which were working within the English Education Department. Since 1872, the Scotch Education Department had been attempting to anglicise Scottish education and was against its transfer to the Scottish Secretary. A curious ally of the SED was the Educational Institute for Education, nowadays the largest teachers' union and a staunch defender of the autonomy of Scottish education! Much of Scottish opinion, though, was in favour of the transfer.

When the education clause of the Secretary for Scotland Bill reached the House of Commons in 1885, there was a fierce debate over the merits of including education in the powers transferred to the Scottish minister. Sir Lyon Playfair, one of the two MPs representing the Scottish Universities, attacked the proposal as a backward step:

"This Bill is intended to accentuate the differences between England and Scotland for the future and, in my opinion, it will tend to convert Scotland into a Province, with the narrower peculiarities of Provincial existence. No country can less afford than Scotland to narrow the ambition of its educated classes or to parochialise its institutions. If it separates itself from England in administration and education, it need not be surprised if in time England becomes less of an outlet for Scotch enterprize." (HJ Hanham *The Creation of the Scottish Office* in *Judicial Review* p. 219, 1965)

Despite this dire warning, the Bill was passed intact and the Secretary for Scotland became Vice-President of the Scotch Education Department - in effect, the minister for Scottish education.

The other important dispute which arose out of the Act was over the question of law and order. Both the Home Office and the Scottish Office appeared to have responsibilities in this area and almost immediately the two were to clash over the handling of the 'Crofters' War' in the Western Isles. The Home Office claimed that its role was to maintain law and order, including the suppression of disturbances such as those occurring in the Highlands. The Scottish Office, on the other hand, now had responsibility for control of the local police and for local government in the areas where the disturbances were taking place. In the end, the Home Office took charge, leaving the Scottish Secretary, Arthur Balfour, with the unenviable task of having to defend the Home Secretary's policy over which he had no control. Eventually, Balfour referred the matter to the Cabinet in September 1886. He argued that law and order in the Highlands should come under his control alone and that the present arrangement was intolerable:

"At present, the Scottish Secretary is supposed...to be responsible for the action of the Central Government in dealing with the disorders now prevalent in the West of Scotland. But...the Secretary for Scotland has no more to do with restoring law and order in Skye and in Tyree than he has in restoring order in Belfast and Kerry. The whole duty lies with the Home Secretary and with the Lord Advocate who are not required to consult, or even to keep informed, the (Scottish) Secretary at Dover House." (HJ Hanham *The Creation of the Scottish Office* in *Judicial Review* p.224, 1965)

The Cabinet agreed with Balfour and transferred the control of law and order from the Home Office to the Scottish Office. This transfer was brought into effect by the *Secretary for Scotland Act (1885) Amendment Act, 1887*. The Act also transferred all the other residual powers to the Scottish Office, with the exception of responsibility for mines and explosives, workshops and factories. Now that it had 'won' its various battles, the Scottish Office could settle down to become "the unchallenged agency of the central government for 'purely Scottish affairs', and the Scottish Secretary was regarded as 'Scotland's Minister'." (James Kellas *Modern Scotland* p. 96)

1887 - 1939

The period up to the outbreak of the Second World War saw the steady growth of the Scottish Office and a corresponding increase in the status of the Scottish Secretary. In 1885, the Scottish Office inherited a staff of 4 to deal with Scottish correspondence. As table 11.1 shows, the volume of work immediately shot up after the creation of a separate office and the staff were forced to forego holidays for 3 years until extra clerks were appointed. This was in marked contrast to the SED which had a staff of 30.

Scottish Correspondence		
Date	**In Letters**	**Out Letters**
Home Office		
1885	3111	
1886	4998	4134
1887	6387	4778
Scottish Office		
1888	9041	6234
1889	9098	6394
1890	9617	6718

Table 11.1 (Source: H J Hanham *The Creation of the Scottish Office* in *Judicial Review* p. 209, 1965)

By 1939, the role of government had expanded considerably and this was reflected in the increase in the Scottish Office staff to 117. If the various Departments and Boards are added, the figure rises to over 2000. (By the late 1970s, the Scottish Office had 10,000 civil servants).

The position of the Scottish Secretary also improved during this period. After 1892, all Scottish Secretaries were, in practice, members of the Cabinet, although it was 1926 before the post was officially upgraded to Secretary of State for Scotland with automatic Cabinet status. Incredibly, another 11 years passed before the Scottish Secretary of State was paid the same salary as his Cabinet colleagues of similar rank. In 1926, Sir John Gilmour was getting £3000 less than the UK Secretaries of State. Along with the new political and financial status of the Scottish Secretary, the Scottish Office Headquarters were finally transferred from London to St Andrew's House in Edinburgh.

The 19th century administrative Boards came in for scrutiny in 1914. The Royal Commission on the Civil Service recommended that Boards should be reorganised into Government Departments with a civil service recruitment and career structure. At this time, top Board members could be appointed with little or no administrative background. Eventually in 1928, the Commission's recommendations were put into practice. All except two of the Boards were transferred into Scottish Office Departments. The Gilmour Report in 1937 finally brought all the Scottish agencies under the direct political control of the Secretary of State, and the Scottish Office was reorganised into 4 large Departments - Health, Education, Agriculture and the Home Department. The Gilmour Report reorganised the Scottish Office into a recognisably modern form.

1707 Office of Secretary of State for Scotland retained by Act of Union.

1746 Office of Secretary of State dropped in the aftermath of the Jacobite rebellion. Lord Advocate now the only official Scottish government minister.

1828 Home Secretary takes over responsibility for Scottish affairs.

1885 Creation of Scottish Office and Scottish Secretary. Over the next two yearsthe Scottish Office takes over most of the existing Home Office functions.

1892 Scottish Secretary thereafter always a Cabinet member.

1926 Scottish Secretary elevated in rank to Principal Secretary of State with automatic Cabinet status.

1928 The various Boards absorbed into the Scottish Office.

1937 Gilmour Report reorganises the Scottish Office into 4 large Departments.

1939 -1979

Since the Gilmour Report, the trend has been for the Scottish Office to acquire further functions to administer. During the Second World War, Thomas Johnstone, the Scottish Secretary set up the North of Scotland Hydro-Electric Board and that, along with Crown Lands and the Forestry Commission was added to the Scottish Office remit. Given that the Government was busy running the war, the energetic Johnstone and his team were allowed unprecedented scope to govern Scotland. All this changed, though, with the advent of the post war Labour Government, which was more concerned with national ie. British policies. Nevertheless, there was a recognition that officials should be sensitive to Scottish opinion. A Treasury memo issued in 1946 to UK Departments stressed the need to "devolve upon their Scottish representatives sufficient authority to enable Scottish business to be settled on the spot, with the minimum of reference to London, and should ensure that in the settlement of large matters of principle, Scottish aspects are fully considered". (James Kellas *Modern Scotland* p. 102) However, no additional functions were devolved to the Scottish Office during the Labour period from 1945 - 51.

Under Churchill's Conservative Government from 1951-5, another Minister of State was added to the Scottish Office team. In 1952, the government set up the Balfour Commission to look (again) at the administration of Scotland. This was on a smaller scale than the Gilmour Report and Balfour recommended that highways, the appointment of JPs and control of animal diseases should be devolved to the Scottish Office. This was duly carried out over the following 4 years.

Scotland was to come under the spotlight once more in the late 1950s due to the downturn in its economic fortunes. In 1959, Scotland's unemployment rate of 4.4% was double the UK rate. Clearly, devolution of some administrative functions had not helped the Scottish economy. An enquiry into the state of the economy was now started. The Toothill Report (1961) recommended the setting up of a new department in the Scottish Office to oversee planning and development and that to advise on economic and

industrial policy. This was carried out in 1962. The new Scottish Development Department took responsibility for industry and development, roads, railways, electricity, local government, housing, town and country planning and environmental services. From then onwards, the Scottish Office began to expand its role in economic affairs. The following organisations were established:

- 1965 Highlands and Islands Development Board
- 1966 Scottish Economic Planning Board and Council
- 1973 Scottish Economic Planning Department
- 1975 Scottish Development Agency

In addition to an increased role in the Scottish economy, the trend was for the Scottish Office to gain more and more functions at the expense of the UK Departments. On the other hand, when one compares the Scottish Office functions with those of the UK Departments in Scotland, it is clear that the really important powers are still in the hands of the UK Departments.

The Principal Functions of Central Government in Scotland (1979)	
British Departments	**Scottish Departments**
Treasury	Dept. of Agriculture & Fisheries
Board of Inland Revenue	Scottish Development Dept.
Board of Customs & Excise	Scottish Economic Planning .
Dept. of Trade	Scottish Education Dept.
Dept. of Industry	Scottish Home & Health Dept.
Dept. of Energy	
Dept. of Employment	
Dept. of Transport	
Dept. of the Environment	
Dept. of Health & Social Security	
Dept. of Education and Science	
Ministry of Defence	
Ministry of Agriculture, Fisheries & Food	
Home Office	
Foreign & Commonwealth Office	
Cabinet Office	

Table 11.2   (Source: Adapted from James Kellas *Scottish Political System*, 4th ed., p. 34-6)

Conclusion

Throughout this section, we have seen that administrative devolution has meant the transfer of powers from UK Departments to the Scottish Office. Does this mean then, that Scotland has achieved a measure of autonomy or independence from the rest of the UK in the way that it is governed? The answer, according to most writers on the subject, is no.

"...it is a fact that despite the proliferation of Scottish government agencies since (the 1880s), government is more centralised today. The increase in government activity has strengthened the real policy-makers (the principal UK ministers) who have the substance of power. The shadow is left to the Scottish departments...

Thus, the lack of a Scottish Office in 1870 did not mean that Scotland was more governed from London than it is today. On the contrary, such government as then existed was in the hands of local leaders in church,

New St. Andrew's House, Edinburgh

school and castle. Assimilation throughout Britain has proceeded ever since, by popular demand, and in essentials will continue."
(James Kellas *Modern Scotland* p. 111)

"The Scottish Office... is exceptional among British Government departments in being organised on the 'area' principle. This arrangement (is) a peculiar way for central government to organise its own structure and activities, rather than the handing over of responsibilities and powers to bodies outside central government. For the Scottish Office is an integral part of central government...

Recent research has demonstrated that the structural differences in Scottish Office administrative arrangements have not resulted in substantive policy autonomy. The British political system is a unitary one and the pressures for alignment of policy within the Whitehall network are considerable."
(M Keating & A Midwinter *The Government of Scotland* p. 13 & 25)

"The great pride of the civil service is not that it has developed special methods or a different emphasis in Scotland, but rather that no gap can be found between Edinburgh and London methods."
(JP Mackintosh *The Devolution of Power* p. 132)

"One of the more facile jibes of the opponents of the case for independence is that, in view of the extent of administrative devolution in Scotland, many of the important decisions in Scottish affairs are already taken in Scotland. Hence, there is no need for any kind of self-government for Scotland...

The weakness of the argument lies in the nature of the decisions made by the Secretary of State for Scotland. Obviously, such decisions cannot be of principle. Decisions of principle are made by the government and enacted by parliament, and the Secretary of State's function is to make the relatively minor decisions which transform government policy into action...He is a member of the Cabinet and shares responsibility for its decisions, almost all of which are made to suit English conditions."
(Iain MacCormick *The Case for Independence* in Iain MacCormick *The Scottish Debate* p. 97)

"A different kind of limitation upon the value of administrative decentralisation in Scotland lies in the fact that expenditure on Scottish Office functions is limited by the need to ensure comparability with expenditure in England. Decisions upon expenditure are taken on a functional and not a geographical basis. The criterion on which they are judged is that of need, rather than geography...This means that it is very difficult for the Scottish Office to determine its own priorities for Scottish expenditure."
(V Bogdanor *Devolution* p. 84)

Simply put, the sources indicate that the Scottish Office policies and procedures for Scotland are not much different from those of the equivalent government departments for the rest of the UK. However, there is no doubt that there has been a substantial amount of administrative devolution since the 1850s. Administrative devolution, though, should not be confused with freedom of action. This was brought home most clearly in the 1980s when Conservative policies were being administered by the Scottish Office on a population, most of whom had rejected those policies at the polls. As one writer comments:

"...a Conservative Secretary of State's claim to be Scotland's Minister becomes rather transparent when his government persists with policies affecting Scottish domestic administration that would be rejected by Scotland's elected representatives."
(AW Bradley in H Calvert *Devolution* p. 100)

It is little wonder, then, that the demand for legislative devolution has never been far from the top of the Scottish political agenda in the last 20 years.

LEGISLATIVE DEVOLUTION

The growth of the Home Rule movement from 1850 onwards has already been covered to some extent in chapter 10. There, we looked at the Home Rule groups which preceded the setting up of the National Party of Scotland in 1928. These organisations, the National Association for the Vindication of Scottish Rights (NAVSR), the Scottish Home Rule Association (SHRA) and the Young Scots Society (YSS) were what are nowadays known as pressure groups. They were attempting to persuade the existing political parties to adopt devolution as party policy.

In this section, we will look briefly at the demands of the various groups and the reasons for their demands and at the attitudes and actions of the parties to pressures for devolution.

1850 - 1968

The earliest evidence of dissatisfaction with the existing Parliamentary arrangements came from the NAVSR in 1853. This non-party organisation attracted crowds of 2000 and 5000 at its first meetings in Edinburgh and Glasgow. At the Glasgow meeting, one of the principal speakers, PE Dove, a Radical, called for "some Scottish assembly for the direction of those matters which are exclusively Scottish". (Sir R Coupland *Welsh and Scottish Nationalism* p. 286) This was to be an administrative, not a legislative body. Exactly what Dove meant by this is not clear. His rather vague proposal did not find favour with any of the Scottish MPs, who remained aloof from the NAVSR.

Another of the organisation's proposals, "That the representation of Scotland in Parliament be increased", was more successful. (ibid p. 286) In 1863, the number of Scottish MPs was increased from 53 to 60.

However, the demand for a measure of legislative devolution really hardened and took shape as a direct result of the agitation for Irish Home Rule from the 1870s onwards. In 1877, the issue was raised in the House of Commons by the Scottish Liberal MP, Sir Graham Campbell. He stated that Scotland's claim to Home Rule was as valid as the Irish one, but that at the moment, the Scottish people did not fully support devolution or federation. In the meantime, he proposed the setting up of a 'Grand Committee' to deal with Scottish Bills. Campbell's complaint was that Parliament was not spending enough time on Scottish legislation - a technical argument in other words, not a nationalist one.

The Scottish people apparently were unmoved by such matters. Two years later though, Home Rule for Scotland was brought very publicly and powerfully to the attention of the voters by no less than Gladstone himself during the 'Midlothian' campaign in 1879. There, he advocated devolution for all the nations of the UK:

"We have got an overweighted Parliament...and, if we can make arrangements under which Ireland, Scotland, Wales and portions of England can deal with questions of local and special interest to themselves more efficiently than Parliament now can, I say, will be the attainment of great national good".
(ibid p. 297)

Note again that efficiency and not national sentiment, is the reason for contemplating devolution of legislative power.

Gladstone's policy on devolution changed significantly in 1885. Home Rule for Ireland was now his major preoccupation and only after achieving this would he contemplate devolution of a less powerful form for Scotland and Wales. Gladstone's commitment to Irish Home Rule had a direct bearing on the future progress of devolution for Scotland. His policy had the effect of splitting the Liberal Party, with the Liberal Unionists eventually joining the Conservatives. The Conservative and Unionist Party were now implacably opposed to Home Rule for Ireland and clearly could not support similar measures for the Scots. With the Liberals weak and divided, British politics entered a period of Tory ascendancy from 1885 - 1906. During that time, although several Scottish Home Rule Motions and one Bill were introduced in the House of Commons, none of them had the slightest chance of getting government backing. It can perhaps be said that if Gladstone was the friend of Irish Home Rule, he was also inadvertently and indirectly the 'enemy' of progress towards Home Rule for Scotland. A further hindrance to the Scottish cause was the militancy of the Irish Home Rulers who, by dominating the Parliamentary debate, effectively kept the Scottish issue in the background as well as alienating moderate support in Scotland.

The Conservatives were now firmly opposed to legislative devolution in any shape or form, and yet it was a Conser-

vative government under Lord Salisbury who presided over the introduction of the first measure of administrative devolution for Scotland - the creation of the Scottish Office and the reintroduction of the post of Secretary for Scotland between 1885 and 1887. In 1886, the Scottish Home Rule Association was formed, modelled on its Irish counterpart. Its aim was to continue the momentum for legislative devolution, mainly by applying pressure on the Liberal party. Lloyd George, a future Liberal Prime Minister, attended an SHRA conference in Aberdeen in 1891 and seconded a Scottish Home Rule motion. However, such pledges of support at this time were less meaningful with the Liberals out of power. The SHRA soon developed links with the emerging Scottish Labour Party. Keir Hardie, co-founder of the SLP was also vice-President of the SHRA in the early years. He spoke out in favour of Home Rule on numerous occasions. The following is from his address during the Mid-Lanark by-election in 1888:

"I am strongly in favour of Home Rule being convinced that until we have a parliament of our own, we cannot obtain the many great reforms on which I believe the people of Scotland have set their hearts."
(J Brand *Parties and Politics in Scotland* A Paper prepared for the ECPR Workshop on Social and Political Movements in Western Europe, Berlin 1977 p. 5)

Although there was fairly widespread support within the ranks of the Liberal Party and the Labour movement, it counted for nothing during the period of Conservative rule. The classic Unionist position was stated by Balfour in 1895:

" We object to Home Rule whether it begins with Ireland and ends with Wales or begins with Wales and ends with Ireland. We object to the whole thing."
(Sir R.Coupland *Welsh and Scottish Nationalism* p. 302)

When the Liberals came back to power in 1906, it was considered to be a possibility that the devolution issue might be treated more sympathetically. However, the introduction of social legislation and Irish Home Rule took precedence over Scotland. As table 11.3 shows, two Scottish Home Rule Bills were introduced in 1908 and

Scottish Home Rule Bills and Motions 1889 - 1914			
Date	Motion or Bill	Proposer	Result
1889	Scottish Home Rule Motion	Dr Clark	Defeated by 200 to 79
1891	Federal Home Rule Motion	Dr Clark	Counted Out
1892	Federal Home Rule Motion	Dr Clark	Defeated by 74 to 54
1893	Scottish Home Rule Motion	Dr Clark	Defeated by 168 to 150
1894	Scottish Home Rule Motion	Sir Henry Dalziel	Carried by 180 to 170
1895	Federal Home Rule Motion	Sir Henry Dalziel	Carried by 128 to 102
1899	Scottish Home Rule Bill	DV Pirie	Defeated at First Reading
1908	Government of Scotland Bill	DV Pirie	1st Reading carried 257 to 102
1911	Scottish Home Rule Bill	Sir Henry Dalziel	1st Reading carried 172 to 73
1913	Scottish Home Rule Bill	Sir WH Cowan	2nd Reading carried 204 to 159
1914	Scottish Home Rule BillI	I Macpherson	Adjourned at 2nd Reading

Table 11.3

1911. Both Bills were supported by a majority of Scottish MPs, but the government was not willing to take the matter further until the Irish problem was settled.

In the few years before the First World War, the Young Scots Society had taken over from the SHRA as the chief Home Rule pressure group working within the Liberal Party. It seemed to be working effectively. In 1908, the Scottish Liberals officially adopted devolution as party policy. Four years later, it helped to form the Scottish Home Rule Council, comprising the Liberal MPs and the Scottish Liberal Association. Nevertheless, despite the apparent commitment of the party, nothing much was being done. As Brand points out,

"It is ... significant that these organisations were brought into being. If the Liberal Party had been solidly behind Home Rule, there would have been no need for them. Their presence is a strong indication of the marginal nature of devolution for the party as a whole." (J Brand *The National Movement in Scotland* p. 41)

We have already seen that Prime Minister Asquith introduced the Third Irish Home Rule Bill in 1912 with the promise that it was "only the first step in a larger and more comprehensive policy". (see chapter 10) Yet, it was fairly clear from another of his speeches in 1908 that he did not intend to see Scotland gain similar devolved powers to those envisaged for Ireland:

"... there is no other solution of the congestion of the Parliamentary machine, in which it may be Scotland suffers more than any other part of the United Kingdom, than by some form of delegation of Parliamentary business in regard to local matters to local authorities with local knowledge and local responsibilities." (*Sixty Points for Scottish Home Rule* Young Scots Society pamphlet 1912 p. 61)

This vague and rather weak proposal contrasts sharply with the aims of the Young Scots:

"Home Rule for Scotland means:
1 The creation of a Scottish Parliament, to sit in Scotland and pass laws on matters affecting Scotland, and Scotland only;
2 The creation of a Scottish Executive or Ministry, to control the administration of Scottish affairs, subject to the Scottish Parliament." (*Sixty Points for Scottish Home Rule* Young Scots pamphlet 1912 p. 7)

In the end, of course, the First World War interrupted progress on all fronts. Some historians have speculated that had it not been for the war, Scotland would have gained some measure of legislative devolution. The irony here is that it is doubtful if many of the Scottish public were interested in or acquainted with the issues involved. At this time, the nationalist movement was still a "somewhat dry and academic affair". (Sir R Coupland *Welsh and Scottish Nationalism* p. 307) While it is true that two Home Rule Bills did reach Second Reading stage in 1913 and 1914, the debates on them were characterised by the Secretary for Scotland as "good-humoured and passionless" (ibid p. 307) in stark contrast to the heat and fire of the Irish debates:

"Appeals to patriotic sentiment were rare. No Scot complained that the neglect of Scottish affairs was an intolerable insult to Scotland or foretold the extinction of Scottish nationhood if the Union stood unchanged." (ibid p. 307)

There was further disappointment and frustration for the devolutionists after the Great War when two Scottish Home Rule Bills were defeated in 1924 and 1927. Both Bills were introduced during the period of a Labour Government and under a Prime Minister, Ramsay MacDonald who in the past had publicly supported Home Rule for Scotland. In mitigation, it could be said that the 1924 Bill was introduced at a difficult time when the Labour Government was in a minority in Parliament, but if the political will had been there, a deal could undoubtedly have been done with the Liberals in order to carry the measure through. Like the Liberals when in government, Labour did not consider Home Rule for Scotland to be of sufficient importance to commit government time to it. The pattern was familiar, namely "...approval of Home Rule when out of office, inaction when in office". (Gordon Donaldson et al in JN Wolfe *Government and Nationalism in Scotland* p. 11) With the downfall of the 1927 Bill, we come to the end of an era. From 1889 up until this time, Scottish Home Rule had been debated in Parliament just about every year except during wartime. Now there was to be a Parliamentary lull of 40 years.

During the 'wilderness years', the Liberals kept up their policy on Home Rule, but as we have indicated, they could afford to do this now that they were an insignificant political force. To be fair, the Scottish Liberals were genuinely in favour of Home Rule and as we saw in the previous chapter, there were talks with the infant SNP concerning an electoral pact. As for the SNP, it made no headway during these 40 years and it was only when the party made real progress in the mid-1960s that the others began to re-examine their policies (or lack of them) on devolution. The Conservative Party, up until 1967, was solidly unionist. During the 13 years of Tory rule from 1951-64, calls for Home Rule were certain to fall on deaf ears. As for Labour, there was no mention of devolution in their election manifestos between 1935 and 1966. In 1945, Labour's priorities were economic reconstruction and the building of the welfare state; in 1964, it was the 'technological revolution'. Devolution, apparently, had completely fallen off the political agenda.

1968 - 1979
In the autumn of 1968, the Labour Home Secretary, James Callaghan, set up, under Lord Crowther, a Royal Commission on the Constitution. Its remit was, "to examine the present functions of the central legislature and government in relation to the several countries, nations and regions of the United Kingdom." (H Drucker and G Brown *The Politics of Nationalism and Devolution* p 55)

Nowhere did this document mention the words 'Scotland' or 'devolution', even although it was clear to everyone that the Commission's purpose was to come up with proposals for the creation of an Assembly for Scotland.

Perhaps the reason for the Labour Government's omission of the term 'devolution' was that it was not a popular word in the vocabulary of party activists and members, especially in Scotland. Prime Minister Harold Wilson would not have cared to admit that the spectacular rise of the SNP had something to do with the decision to consider devolution for Scotland after 40 years of studied neglect of the issue. Nevertheless, there is ample evidence to show that Labour were reluctant advocates of legislative devolution and were pushed into it by the nationalists. The most telling evidence comes from an 'insider' - Tam Dalyell, Labour MP for West Lothian and a leading opponent of devolution. In his book, *Devolution - The End of Britain?*, he sees the SNP victory at the Hamilton by-election in 1967 as a turning point in Labour's attitude towards the nationalists, who, up until then, had been dismissed out of hand.

> "The election of Mrs Ewing went off like an electoral atom bomb in the Labour establishment. To say that party leaders were shell-shocked for weeks is an understatement. After all, Hamilton was not just any old Labour seat...it embodied the socialist heartland."
> (T Dalyell *Devolution - The End of Britain?* p. 76)

Dalyell also reveals that Wilson and Callaghan decided on the setting up of the Commission on their own without consulting the Scottish Labour Party or MPs. Given that most of the Scottish party were hostile anyway, we can understand why no consultation took place. It is also clear that the Commission would serve to placate both the SNP and buy valuable time. The Government "... wanted an excuse to do nothing in the face of Nationalist success ... For the period that the Commission sat, the Government had an unimpeachable excuse for taking no action and producing no plans". (H Drucker and G Brown *The Politics of Government and Nationalism* p. 54) Indeed, it took the Government over 6 months to appoint the members of the Commission and another 4 years went by before the Commission reported. In the meantime, the Chairperson, Lord Crowther died and was replaced by Lord Kilbrandon. The final report became known as the Kilbrandon Report.

The Conservative response to the Nationalist challenge also seems to have been fairly cynical. When in Opposition, they became pro-devolution (1967-70) but in government (1970-74) they did nothing to carry out their policy. In 1955, the Tories had been at their peak in Scotland, gaining 50% of the votes at the General Election. However, their fortunes declined steadily over the next 11 years. In 1966, their share of the vote had gone down to 37.7%. They had lost 16 seats since 1955. Two initiatives arose out of the party crisis. Firstly, a new pro-devolution faction emerged within the Scottish party called the Thistle Group. Then, a committee under Sir William McEwan Younger was set up to look into the workings of government in Scotland. The real breakthrough, though, came at the Scottish Party conference in 1968 when the party leader, Edward Heath, announced himself in favour of a directly elected Scottish Assembly. A committee was formed to investigate the details of Heath's proposals, chaired by former Prime Minister Sir Alec Douglas Home. In 1970, the committee proposed the idea of a 'Scottish Convention'. This body would take over the work of both the Scottish Grand Committee (ie. take the Committee stage of Scottish legislation going through the House of Commons) and the Standing Committee on Scottish Affairs (i.e. have the right to question Scottish Ministers). Since the Convention would merely be, in effect, a Committee of the House of Commons with no right to initiate legislation, it would be misleading to call the Home proposal the devolution of legislative power. One writer called the proposed Convention "no more than a powerless, debating chamber" (John Mercer *Scotland: The Devolution of Power* p.178) Even two of the Home Commission members dissented, claiming that the Convention would have little to do.

Nevertheless, the Home Report became party policy and the Conservatives fought and won the 1970 General Election with a manifesto pledge to place these proposals before Parliament. In the event, devolution was quietly shelved by Prime Minister Heath. Why? The SNP challenge which had been threatening in 1967/8 seemed to evaporate at the General Election - the party returned only 1 MP. In 1973, the Conservative Party conference drew back from its stance on devolution and threw out the Home Report proposals. What about Heath himself? Dalyell claims that Heath genuinely wanted to get legislation through, but it was low on his list of priorities and he got sidetracked. Heath's first concern was gaining British entry to the EEC; his Government was bedevilled with industrial relations problems; and he could not introduce devolution proposals until the Kilbrandon Commission reported in October 1973. In the meantime, the Government was reorganising Scottish local government and it would have been unwise to do anything until the system was in place. None of these distractions, of course, would have been insurmountable if the political will had been there.

The Liberals had been more consistent than both Labour and the Conservatives in advocating the decentralisation of power to Scotland. On the other hand, they were never to be put to the ultimate test ie. governmental office. The two main platforms of the Liberals in the 1960s and 1970s were proportional representation (PR) and federalism, with PR at the forefront. However, the Scottish Liberal Party were independent of the UK Liberals. On 3 occasions in the 1960s, the Scottish Liberals were offered a pact with the SNP. In each case, the creation of a Parliament was the core issue. In 1964, William Wolfe, later to become Chairperson of the SNP, invited the Scottish Liberals to "put self-government at the head of its electoral programme". (W Wolfe *Scotland Lives* p. 39) The offer was rejected. Two years later, Ludovic Kennedy (better known as a TV broadcaster) got a motion passed at the Scottish Liberal conference demanding that Home Rule should be the Liberals' top priority. The resolution was never put into practice. Finally, after the SNP's Hamilton by-election triumph in 1967, David Steel, the future Liberal leader, again tried to secure a pact with the SNP. It too failed when the SNP insisted on top billing for Home Rule in the Liberal manifesto. At the 1970 General Election, the Liberal Party's share of the vote in Scotland fell to 5.5% and it lost 2 of its 5 MPs. For the first time, the SNP overtook the Liberals - in fact, they now had double the Liberals' vote. For the next decade, the Liberals played only a peripheral role in the devolution debate.

The Kilbrandon Commission Report was duly published in 1973. Not all the Commissioners agreed about the best proposals, so there had to be Majority and Minority Reports. The following are the Majority Report recommendations:

"a.	A directly elected assembly, consisting of a single house of about 100 members, sitting for 4-year terms. Proportional representation was proposed.

b.	Power to decide policy on devolved subjects - roughly those at present in the hands of the Scottish Office - and to enact the appropriate legislation and to set up the machinery to carry the policies through

c.	Executive power would remain with the ministers of the Crown

d.	Scotland would retain its seats in the UK parliament, a contentious issue.

e.	The office of Secretary of State for Scotland would end..a power of veto would be held by the UK parliament

f.	Although limited power to raise revenue locally was feasible, the bulk of 'regional' funds would still come, as a block grant, from the centre."

(Extracted from John Mercer *Scotland: The Devolution of Power* pp158-9)

The Kilbrandon Report was given a brief debate in the House of Commons, but its authority was undermined because of the variety of views expressed in the Report. The Government took more notice the following week when the SNP won a spectacular by-election victory at Govan. Labour's 16,000 majority in the constituency was overturned by Margo MacDonald. Dalyell says that the timing of the SNP victory coming hard on the heels of Kilbrandon "helped to determined Wilson's response to the Kilbrandon proposals and marked the beginning of the Prime Minister's conversion to Devolution." (T Dalyell *Devolution: The End of Britain?* p. 94)

The final part of the devolution story is complex and tortuous. The main points are summarised in the following chronological table.

Legislative Devolution in Scotland 1973-79

February 1974	Election of a Labour Government but with a minority of seats in Parliament. SNP gained 22% of the votes and 7 seats in Scotland. Neither Labour nor Conservatives had put devolution in their election manifestos, but SNP gains plus the likelihood of another General Election in 1974 hardened the two parties' commitment to devolution. Prime Minister Wilson promised to produce a White Paper and a Bill on devolution.

June 1974	The Government produced their first White Paper - *Devolution within the United Kingdom - Some Alternatives for Discussion*. Usually, White Papers contain definite Government proposals for legislation, but this one did not commit the Government to anything.

September 1974	The Government issued a second White Paper called *Democracy and Devolution: Proposals for Scotland and Wales*. Scotland was to gain a Scottish Development Agency and the proposed Scottish Assembly would be granted legislative powers. Shortly after this, Wilson called a General Election for October.

October 1974	Labour were returned to Government with a small majority, but in Scotland the SNP increased their share of the vote to 30% and gained 4 MPs. Most worrying for Labour was that the SNP came second in 35 of Labour's 41 seats in Scotland. It was estimated that with only another 6% of the vote, the SNP would gain a majority of Scottish seats and give them the right to demand an independent Scotland.

February 1975	Margaret Thatcher replaced Heath as leader of the Conservative Party. She was opposed to devolution.

November 1975	The Government published a new White Paper - *Our Changing Democracy: Devolution to Scotland and Wales*. It caused a furore in Scotland because of its watered-down proposals. There was no mention of the SDA being devolved to the Scottish Assembly; it seemed that the Scottish 'block grant' would be settled at the Treasury; the Assembly would not have strong economic powers.

March 1976	Wilson resigned as Prime Minister. Replaced by Callaghan.

August 1976	The Government produced another White Paper - *Devolution to Scotland and Wales: Supplementary Statement*. The Scottish Assembly was now to have control over the SDA and the provision that the Secretary of State for Scotland could overrule an Assembly Bill on policy grounds, was removed.

December 1976	The Scotland and Wales Bill started its progress through Parliament. It passed its Second Reading but by a narrow majority. As a concession to those Labour MPs who did not vote for the Bill, the Government agreed to hold referendums in Scotland and Wales if the Bill went through all its stages.

February 1977	The Government had allowed 30 days for the passage of the Bill. However, they had already used up 4 days on the Second Reading debate and 10 days on the Committee stage. The Committee stage looks at the Bill clause by clause. Since only 4 of the 115 clauses had been debated, the only way the Bill could be saved was for the Government to ask for a vote on a timetable motion or guillotine. The guillotine allows the Government to cut short debate on each clause at a prearranged time, thus allowing the Bill to get through its stages on time. But the guillotine motion failed by 312 to 283 votes. The Scotland and Wales Bill was now effectively dead.

March 1977	The SNP withdrew support for the Government. Labour concluded a Parliamentary pact with the Liberals (the Lib-Lab pact). This would allow the Government to carry out its devolution commitment.

July 1977	The Scotland and Wales Bill was separated into two Bills. As a concession to the Liberals, the Government allowed for a free vote on proportional representation for the Scottish Assembly.

November 1977	The Scotland Bill passed its Second Reading and the motion to guillotine the Bill at the Committee Stage succeeded by 313 to 287 votes. However, the Government was forced to accept a new amendment to the Bill. This was the '40% rule' ie. if less than 40% of the total electorate did not vote 'Yes' at the referendum on a Scottish Assembly, then the Scotland Act would be repealed. (See p. 61)

July 1978   The Scotland Bill finally passed all its stages through Parliament.

1 March 1979   The referendum on a Scottish Assembly was held. Although a majority voted 'Yes', the 40% was not achieved. The result was: 32.5% Yes, 30.4% No, 37.1% did not vote. For a major constitutional issue, this was a high percentage of nonvoters. The anti-devolutionists claimed that the stay-aways had effectively voted 'No', as not voting had the same effect as voting 'No'.

The referendum drew the curtain on devolution for Scotland for the foreseeable future. Two months after the vote, the Labour Government was defeated at the General Election. ushering in 11 years of Conservative rule under Mrs Thatcher. As long as Thatcher remained at the helm, devolution for Scotland was out of the question. Given the long history of failed attempts to gain devolution of legislative power to Scotland, it will take a much clearer political signal from the Scottish people to make significant progress on this issue.

Bibliography

The Labour Movement

Labour and Socialism by James Hinton (Wheatsheaf Books)
Origins of the Labour Party by Henry Pelling (Oxford Paperbacks)
A History of British Trade Unionism by Henry Pelling (Pelican)

Women

A 'GUID' CAUSE - The Women's Suffrage Movement in Scotland by Lealy Lerieman (Aberdeen University Press)
Out of the Doll's House by Angela Holdsworth (BBC Books)

Peace Movements

Protests and Visions by James Hinton (Hutchinson Radius)
The Abolition of War by Keith Robbins (University of Wales Press)

The Growth if Democracy

Democracy and Reform by DG Wright (Longman)
The Common People by GDH Cole & Raymond Postgate (University Paperbacks)
English History 1914 - 45 by AJP Taylor (Pelican)
A Century of the Scottish People by TC Smout (Collins)

General Books on the Growth of the Welfare State

The Shaping of the Welfare State by RC Birch (Longman)
The Coming of the Welfare State by M Bruce (Wiedenfield & Nicholson)
The Rise of the Welfare State by M Bruce [ed.] (
The Evolution of the British Welfare State by D Fraser (Macmillan)
The Development of the British Welfare State by JR Hay (Macmillan)
The Foundations of the Welfare State by P Thane (Longman)

Victorian Origins of the Welfare State

Gladstone, Disraeli and Later Victorian Politics by P Adelman (Longman)
Victorian Social Reform by EC Midwinter (Longman)
Laissez Faire and State Intervention in 19th Century Britain by AJ Taylor (Macmillan)

The Liberal Welfare Reforms 1906 - 14

The Evolution of National Insurance by BB Gilbert (Michael Joseph)
The Origins of the Liberal Welfare Reforms by JR Hay (Macmillan)
Human Documents of the Lloyd George Era by E Royston Pike (Unwin Hyman)

The National Governments of the 1930s

No Mean Fighter by Harry McShane (Pluto)
Politicians and the Slump by R Skidelsky (Penguin)
English History 1914 - 45 by AJP Taylor (Penguin)

The Arrival of the Welfare State

Now the War is Over by P Addison (Cape)
The Road to 1945 by P Addison (Quartet)
The 1945 - 51 Labour Governments by R Eatwell (Batsford Books)

General Books on Scottish Nationalism and Devolution

Scottish Nationalism by HJ Hanham (Faber)
Modern Scotland by J Kellas (Allen & Unwin)
The Scottish Political System by J Kellas (CUP)

Scottish Nationalism

The National Movement in Scotland by J Brand (RKP)
The Growth of Nationalism in Scotland by K Webb (Molendinar Press)
Scotland Lives by W Wolfe (Reprographia)

Scottish Devolution

Scottish and Welsh Nationalism by Sir R Copland (Collins)
The Politics of Nationalism and Devolution by H Drucker and B Brown (Longman)
Scotland : The Devolution of Power by J Mercer (J Calder)

Agricultural marketing Act (1931), *19*
Agricultural marketing Act (1933), *90*
Anomalies Act (1931), *92*
Artisans Dwellings Act (1875), *65, 70*
Asquith HH, *33-4,59, 73, 78*
Attlee C, *20-2, 100*

Baldwin S, *16, 87-8*
Balfour A, *123*
Ballot Act (1872), *9,71*
Banking Crisis (1930-1), *87*
Bentham J, *62-4*
Bevan A, *22, 100-1, 103*
Beveridge W, *73, 82*
  -Report *20, 97-98*
Booth C, *68-9*

Callaghan J, *24, 124-5*
Campaign for Nuclear Disarmament, *50-2*
Campbell-Bannerman H, *59, 73, 76*
Cattle Industry Act (1934), *90*
Chamberlain J, *57, 65-66, 78, 89*
Chamberlain N, *88-9, 96*
Champion HH, *10*
Charity Organisation Society, *67*
Children Act (1908), *76*
Churchill W, *20, 33, 61, 71, 76-7, 82-3, 85, 97-100, 104, 121*
Coal Industry Nationalisation Act (1946), *21*
Coal Mines Act (1908), *74*
Coal Prices Act (1929), *19*
Combination Acts (1799 & 1800), *6*
Committee of 100, *52*
Conscientious Objection, *46-7*
Conservative Party, *70-1, 100*
Conspiracy & Protection of Property Act (1875), *70*
Cook AJ, *17*
Corrupt & Illegal Practises Act (1883), *57*
Criminal Law Amendment Act (1871), *71*
Cunningham-Graham RB, *10, 106-8*

Dalyell T, *113, 125*
Determination of Needs Act (1941), *97*
Devolution, *24, 61, 117-127*
Disraeli B, *7, 32, 55-6, 119*
Divorce, Royal Commission on (1912), *30*
Donaldson A, *112-3*
Dundas H, *118*

Education, *29, 31-2, 102-3*
Education Acts (1870) *71;* (1876) *70;* (1891) *71;* (1944) *99*
Education (Administrative Provisions) Act (1907), *74-6*
Education (Provision of Meals) Act (1906), *74-5*
Education (Scotland) Acts (1872) *71;* (1908) *76;* (1946) *99*
Emergency Powers Act (1920), *15*
Employees and Workmen Act (1875) *70*
Employment Protection Act (1975), *42*
Enclosure Act (1876), *70*
Equal Franchise Act (1928), *36*
Equal Pay Act (1970), *42*

Fabian Society, *5, 62, 70*
Factory Acts (1847 & 1850) *5;* (1844) *62;* (1874 & 1878) *70*
Family Allowance Act (1945), *99*
Free Trade, *59, 89-90*
Friendly Societies, *78-9, 81*

General Strike (1926), *15, 16-18, 84*
Gibson TH, *108-9, 111*
Gilmour Report, *120-1*
Gladstone WE, *7, 54-7, 59, 71, 119, 123*

Glasgow University Student Nationalist Association, *109-110*
Gold Standard, *84-5, 89*
Guardianship of Infants Act (1924) *36*

Hardie K, *9, 11-12, 43*
Health, *94-5, 99-102*
Heath E, *23, 125*
Home Rule Bills, *123-4*
Housing , *95, 103*
Housing Acts, (1890) *71;* (1930) *19;* (1932) *91*
Hyndman HM, *10, 68, 70, 74*

Independent Labour Party, *11, 14*
Industrial Relations Act (1972), *23*
Iron and Steel Act (1949), *21*

Jarrow, *93-4*

Keynes JM, *85-6*
Kilbrandon Report, *125-6*

Labour Exchanges Act (1909), *82*
Labour Party, *9-24, 85-8, 96-104*
Laissez Faire, *4, 28, 62-72, 77, 79, 85-6, 88*
Law Reform Act (1935), *36*
League of Nations Union, *48*
Liberal Party, *11, 58-60, 73-83, 89*
Life Expectation, *3*
Life Peerages Act (1958), *61*
Living Standards, *93-4*
Lloyd George D, *14-5, 58-60, 76-7, 79-81, 83, 86, 89*
Local Government Act (1894), *71*
Local Government Board Act (1871), *71*
Loch CS, *66*
London Dock Strike, *8*
Lords, House of, *60-1, 80*

MacCormick J, *109-113*
MacDonald R, *14, 16, 18-9, 85-9, 106*
Married Women's Property Acts (1870 & 1882), *30*
Marx K, *5*
Match Girls Strike (1889), *28*
Matrimonial Causes Acts (1857 & 1873), *30;* (1923) *36*
Maxton J, *92*
May Committee, *19, 87-8*
McDowall JK, *110*
Means Test, *92-3*
Military Services Act (1916), *46*
Mill JS, *32, 54, 62-4*
Mines Act (1842), *62*
Montrose, Duke of, *108, 110-1*
Morris W, *10*
Mosley O, *86*
Muirhead RE, *107, 109, 112*
Munitions Act (1915) *14*

National Assistance Act (1948), *101*
National Association for the Vindication of Scottish Rights, *105-6, 122*
National Governments, *19, 84-95*
National Health Service Act (1948), *102*
National Insurance Acts (1911), *74, 80, 82, 94;* (1946) *101*
National Insurance (Industrial Injuries) Act (1946) *101*
Nationalisation, *20-1*
Nationalism, *5, 105-117*
National Milk Scheme (1940), *97*
National Party of Scotland, *109-110*
New English Law of Property (1926), *36*
No Conscription Fellowship, *46*

Occupational Groups, *3-4, 26, 35, 41*

Old Age and Widows' Pension Act (1940), *97*
Old Age Pensions Act (1908) *74, 77-9*
Out-Door Relief (Friendly Societies) Act (1894), *71*
Owen R, *6*

Pacifism, *43-52*
Parliament Act (1911), *13, 60, 80*
Peace Pledge Union, *49*
Peerages Act (1963), *63*
People's Budget (1909), *60, 81*
People's Charter, *54*
Police Act (1915), *15*
Poor Law, *66-7,69, 77, 80-1, 97*
Population, *3*
Proportional Representation, *61*
Public Health Acts (1848) *5, 62;* (1875) *70;* (1936) *94*

Red Clydeside, *45*
Redistribution of Seats Act (1885), *57*
Referendums, *24, 61*
Reform Acts (1832) *6, 53-4;* (1867) *9, 32, 55-7;* (1884) *9, 32, 57;* (1918) *15,58*
Roseberry Lord, *59, 83, 119*
Rowntree S, *26-7, 68, 94*

Salisbury Lord, *71*
Sale of Food and Drugs Act (1875), *70*
Samuel Sir H, *17-8*
Sanitation Act (1866), *62*
School Meals Act (1906), *73*
Scottish Convention, *110*
Scottish Home Rule Association (I), *106-7;* (II) *107-110, 123-4*
Scots National League, *108-110*
Scottish Office, *119-122*
Secretary for Scotland Act (1885), *119*
Sex Discrimination Act (1975), *42*
Sex Disqualification (Removal) Act (1919), *36*
Shops Act (1911) *74*
Smiles S, *64*
Smith A, *62-3*
Snowden P, *19, 86, 88-9*
Social Contract, *24*
Social Democratic Federation, *9-10*
Social Security, Pensions Act (1975), *42*
Special Areas Act (1934), *90*
Suffragettes, *32-6*
Sugar Industry Act (1936), *90*
Syndicalism, *13*

Ten Hours Act (1847), *62*
Trade Boards Act (1910), *29. 74*
Trade Disputes Acts (1906) *12;* (1927) *18, 21*
Trade Unions, *6-9, 14, 23, 26-7, 39*
Trade Union Acts (1871) *7, 71;* (1913) *13*
Trade Union Congress, *7, 9, 11, 17-9, 28-9, 41*

Unemployment Workmen's Act (1905), *81*
Unemployment, *14-15, 20, 81, 85, 90-3, 104*
Unemployment Insurance Act (1930), *88*
Union of Democratic Control, *45*

Vaccination Act (1871), *71*

Webb S & B, *10, 16, 66, 70, 73*
Welfare Reforms, *73-104*
Wilson H, *22-4, 124-5*
Women's Movement, *25-43*
World War One, *13-15, 35-36, 45-47*
World War Two, *20, 39-40, 49-50, 96-100*
Workmen's Compensation Acts (1897 & 1900) *71;* (1906) *74*

Young Scots Society, *107*